WALLENBERG:
MISSING HERO

WALLENBERG:
MISSING HERO

Kati Marton

ARCADE PUBLISHING • NEW YORK

FIRST ARCADE EDITION 1995

First published in 1982 by Random House, Inc.

ISBN 1-55970-276-1
Library of Congress Catalog Card Number 94-79600
Library of Congress Cataloging-in-Publication information is available.

Published in the United States by Arcade Publishing, Inc., New York
Distributed by Little, Brown and Company

10 9 8 7 6 5 4 3 2 1

BP

PRINTED IN THE UNITED STATES OF AMERICA

To the memory of those Hungarians for whom
Raoul Wallenberg arrived too late

Acknowledgments

During the six months he spent in Budapest, Raoul Wallenberg evinced qualities one rarely encounters outside fiction. Courage, steadfastness, unselfishness—the words fall flat perhaps because we so seldom associate them with real, living people. They are the stuff of epic poems, novels and films, not life. Yet Wallenberg is very much a human figure. Under ordinary circumstances he may not have called much attention to himself. He is the kind of man one would easily pass on the street and continue walking.

The story of what he accomplished in Budapest needs no embellishment. There are fortunately enough eyewitnesses left to enable us to let his deeds speak for themselves. In fact, the dialogue throughout the narrative is from documented eyewitness accounting of events.

Piecing together Wallenberg's story required extensive travel. During my research I made three trips to his native Sweden. I spent time in Budapest, Vienna, Munich, Brussels, London and New York. In all of those places I found people who had known the man and were willing to talk about this dramatic period in their lives. A trip to Moscow provided only local color, no new information.

To discover what has happened to Wallenberg since January 1945, when the Soviets took him prisoner, is almost too painful to bear. The screaming injustice of his brutalization since Budapest is what enrages one. It makes one wish Wallenberg were a piece of fiction, so one could slam the book shut and go back to life. But he is there all the time to remind one of man's capacity for inhumanity to his fellow-man.

As a Hungarian whose parents lived through the Wallenberg

period, I learned, in the process of writing this book, things about my former homeland and its history that I would have been happier not knowing.

I am grateful, first of all, to my mother and father, Ilona and Endre Marton, for bringing this period to life for me. I was aware of their courage during the subsequent "liberation" of Hungary by the Red Army. I knew the details of their imprisonment by the Communists. That was my childhood. I was not familiar with the hell they lived through under the Nazis. That was, and still is, too agonizing for conversation.

Thanks are also due the Baroness Elisabeth Kemény for sharing for the first time the story of her special relationship with Raoul Wallenberg, and of how, together, they were able to help the people of Budapest. Aladár Szegedi-Maszák, a member of Regent Horthy's Foreign Ministry and Hungary's last ambassador to Washington prior to the Communist takeover, and George Schöpflin, professor of Eastern European History at the London School of Economics, were both patient in backgrounding the period. Elizabeth Eppler, librarian of the Institute for Jewish Affairs in London, shared her personal recollections of the Budapest underground movement. Thomas Veres, once Wallenberg's photographer and today a successful New York City commercial photographer, contributed observations about the personality and character of Raoul Wallenberg. So did Miklós Kalmar and Stephen Radi in New York, and George Wilhelm in Brussels, all vital players in the larger drama.

The tireless correspondence from Claremont, California, of another Wallenberg associate, Dr. Francis Zöld, provided insights into both the man and the times, and deserves the author's deepest thanks. Susan Tabor's personal rendering of the death march was invaluable.

Nina Lagergren, Raoul Wallenberg's half-sister, gave generously of her time and made available the family correspondence I have used throughout the book. Elie Wiesel put the Wallenberg story in the larger perspective of the Holocaust and Jewish history. Simon Wiesenthal, in his cluttered office in Vienna, made the Gulag Archipelago seem less unreal but no less repellent. Lena Biörck-Kaplan, head of the American Wallenberg Committee, was a tireless source of information.

Robert D. Loomis, vice president and executive editor of Random

House, deserves a special note of appreciation for his encouragement and many helpful suggestions. I am grateful for the early faith shown by Gilbert Kaplan.

My deepest thanks for his grace and invaluable editorial and human support go to my husband, Peter Jennings.

K. M.

Contents

WALLENBERG:
MISSING HERO

Prologue

here was a bite of winter already in the air during those early days of November. Budapest smelled of fear. The Jews in the capital realized that the Nazi coup, which two weeks earlier had driven a weary old man from power, had also swept away their last layer of protection. Until mid-October they had lived in a hypnotic state, entranced by their own ability to endure while Jewish communities in neighboring countries were systematically erased from the map. In the early morning chill of November 5, 1944, the city's Jews awoke to find that their time, too, had run out.

Like most Budapest houses, the rear of the five-story apartment house on Sass Street, just behind the Basilica, faced a courtyard. In the old days, before the Nazi putsch, before the Germans had marched in last spring, before someone smeared a crude yellow star on the front gate, this courtyard, like the others, hummed with the laughter of children and the cacophony of clanging pots as housewives prepared dinner, their kitchen windows flung wide open. Now there was silence in the courtyard. All the windows were shut tight.

The brisk stride of the black-booted, green-shirted member of the Arrow Cross, the Hungarian Nazi party, just two weeks in power, echoed across the cobblestoned courtyard. He raised a huge megaphone to his lips. "You have twenty minutes to come downstairs," he blasted through windowpanes which hid large eyes, afraid to blink.

Many of the Jews behind their curtained and sealed windows had already lost family members during the summer, when Adolf Eichmann beat his own record for speed and efficiency in exterminating the Jews—this time Jews of the Hungarian countryside.

They had even heard that just a twenty-minute subway ride from
the Basilica there were no Jews left in the suburbs. They, too, had
been taken by train to one of the death factories that dotted the
Reich's landscape. Still, when the Sass Street residents staggered
into the courtyard twenty minutes later, the women wore wobbly
high-heeled shoes and light coats. Few of the men carried knapsacks with life-saving bits of bread or sausage inside. They still refused to read the message that was as plain as the death's-head on
the Arrow Cross recruits' armband. For this final illusion some of
them would pay with their lives.

With rifle butts prodding them to be quick about it, the residents
stumbled into the street. They were mostly women with small
children, and old men; the young and fit had been taken away
months before into forced labor. The women blinked in disbelief
as they emerged into the bright light of the street. As far as their
blurred vision could penetrate they saw themselves reproduced, a
hundred, a thousand fold. A sea of dark, reeling humanity was
being led by a battery of armed youth, yesterday's outcasts, freshly
uniformed and arrayed for battle. They now owned the streets of
Budapest. The speed of the march was more than many of the old
could bear. Shots rang out and slumped bodies were left behind.
No one dared stop to mourn or protest. Their captors did not bother
to mask their impatience to use their new weapons at the slightest
excuse.

By the time the group reached the Óbuda brickworks on the
outskirts of the city, the marchers had been transformed. They
looked now like frightened animals, passive and ready to accept
their fate. Thousands of them from all corners of the city were
herded into a vast shed that not long before had been used as a
place to dry bricks. In the darkness, there was no way for the
tottering marchers to see the large holes—hot-air vents to dry the
new bricks—which dotted the entire floor. Driven impatiently by
their guards, the Jews tripped and fell into these holes and were
trampled by an endless rush of people. Ankles were sprained, legs
broken, and still no one was allowed to hold out a helping hand.
By the time the shed was filled, there was not enough room for
most people to sit. Nor was there any food, or water, or sanitary
facilities.

After a while people slumped indifferently against one another or sat in their own dirt without noticing. They had stopped caring. The veneer of civilization and breeding had already started to peel away. The soldiers strutted among them, and if a hand or an arm got in their way, they would step on it as though it were an inanimate object. An old woman started weeping in a corner. A rifle butt in her face dried her tears. From another corner a rumor was passed that the next day they were to march to Austria, toward Strasshof or Mauthausen, death camps that were more accessible than Auschwitz. The Reich's rapidly deteriorating war effort ruled out the use of trains for human transport—that much they had heard. But the Jews of Budapest had once again underestimated the Nazis' zeal and ingenuity to finish the job and make this part of Central Europe *judenrein*.

Those who dropped off to sleep during the night awoke the next morning to find the previous day's nightmare unchanged. There was still nothing to eat, still not even a bucket for human waste.

In the early afternoon there was a ripple in the vast sea of misery. A man in a dark-blue winter coat and the wide-brimmed hat that was the fashion in those days was carefully making his way through the crowd. He mumbled "Pardon me" in German each time he was forced to jolt or displace someone. When he reached the center of the shed he, too, used a megaphone to speak to them. In the half-light it was impossible to make out his features. But his voice, even through the crude loudspeaker, was soft and even. His German was modulated by a strange accent. *"Ich bin Wallenberg,"* he told them. He said it with quiet simplicity, in a matter-of-fact tone, as if they were all gathered at a diplomatic reception. The people began to stir slowly from their trance.

The name was known to most of them. For the last four months it had been associated with miracles. But these people thought they were beyond miracles. "I shall return tomorrow," the Swede told them. "And those of you who have Swedish or Swiss protective passes I shall return to the city in trucks." So there was someone left who had not already crossed out their names from the list of those who had a right to live! "The Hungarian government has given permission for doctors and nurses to come and take care of you," Wallenberg told them. "If you are unable to walk, your neighbors must help you." He spoke to them as though they were still responsible people, human beings, not anesthetized shells of despair.

And they responded. The slumped backs became a little bit straighter. Those who had managed to squirrel away a bit of meat or cheese started now to distribute it, precious slice by precious slice, among their neighbors. There was not enough to fill anybody's stomach, just enough for every mouth. Their captors introduced latrine buckets. By the time Wallenberg left, a team of Jewish doctors and nurses was tending the sick.

From the dark depths of the cavernous shed someone started a prayer: "Shema Yisrael, Adonai Eloheinu, Adonai Echad"—"Hear, O Israel: The Lord our God, the Lord is One . . ." The prayer was picked up until every corner of the dimly lit place hummed with its soft, dirgelike rhythm. The Shema is the Hebrew prayer before death. If death was to come, several thousand Jews huddled in the Óbuda brickworks silently decided, they would face it with dignity. And perhaps, just perhaps, death was not inevitable.

Who was this Wallenberg, the mention of whose name was enough to stir life into the half dead? He was not a diplomat—his was merely a title of convenience. He was a son of neutral Sweden, product of a family of privilege and position. Why, then, had this young man chosen to stride into the Kafkaesque nightmare of Budapest, 1944?

He did not need to go. He went and proved that one man could make a difference. All the solid reasons the rest of the world gave to sit with its arms primly folded while cattle cars swallowed entire towns did not really hold up. He proved that if the givers of life showed as much enthusiasm for their job as the merchants of death, humanity had an even chance.

Wallenberg was a man who broke laws when he had to. He was operating in a world where practically all the usual codes of conduct were absent. The only law he obeyed was that of survival, the survival of a people written off as expendable by a large portion of humanity. What appalled Raoul Wallenberg was that these people, the Jews of Hungary, seemed themselves to assume the right of their fellow-man to deal with them as they chose. This was the supreme victory of the Nazis, and the unspeakable tragedy of the

Jews. They were no longer outraged by their own extermination. They were entranced by their own doom.

What gave the genocide of Hungary's Jews its particularly cruel edge was that the end of the war and of the Nazis was in sight. By late 1944 only the most deluded fanatics of the Third Reich believed in Hitler's future. The slaughter of Hungary's Jews took place before the eyes of a world that could no longer plead ignorance. It was carried out by a driven people who no longer gave a damn about world opinion. They were determined to finish the job they had started.

The story of Raoul Wallenberg is a double paradox. Why was his reward for unmatched humanity to be life as a silent inmate of that impenetrable continent, the Gulag Archipelago? Why did the Russians take the Swede in the first place? Even more paradoxical, why did they keep him for so many years and lie about his fate?

The overwhelming evidence points to Wallenberg's being alive in the fifties, sixties and mid-seventies. The tracks fade after that, but they have never been completely obliterated. International opinion has been agonizingly slow to mobilize on his behalf. By the time the world decided to be outraged, it may already have been too late for Raoul Wallenberg.

The Soviets nearly got away with it. There is not a shred of doubt that they have lied about Wallenberg. They have come up with three versions of the Wallenberg story: Wallenberg safe and sound under Soviet protective custody; Wallenberg the ghost who does not exist in the Soviet Union; Wallenberg dead, the victim of sudden heart failure. Neither a body nor a death certificate has ever been produced by them.

Raoul Wallenberg is one of a small handful of heroes to have emerged from modern history's most squalid chapter. He was a young man whose epic lasted only six months. His story, cut short, is brief. His name should today stand for humanity and justice. Instead it has become a symbol for indifference and injustice. Wallenberg has spent more than half of his life a captive of his would-be allies, an inmate of that gray world, beyond the reach of those who owe him their survival.

If Raoul Wallenberg can be faulted *with* anything, it may be an excess of hubris. He had observed his own miracles and in the end perhaps he had begun to believe them. He confronted the new masters of Hungary, the Red Army, with too little caution, as though he were an indestructible force; he had, after all, extracted unbelievable concessions from the Nazis. He had outlived a battalion of would-be assassins. He had lost a sense of his own mortality. He sought out the Soviets, when he should have been underground with the other, more wary diplomats.

He was a man with a mission. He now understood how much he could accomplish, and how few others could be counted on. The community he had salvaged was in ruins. "His" Jews, the ones he had snatched from the thugs who were now on the run, were too shell-shocked to do much for themselves. He, Raoul Wallenberg, wanted to lead them toward the future.

But his magic ran out. His journey ended on January 13, 1945, the day he introduced himself to a Soviet street patrol and asked to be taken to Red Army headquarters. He has since become a faceless, voiceless citizen of the Soviet penal system. In the Gulag Archipelago there are no heroes or villains. No prince or pauper. It is the most democratic of all societies. Everyone is an inmate.

1   The Legacy

n Sweden the name is synonymous with capitalism, power
and service. Raoul Wallenberg was born into a family of
extraordinary achievers. The Wallenbergs are, and have
been for over a century and a half, the Swedish Establishment. It was
in the middle of the nineteenth century that they began to carve out
a place for themselves as one of the most successful capitalist dynas-
ties in history, to rank alongside the Medicis, the Rothschilds and
the Rockefellers. Like those other great clans, they first gathered
power and prestige within their own societies, then cast their net
over a wider, international sea.

The wealth they amassed along the way was never displayed.
They preferred to hold it in reserve, quietly, unostentatiously. The
last thing the Wallenbergs wished for was the envy or resentment
of their peers. Their strait-laced Lutheranism frowned on a splashy
show of property and possessions. "To be, and not to seem" is the
family motto. For the past five generations they have never really
departed from its message.

A bishop named Marcus really started it all. This patriarch was
more interested in Homer and the classics than in making money,
but his curiosity about the world beyond his provincial capital of
Stockholm encouraged his son André Oscar to sail to the New
World. There the young Wallenberg found a country bursting at
the seams with freshly tapped vitality and newly released capital.
It was the eve of the Industrial Revolution. André Oscar Wallenberg was impressed by the crucial role America's banks were playing in the transformation of this rough, sprawling former colony
into a modern industrial power. He took the lesson home to Stockholm.

Shortly after his return, Wallenberg founded Stockholms Enskilda Bank. Today, merged into Skandinaviska Enskilda, it is one of the country's largest and most respected banks. This was the beginning of the family's intimate involvement in their country's capitalist expansion. From shipping to railroads, tobacco and electronics, the Wallenbergs began stitching together their empire, which today embraces fifty thriving enterprises. As Sweden rode the crest of the Industrial Revolution, so did the Wallenberg family fortunes.

The old bishop saw nothing wrong with that. Not as long as his sons and their own children, who would carry on after him, remembered the country whose energy and resources had allowed them to prosper. Ultimately, when the Wallenberg family fortunes were safely sheltered, the progeny were expected to serve Svea Rike, the Swedish kingdom. This they have done with distinction for over a century. With one cautious hand on the tiller of their empire, the Wallenbergs have been bishops, diplomats, counselors to their king and ambassadors-at-large for their prime minister. They made certain Sweden steered a moderate and neutral course. That was good for Sweden and certainly healthy for the Wallenbergs.

If today helicopters collect young Wallenbergs to transport them from boarding schools to their elders' retreats on the French Riviera, they no longer feel shy about this show of wealth and privilege. When the country needed them, the Wallenbergs were ready to serve. Anyway, Marcus, the current head of the family, who was named after the founding father of the dynasty, still drives his own Saab to work, to prove both to himself and his peers that the family motto is alive and well.

The banker André Oscar laid the foundations for today's dynasty. His two sober, purposeful wives gave birth to a total of twenty children. Banking, diplomacy and the church were all equally well served by the next two generations of Wallenbergs. The Wallenberg women were not content to be mere breeders of perfect upper-middle-class children. Like the female members of other families in their social class, they played music and painted. Only these ladies did both extremely well. Wallenbergs are not supposed to do anything by halves. Some of the landscapes and portraits these ladies produced would not look out of place in an art gallery.

For generations the Wallenbergs have been seafaring people, with an eye on the rest of the world and an immense curiosity about how other people manage their affairs. Just as the Wallenberg family insists on discretion and reserve, so the family demands of its members an internationalism that stretches far beyond the European mainland.

When the children are gathered together for family reunions at one of several Wallenberg mansions, they are expected to show a command of several languages and cultures. The Wallenbergs are not meant to see the world as spectators. They have always been expected to participate, to learn to live in discomfort if necessary and then to return to Stockholm armed with the newfound knowledge. The price of privilege is hard work.

One of André Oscar's sons, the bulky-framed, bearded Knut Agathon Wallenberg, became Sweden's Foreign Minister during World War I. He already had an astonishing record in business and diplomacy behind him. "K.A.," as he was known, steered his country between the two hostile powers and helped it to emerge in remarkable financial health at the end of those cataclysmic years. The family's own wealth, managed by K.A.'s brothers, kept in step with the country's sturdy finances.

André Oscar, the patriarch whose face of pale leather stares down at his large brood at family gatherings, would be pleased at the Wallenbergs' contemporary image. Their own countrymen know precious little about the famous family's private life. Depending on a Swede's own politics, he utters the Wallenberg name with either reverence or distaste. No Swede is oblivious to the special role the family continues to play in shaping modern Swedish society. The Wallenbergs are inextricably entwined with the transformation of Stockholm into a graceful, cosmopolitan city, combining the colors of Central Europe with the architectural elegance of the West.

Nor are Swedes remotely aware of how the Wallenbergs live, where their homes are, or who designs the women's wardrobes or coiffes their prematurely gray heads. No sign marks the imposing Renaissance fortress on Stockholm's prestigious Kungsträdgårdsgatan, the headquarters of Skandinaviska Enskilda Banken, the family's flagship enterprise. They do know that when Marcus, or before him his brother, Jacob, makes a statement about Sweden's role in the world, he is reflecting the view of both the Crown and the Cabinet. It is impossible to imagine either of those two institutions ignoring the advice or the interests of this influential family.

Today it is no longer the bishop or the foreign minister or the banker who is most respected by his countrymen. The Wallenberg who is best known and most admired in this family of remarkable characters is one who was never fully accepted into their ranks. Raoul Wallenberg did not have the total support of his powerful relatives in his early professional struggles. More tragically, the Wallenbergs failed to play a vital, positive role in the life of their cousin, the Soviet captive. They have done precious little to win his freedom.

When, in 1947, President Harry Truman offered Marcus Wallenberg his personal help in extricating Raoul from Soviet custody, the elder Wallenberg thanked the American but declined the offer. "Raoul," he told Truman, "is probably dead by now." There is no record of Marcus Wallenberg ever urging his old friend Finnish President Urho Kekkonen, a confidant of Leonid I. Brezhnev, to intervene on Raoul's behalf. Is it pure pragmatism on the part of a family that owes its name and fortune to practical, profitable decisions and to neutrality to have literally written off one of its own members? The Soviets are important Wallenberg trade partners. But the West is even more important to the family. The fact remains that outside Raoul's immediate family—his mother, his stepfather, half-brother and half-sister, the dynasty has a record of callous indifference to his fate.

Raoul's mother, Maj, the great-granddaughter of a highly successful German Jewish jeweler who emigrated to Sweden, never recovered from her son's imprisonment. Though she was blessed with a devoted husband and two talented, loving children, Raoul, her firstborn, was never out of her thoughts. Toward the end of her life, Stockholm society avoided this sad woman. Her almost obsessive preoccupation with her missing son made many uncomfortable. Maj likened herself to a handicapped person. "People are afraid to talk to me about Raoul," she used to say, "but they are also afraid not to talk to me about the one subject which I live for. So, really, it's much easier for them just to avoid me." Until the very end she never stopped fighting to get him free. She never hesitated to touch the powerful, to write letters to Brezhnev or

Kissinger, a mother who wanted to hold her son in her arms one more time. But the letters of an old lady are easy to ignore.

She and her husband died within just a few days of each other in 1979. They were both in their eighties, weary of the fruitless campaign to jar the world from its apathy, tired of life without Raoul.

The recent family elder, Jacob Wallenberg, who died the following year, attended the funeral of Raoul's mother and stepfather. The prisoner's childhood hero and godfather spent an unusually long time taking his leave of the old couples' twin coffins. Some who were present felt Jacob was apologizing to them for his many years of indifference.

In 1976 Simon Wiesenthal, the Nazi hunter who led Adolf Eichmann to his final judgment in Jerusalem, traveled to Stockholm. Years before, he had joined Raoul's mother's campaign to free her son. "If you could find Eichmann," she had written to Wiesenthal, "surely you could locate my son." He agreed to try, and has been devoted to the cause ever since. So, when he went to Stockholm he wanted to form a high-powered international commission which, under one letterhead, would take over the mother's lonely, fruitless efforts. Wiesenthal telephoned Marcus Wallenberg, the other head of the family, and an obvious choice to lead the influential commission. Wallenberg asked Wiesenthal to send him a memo on the subject, before he would give an answer. Wiesenthal drafted a long, carefully composed proposal. He already had several Nobel Prize-winners as volunteers to head a Free Raoul Wallenberg Committee. His memo to Marcus Wallenberg was never answered. Simon Wiesenthal abandoned the idea of the commission.

If the Wallenbergs' prestige and influence have not done the prisoner much good, the name may in fact have done him harm. During the war Marcus, who lived in London, and Jacob, in Stockholm, were the major Western contact points for the German anti-Nazi underground. Through their vast global business connections the Wallenberg brothers had formed a close friendship with Karl Goerdeler, the mayor of Leipzig. This headstrong, upright conservative was among the first German public figures to break with the Nazis. He became disenchanted with them in 1936, when their anti-Semitism began to show the first signs of the barbaric form it would eventually assume.

Goerdeler then started a rather futile campaign to arouse the Western powers to the danger of Hitler's anti-Semitism to all, not just to Germans. Dashing between European capitals, he was almost universally greeted with bland indifference. But Goerdeler never abandoned the idea of ridding the world of Hitler. By 1942 he had a plan. He could still travel, so he went to see his powerful friend Jacob Wallenberg in Stockholm and asked him to act as liaison between the underground and Winston Churchill. Goerdeler and his fellow conspirators needed advance assurance from the Allies that they would make peace with Germany if Hitler was overthrown. The assurance was not forthcoming, but even so, by February the following year Goerdeler and his companions were ready to unleash Operation Flash, their carefully planned coup against Hitler.

Goerdeler again traveled north to see Wallenberg and gave his friend precise details of the plot. The conspirators were pinning their hopes on Hitler's disillusioned generals to help topple the Führer. Wallenberg made sure the Allies had advance notice. But the Goerdeler plan, like several others, was unmasked by infiltrators inside the conspiracy. Hitler took his bloody revenge and put a price of one million reichsmarks on Goerdeler's head. The former mayor of Leipzig assumed a new name and identity and waited for the war to end. He changed residences every few days. He trusted no one.

One day an old family friend spotted the bearded, run-down fugitive sitting in a small roadside tavern. The Gestapo arrived before Goerdeler had finished his meal. A People's Court sentenced Goerdeler to death in September 1944. The intervention of Heinrich Himmler kept the prisoner alive until the last days of the war. Himmler himself was looking for a way to get off the sinking Nazi ship in those days. He had hoped to use Goerdeler's contacts with the West, and particularly with the Wallenbergs, to reach some kind of eleventh-hour unconditional-peace agreement. The Reichsführer SS had even made his own overtures to the Wallenbergs. The Allies showed no interest in striking a deal of any sort with representatives of a country that was fast crumbling.

On February 2, 1945, three months before the official end of the war, Himmler gave the order to have Karl Goerdeler executed.

There is little doubt that SMERSH, the energetic Soviet counter-intelligence service, followed these attempts at a separate peace between the Allies and the Third Reich. They were, in fact, one of the main reasons for Stalin's paranoia toward his allies at war's end: he feared that the Anglo-Americans would leave him out in the cold and arrange their own armistice with the Germans.

When Raoul Wallenberg was led to his first interrogation by the NKVD (the predecessor of the KGB), the plain-clothes major he faced greeted him with an ironic expression. "Ah yes, Wallenberg. That capitalist family is well known to us."

2   The Youth

R aoul Wallenberg Sr., grandson of the patriarch André Oscar and the son of one of Sweden's most distinguished ambassadors, was young, gifted and in love. That he was blessed with wealth and good looks did not hurt. He followed the tradition of service in the Royal Navy before marrying one of Stockholm's prettiest girls.

Raoul was only twenty-one when his ship was struck by an epidemic off the French port of Cherbourg. Wallenberg's commanding officer wrote the young man's parents of "the exceptional courage and sangfroid" with which Raoul cared for his stricken shipmates. Using his fluent French to interpret for the medics that had come on board, Raoul often kept vigil through the night at the bedside of his ill comrades, and displayed "a rare energy." Thirty-five years later, precisely the same adjectives would be used to describe his own son combating an even deadlier epidemic. But Raoul Wallenberg Sr. would not be alive to hear those words, or even to see the birth of his first son.

Two years after the Cherbourg episode, the naval officer with the brilliant future ahead of him finally married his beloved Maj Wising. She was the daughter of a celebrated neurologist and had gone to school with her fiancé's cousins. The best of Stockholm society toasted the young couple at the elegant Grand Hotel. The union was considered acceptable, if not brilliant, by the exigent Wallenbergs. It was a genuine love match between the twenty-one-year-old Maj and her Raoul. The naval officer with the far-off, dreamy expression had inherited much of his grandmother's artistic ability—that was clear from the graceful, Doric-columned family tomb which he designed shortly after the wedding. It was a prophetic work. Two months later a tumor in his abdomen was diagnosed as malignant. Raoul Wallenberg, aged twenty-three, died of cancer three months before the birth of his son.

For the young, newly married Maj, her confinement was a time of deep gloom, a feeling that life would hold nothing more for her. It had all happened so quickly. The wedding, her darling Raoul's illness and death, and now the baby. On black-bordered stationery the young widow wrote her mother, "I feel an enormous emptiness inside," an emptiness not filled by the daily growing child she was carrying. "I don't know if I will be competent to raise this child," she confessed to her mother.

On August 4, 1912, Raoul Gustaf Wallenberg came into the world without much struggle. He was born in the Victorian comfort of his maternal grandparents' summer home in Kapptsta, in the archipelago outside Stockholm. The house is long gone, mysteriously burned down sometime in the thirties. Only the foundation is left, overgrown with moss and lush white anemones. The view from the island, with a minuscule Stockholm off in the distance, is nearly unspoiled and hypnotically calm. The rough, sloping terrain has not changed much since the little boy stumbled among the beech trees, nearly seventy years ago.

Little Raoul, as the child was called, loved this bit of land at the mouth of the Baltic. It was here that his mother returned to life, transformed by the birth of the son she had not been sure she wanted to bear alone. "I have never known such happiness could exist," the new mother wrote her own mother, no longer on black-edged stationery. The little boy did not have his father's dreamy, far-off look. The boy's eyes seemed to fix on every detail of the world around him.

It did not take the child long to discover his special role in his widowed mother's life. "He is already taking care of me," young Maj wrote her mother-in-law before the boy was even walking. There were two women now looking after Raoul: his grandmother had also recently been widowed. Mother and daughter shared the clapboard gingerbread house, and the cherished infant.

Maj turned out to have very firm views about motherhood. She proved herself more than equal to the task. Her son would not be spoiled, despite the constant presence of two adoring women and devoted governesses. He must always sleep with his window open. He would love the outdoors, feel comfortable in the woods, alone

or in company. Maj Wallenberg found amazing resources in herself for raising this half orphan. She was convinced from the start
that an extraordinary fate was operating around her son, born so
quickly after the death of her beloved husband. She drew on reserves of energy, intelligence and fantasy even she did not know
she possessed. Raoul responded to all of this love and imagination,
and reinforced Maj's conviction that he was special. Her greatest
gift to him was a totally unconfining love, a love which encouraged him to take his first hesitant steps away from her and from the
warm, dappled world of Kapptsta.

Maj wanted her little boy to know what it meant to be a Wallenberg. Raoul's paternal grandfather offered to take the child's education in his hands. This imposing ambassador to China, Japan and
Bulgaria was going to initiate him into the rites of the demanding
dynasty. Gustav Wallenberg found a remarkably responsive student in the child of his deceased only son. All of the hopes and
dreams he had nourished for his own son, all unrealized, he now
poured into this little boy with the unruly locks and the knowing
eyes.

Gustav, with his starched stand-up collars and rough tweeds, was
a Victorian father figure. He loved to cradle the boy in his arms
and tell him endless stories of his own grandfather the banker and
his great-grandfather the bishop, who were both welcome at the
King's table. The little boy understood very quickly that only he
could lift the gloom that his father's death had caused to descend
on the house.

Raoul's grandfather knew very little about children. Nor did he
suffer silliness gladly. He treated his grandson as an equal. Raoul,
flattered by the consuming interest of this portly, forbidding gentleman, was determined not to disappoint him. At the age of eight
Raoul was working his way through the *Nordic Encyclopedia*. He
had reached volume "Z" by the following summer, committing
large enough chunks to memory to dazzle his gratified grandfather.
Business, banking and finance, the boy understood by now, were
all as much a part of his family life as sailing in the waters around
the archipelago or being introduced to His Majesty, King Gustav
V. So Raoul started scooping up the annual reports of the great
Swedish companies, most of them part of the Wallenberg family
empire, and literally memorizing them. His grandfather's reward

was to seek out the boy's views on a broad range of subjects, man to man.

The stories about the "Big Men," as the boy called his Wallenberg forefathers, wove their magic around him. Little Raoul liked to tell his maternal cousins, the Hagströmer boys, tales about his distinguished forefathers. They were like Vikings to him. They had discovered empires, charted unknown waters, always returned to Stockholm covered in glory. He was going to be one of them.

His closest childhood friend, Rolf Klintberg, found him different from the rest; well before Raoul was out of short pants, he seemed more purposeful than boys his own age. He did not like to waste time. Competitive sports were a waste of time. Poetry was for dreamers. Raoul liked to learn something new from everybody he met. He liked to stop construction workers on the streets of Stockholm and question them about bricklaying.

When Gustav Wallenberg took up his post as ambassador to Turkey, he sent for Raoul. The condition for the visit was: no chaperone for the eleven-year-old. Raoul was to make the long train journey from Stockholm to Istanbul on his own. Gustav Wallenberg did not tell his grandson that several train conductors had been handsomely rewarded for keeping an eye on the precocious youngster. When the train pulled into the station in Belgrade for an hour's stop, Raoul wasted no time leaping off and touring this overgrown Serbian village on foot. He barely made it back as the train was building steam, ready to pull out of the station. It had been well worth the risk. Raoul had witnessed several street demonstrations that would make interesting stories with which to regale his grandfather once the Orient Express arrived in Istanbul.

Raoul's mother had remarried by now. Fredrik von Dardel, a promising young Health Department official, would later become director of one of Stockholm's largest and most prestigious hospitals, the Karolinska. A gentle, soft-spoken man of artistic bent, he took a great interest in his stepson and, in fact, treated him like his own, even after the von Dardels' two children were born, Guy and Nina. It was Guy who one day discovered that Raoul was color-blind: the horses he had painted for a school assignment were green, while the grass below them was red. Naval service, part of the Wallenberg tradition, was thus ruled out. But the child loved to draw. No plain surface was safe from his sketches. His fascina-

tion with the way things were put together made him start thinking
of architecture as a possible career.

Raoul never learned to dance because he preferred to talk to
girls. But he had no time for small talk. Once when he returned
from an obligatory school dance Nina asked him if he had enjoyed
himself. "Yes," Raoul answered with more than the usual enthusiasm, "I met a really intelligent girl. We talked all night." Intrigued,
Nina asked what the girl had had to say for herself. "Actually, I
told her about the League of Nations, and why, as a neutral country, Sweden has a certain responsibility toward the rest of the—"
Nina cut him off with a brusque "I see." Raoul's definition of an
intelligent girl was one who knew how to listen.

Raoul liked the company of girls but he was too intense, too involved with his own formation to lose his heart easily. With his
rather full lips and strong nose, his penetrating, inquisitive eyes,
he was not really an ideal Nordic type. He knew he was different
and it did not bother him. One of his partners on the dance floor
in those days, the actress Viveca Lindfors, claims another couple
could easily have found room between her and Raoul when they
danced. "He was very shy. And very serious," she says. Raoul also
felt there would be plenty of time for females later on, when his
very special education had been completed.

He was well aware of his uncanny ability to learn languages.
Most Swedes master English in school, but when he was still a
teen-ager, Raoul spoke not only fluent English but French (a tri-
mester at the University of Poitiers took care of that) and German
(after a summer in Germany). These trips abroad, part of his
grandfather's grand scheme, had made Raoul unusually independent at an age when most boys still look to their parents to take
them by the hand. Raoul's mother never tried to hold him back.

His grandfather thought the time had come for Raoul to embark
on a different adventure. It was time for the American Experience,
yet another time-honored family tradition, going back to the patriarch André Oscar himself. The ambassador ruled out the East
Coast and the Ivy League. Harvard, Yale and Princeton smacked
too much of privilege. Raoul Wallenberg must be exposed to a
broader field. It was to be the Midwest, the University of Michigan
at Ann Arbor.

For the already well-traveled child used to a cosmopolitan Euro-

pean atmosphere, Ann Arbor was less than a compelling environment. The charms of what was then a sleepy one-cinema,
one-business university town quickly wore thin. But the work—to
get an undergraduate degree in architecture—challenged him.

That the nineteen-year-old Wallenberg was anything but a
starry-eyed idealist is clear from a paper he wrote during his first
year at the University of Michigan: "The open-mindedness of
humanity, even in our generation, is a myth. Maybe the individual
is open-minded on one question, but on this question he generally
belongs to the minority. In most other things he generally is extremely reactionary." One of Wallenberg's professors at the time,
Dr. Jean Paul Slusser, later said of him, "He was one of my
brightest and best in thirty years' experience as a professor of drawing and painting."

The most memorable part of his stay took place not in the con-
fined campus world of southern Michigan, but on the asphalt
ribbons and dirt roads which intersect the immense American landscape—a vista that spellbound the Swede. He became an avid
hitchhiker. He wrote dutifully to his grandfather about trips to the
West Coast and down to Mexico, where one of his favorite aunts
lived. "Bus and train trips are predictable," he wrote, "but hitchhiking offers the thrill of the unknown." And, added the shrewd
son of a dynasty of multimillionaires, it is cheap: "I went three
hundred miles on fifty cents." But the best part of hitchhiking, he
claimed, "is the great practice it offers one in the art of diplomacy
and negotiating. You have to be on your guard. And it brings you
into intimate contact with so many different kinds of people."

It was the summer of 1933, between semesters, and the cab of a
bumpy flatbed truck carried Raoul from Ann Arbor to Chicago
and the World's Fair. Adolf Hitler had already taken the oath of
Chancellor of the Third Reich. The Midwest was hot and dusty
and oblivious to the gathering storm a world away. The young
Swede was hungry to take on the big raw land sweeping by the
uncomfortable truck.

Once at the World's Fair, he quickly made himself known as jack
of all trades around the Swedish pavilion. All summer he washed
windows, sold souvenirs, hauled lights, equipment—at three dollars
a day. When it came time to return to Ann Arbor, Raoul was
standing on the interstate highway, looking for a lift. Night was

falling when a Chevrolet with Iowa plates pulled up. The car door swung open and a voice told him to hop in, which he did. Four men in their twenties examined both Raoul and his sturdy leather suitcase with more than casual interest. "How much is it worth to you if we take you all the way to Ann Arbor?" the driver asked Raoul.

"Nothing," the Swede answered without a moment's hesitation, "or I would have taken a bus."

Suspicious now, Raoul turned the conversation to his financial hardships. It is not easy for a foreign student in America, he told them. Jobs were scarce.

His companions were not convinced. A clumsy "breakdown" was put into motion. All four men leaped out of the Chevy and asked Raoul to lend them a hand. Raoul caught the gleam of a revolver in the palm of one of the men. "Strange," he later wrote his grandfather, "but I did not feel any fear the whole time. It was more like an adventure." This quality—not only the absence of panic but the ability to detach himself from moments of high tension and carefully observe his own behavior—was to mark Raoul's adult life.

The thugs demanded all his money. He handed them his summer's earnings. He even told them of a few dollars hidden in his suitcase, in case they decided to make a search. "When they had all my money, I decided it was their turn to be nice," he wrote. "I asked them to give me a lift as far as the main road. They let me sit next to the driver, but put my rather heavy bag on my knees to prevent me from making a move. They had become more nervous. Probably because I was so calm. I actually found the whole situation rather interesting. They probably imagined I was up to something. So, suddenly, they shoved me out of the car and into a ditch and threw my bag on top of me. I hid behind some trees in case they decided to shoot me as a farewell gesture." Raoul closed his letter home saying he had no intention of giving up hitchhiking. "In the future I'll be a bit smarter. I don't think I used good psychology . . ." But he had learned something about himself, his own reactions and those of others when confronted with the calm face of self assurance. It was a useful lesson.

The following summer he made his way to Mexico selling sketches he had made of the American countryside. In California he wrote his grandfather: "I made a point of interviewing all representatives of Swedish trade that my limited time permitted. They were all very optimistic about the future, particularly about the strength and inherent soundness of Swedish shipping. I also inquired about the prospects for an expansion of Swedish trade . . ." He was still desperately trying to impress his grandfather, to prove himself worthy of the future he knew was planned for him. For all that, Raoul also showed remarkable candor and a self-knowledge beyond his years. "I like to take it easy for a week or two," he wrote his grandfather in Istanbul, "then I suddenly pull myself together and study all night. It gives me a little more thrill than just keeping to my everyday routine."

After a four-year absence, Raoul returned to Sweden in 1935, with an honors B.A. in architecture and a fresh dose of self-confidence. He had tackled an entirely different culture and fared exceptionally well. At this point he had already tested himself in ways his friends had not. He had managed without his family and all that was familiar for close to four years. He knew he had a certain way with people. He could take their measure and play on their strengths and weaknesses. He told his sister that he loved to negotiate and felt he had a special flair for it. His greatest enjoyment, he told her, was bringing people around to his way of thinking by subtle and artless dialogue. The young Wallenberg was a passionate student of the human psyche.

Raoul was now also far less intense, seemed less earnest than the anxious-to-please and eager-to-impress young man he had been. A sharp wit and an uncanny talent for imitating others surprised and amused his more conventional family. He was still every bit the passionate conversationalist. He was still drawn to intelligent, serious-minded women, the good listeners! Raoul did not bother masking his boundless energy and ambition. He waited impatiently for the next step in his grandfather's carefully choreographed preparation on the road to becoming one of the "Big Men."

Before the three-week cruise that would take him to Cape Town, South Africa and a banking apprenticeship, Raoul made his first mark on Stockholm. He won second prize in an architectural competition to rehabilitate a seedy, abandoned wharf near the Royal Palace. Raoul's design included an outdoor swimming pool and a public park along the embankment. Today the area looks very

much like his own vision of it. Wallenberg's now famous photograph, the intense young man with the burning eyes and the still
full head of hair, appeared for the first time in the Swedish press
on the occasion of his award-winning design.

In Cape Town, under the tutelage of a Wallenberg family
banker, Raoul discovered that this was not his calling. His greatest
hero, his uncle and godfather, Jacob Wallenberg, was the head
of the family's banking empire. Raoul had nurtured hopes of following the elder Wallenberg's footsteps. Now he wrote home to his
grandfather: "Bankers have to say 'No' too often. I think I am a
more positive person than Uncle Jacob." He had also put architecture aside for the time being. The world recession and the
growing tension throughout Europe made architecture, in even a
neutral country, a difficult field for a young man to enter. His
grandfather thought Raoul needed to be exposed to different worlds
before he made his final choice.

In a letter to a friend his grandfather wrote: "First and foremost, I wanted to make a man of him, to give him a chance to see
the world and through mixing with foreigners give him what most
Swedes lack: an international outlook . . . Raoul is a man. He
has seen much of the globe and has come into contact with people
of all kinds."

After six months in South Africa, the young man was dispatched
to Palestine. Here in the teeming harbor of Haifa, part of the
British Mandate, a Jewish banker friend of Gustav Wallenberg was
manager of a Dutch enterprise. Raoul was to be his apprentice.
The grandfather had still not abandoned hope that Raoul's future
was somewhere in the family's financial empire.

For Raoul Wallenberg, Haifa in 1936 turned out to be an apprenticeship of a different sort. Jews, a short time ago the backbone
of the prosperous and respected middle class of Berlin, Stuttgart
or Hamburg, reduced to ragged beggars by the Nuremberg Laws,
were streaming to Palestine. They were looking for asylum and an
opportunity to make over their shattered lives. Raoul met many of
them through his Dutch mentor and in the kosher boardinghouse
where he was a lodger. He listened to their stories of how they had
gradually been stripped of all rights and turned into non-people,
allowed to exist only at the grace of the Reich.

It was Wallenberg's first exposure to the irrational and poisonous germ of anti-Semitism. Through these refugees he heard about mob rule in the streets of a once civilized country. He sat spellbound listening to stories of upright German citizens, their arms folded, observing the brutalization of their fellow countrymen. Though religion was an entirely private matter with Raoul Wallenberg, he had been reading the Bible before he took on the *Nordic Encyclopedia*. He was a man with closely guarded emotions. The impression this humbled segment of humanity made on him was to be permanent.

He had reached the limit of his appetite for apprenticeship and was restless now for something more substantial, something with a future. "I just don't see what all of this is leading to," he confided to his grandfather, who promised to meet with him at the end of his term in Haifa. But Gustav Wallenberg's health was rapidly declining. He could no longer manage the rigorous journey from Turkey, his final diplomatic post, to Stockholm. The ambassador invited his grandson to join him in his convalescent home in the South of France. It was the last time Raoul would see the ailing ambassador. The devoted grandfather, his surrogate father, who was going to open so many doors for his bright grandson, died suddenly in the spring of 1937. Once again this perfect product of an aged diplomat's carefully crafted formation was alone. In a society that still required sponsors, Raoul Wallenberg, groomed for success, had none.

The young man was about to learn something significant about the Wallenbergs: each branch of the family tree nurtures only its own offspring. Raoul, without a father and now without an influential grandfather standing behind him, found himself a well-liked and admired cousin. One of many. Jacob, his godfather, and Marcus, his uncle, both first cousins of his father, held the keys to the kingdom of power. They were extremely cautious about distributing copies of those keys. Jacob gave Raoul temporary assignments in his bank, but no serious offer was made. One of Jacob's vast multitude of connections finally produced a promising contact for the impatient youth. His name was Kálmán Lauer, a Hungarian businessman.

Lauer ran a small operation with the impressive title of Mellaneuropeiska Handelsaktiebolaget, or the Central European Trading Company, Inc. Known familiarly as Meropa, it was a Stockholm-based export-import firm, trading between Sweden and Central Europe. The bulk of Lauer's dealings in specialty foods was with Hungary, and as a Jew, traveling there was becoming a dangerous proposition for him: Hungary, which had become Hitler's ally in 1941, had recently passed her own anti-Semitic laws. Now, Lauer, whose two-room office was on the same block as one of the Wallenberg family mansions, had already heard about the gifted young linguist with the impressive name who was looking for a job. Raoul accepted Lauer's proposal that he take over the firm's foreign division.

Transshipping grain, poultry and goose-liver pâté from Hungary to Sweden did not completely absorb the energetic young man. The trips he made in place of Lauer were a great diversion for him. In Hungary's capital he found an urbane and stimulating environment. The city's passion for conversation and its irreverent humor matched his own. He made friends without trouble and started picking up the strange Magyar language.

When he was home, life in Stockholm was pleasant. Wallenberg had inherited his grandfather's exceptionally fine collection of wines, which he dispensed freely at small dinner parties in his bachelor apartment. He had a pretty girl, named Jeanette von Heidenstam, twelve years his junior, who liked to keep him company whenever he was in Stockholm. But his life was not focused. He knew there was something missing.

There was no special relationship between Raoul and the man with whom he shared these close quarters. Lauer was, above all, a businessman. Short, squat, with a round face and a flaring temper, Lauer's single-minded obsession was a balanced book. Fundamentally, Lauer and Wallenberg had little in common. Yet this relationship would prove to be fateful.

An exceptionally gifted young man, prepared from infancy for a special future, was straining now to fulfill his early promise. He had to do it on his own. Yet Sweden was not a place where the young and inexperienced could leapfrog into positions of responsibility, not without the determined support of the Establishment. Wallenberg now discovered he would have to prove himself further to open the doors his grandfather was supposed to have opened for him. He was self-confident, ambitious, energetic and a shrewd student of human nature. He was not going to stay Kálmán Lauer's troubleshooter for long. He was on the threshold of wealth, power and prestige. Wallenberg was convinced he belonged inside the door.

3   The Slow Awakening

O n January 20, 1942, the members of the Nazi high command gathered for lunch at a stately villa in the Berlin suburb of Wannsee. Over brandy and cigars the man known as the "Blond Beast," SS General Reinhard Heydrich, pushed his leather chair back from the table and called the attention of his colleagues to the purpose of the luncheon. Heydrich, haunted by rumors of his own Jewish ancestry, was anxious to demonstrate his zeal in solving once and for all the "Jewish problem." Now he began to outline what before had only been whispered: the Final Solution. His energetic assistant, SS Lieutenant Colonel Adolf Eichmann, had prepared the paperwork for the high level meeting. Eichmann sat next to Heydrich and quietly took notes.

In the bloodless vocabulary of Nazism, Heydrich laid out the new policy. Emigration of Jews was no longer feasible. Evacuation to the East would henceforth be put in effect. Europe was to be "combed from west to east" for Jews. They would be cleared "group by group," to be transported ever farther east. No one who sat around the polished mahogany table of the Wannsee villa dining room had any doubts about the real meaning of this "resettlement" project. It was an ambitious plan. Millions of human beings had to be traced, rounded up, transported and "resettled," a pale word meaning "exterminated."

The guests at Heydrich's lunch were undaunted by the task. The machinery of genocide had already been set in motion. Hydrogen and cyanide had been combined to form the amethyst-blue crystal of Zyklon B, a powerful disinfectant that was even more efficient in wiping out human beings than killing germs. The *Einsatzgruppen,* special SS units charged with rounding up Jews and taking them to the killing camps, were ready to go. Less than two months later they earned the admiration of the Führer when the first party of Jews from the Lublin ghetto in eastern Poland reached Auschwitz with unexpected speed. It would be another year before engineer Pruefer, of the I. A. Topf & Sons construction firm of Erfurt, finished the more efficient and spacious crematoria to facilitate maximum usage of Auschwitz.

While Pruefer was putting the final touches on his work, in the spring of 1943, a meeting in a location even more pleasant than Wannsee was under way. The British Crown Colony of Bermuda was the setting chosen by delegates from London and Washington for their own conference on the Jewish Problem. By now Jews from France, Belgium, Holland and Norway were no longer part of the problem. They had already been sealed into railroad cars whose meaning was death. The gentlemen from the State Department and Whitehall came to search for a way to rescue from the Nazi genocide those still left of Europe's Jewish population.

For the past year and a half the White House and Downing Street had known of the plan to exterminate the Jews of Europe. But it was a complicated problem: saving lives while waging war. Some thought rescue was not, in fact, compatible with the Allies' principal war aims. There was so much red tape involved, so many different voices suggesting different solutions. Mostly, objections were raised to those rescue plans already put forward. The delegates to the Bermuda Conference, with their bulging briefcases and their lightweight suits, did not bring the same passion to their task that the smartly uniformed Nazi high command, sitting around the Wannsee conference table, had brought to theirs. The Allies' commitment to save lives was absurdly outstripped by the Nazis' zeal to kill.

Nothing really substantial was agreed on in Bermuda. It marked the fifth year of fruitless search by the advocates of rescue. The only difference this April was that no one could have any illusions left about Nazi intentions. The London *Observer*'s editorial reported from Bermuda:

> Here are the leisurely beach hotels of the Atlantic luxury island where well dressed gentlemen assemble to assure each other in the best Geneva fashion that really nothing much

can be done. The opening speeches of the conference have been widely noted in this country, and noted with dismay and anger. We have been told this problem is beyond the resources of Britain and America combined . . . if they cannot help, who can? What is so terrible about these speeches is not only their utter insensitiveness to human suffering. It is the implied readiness of the two greatest powers on earth to humiliate themselves, to declare themselves bankrupt and impotent, in order to evade the slight discomfort of charity . . .

For the past one and a half years since America joined the war effort, the State Department's motto had been "Rescue through victory." The faster we win this war, the sooner we can help these people, they told their colleagues from London. It would be criminal to divert our resources from the war effort into something as uncertain as a refugee rescue mission.

Breckenridge Long, the Assistant Secretary of State in charge of the refugee question, was proud that the U.S. immigration quotas had been scrupulously upheld, in spite of growing pressures to bend them. But, in fact, between 1933 and 1943 there were 1.2 million unfilled places left on America's immigration-quota list. The Depression and unemployment seemed problems of far greater gravity than the plight of strange people in remote corners of Europe. Isolationism and political quick fixes superseded America's traditional generosity toward the oppressed and the persecuted.

It was also a case of the wrong man in the wrong job. Breckenridge Long, a political backer of President Franklin Delano Roosevelt, was less than enthusiastic about his current political appointment. He had much preferred his previous post as ambassador to Italy. From there he wrote: "Mussolini is a most remarkable man. He is surrounded by interesting people. And they are doing a unique job in an original manner. I am enjoying it all." Earlier this Southern aristocrat of courtly charm had penned this impression upon reading Hitler's *Mein Kampf:* "It is an eloquent opposition to Jewry and the Jews as exponents of Communism and chaos." Under Long's leadership the State Department actually suppressed information about the Nazis' precise scenario for genocide.

By 1943 Long's views on Hitler and Mussolini had altered significantly, but by then he and the entire half-hearted rescue mission had frozen into inaction, having barricaded themselves behind a long list of bureaucratic hurdles. Now it was no longer a problem how to deal with refugees. The opportunity to offer asylum to Jews hoping to emigrate from the Reich had been missed. The question was now far more complicated, and far more urgent.

In the late thirties and early forties, when there was still talk in Washington and London about who could take how many Jews, the Jews themselves were part of the stumbling block. German Jews, the first to feel the effects of Hitler's vision of a *judenfrei* Europe, were among the last to believe his ravings. They were patriotic Germans, particularly reluctant to give up their roots. By the time there was little room for doubt, by the time they finally realized this was not a temporary aberration, they had already been marked, their homes transformed into way stations to death. The Jews of Eastern Europe would have been more willing to accept the offer of asylum had it been forthcoming.

The British kept a cautious lid on Jewish immigration to Palestine, their Mandate. They did not wish to tip the delicate Arab-Israeli balance in their territory. Between 1939 and 1944 they allowed only 75,000 Jews to settle in Palestine. Other schemes, involving Mindanao in the Philippines and Madagascar off the east African coast, had been found lacking in some way. The vast majority of Jewish refugees were over forty, and the countries with land to spare wanted strapping young pioneers. Canada, Uruguay, Colombia and Venezuela were all looking for agricultural migrants. Australia declined to take in Jews, since "we have no real racial problem. We are not desirous of importing one."

When Neville Chamberlain suggested Tanganyika, a former German colony, to Rabbi Stephen Wise, the head of the American Jewish Congress, the rabbi answered, "I would rather have my fellow Jews die in Germany than live somehow, anyhow, in the lands which bear the imprint of yesterday's occupation by Germany in lands which may tomorrow be yielded back to Germany."

The American Jewish community itself failed to mobilize its vast resources for the rescue of its brethren until much too late in the day. American Zionists rejected resettlement anywhere but in Palestine. Jewish migration anywhere else in the underdeveloped world, they claimed, would betray the dream of Jerusalem. American Jewry could not unite behind a single approach to a growing crisis: the American Jewish Congress advocated a militant posture, while the American Jewish Committee believed in watchful waiting. Time was on the killers' side.

Those American Jews, the assimilated and successful, who could have done most to lead the country out of its inertia, often opted to keep their heads down and do nothing. Their view was that they were Americans first and Jews second. Walter Lippmann, the distinguished columnist of German Jewish origin, was among those who adopted a low profile and maintained a remarkably detached view of the plight of European Jews. In 1933, following a rampage of Jewish book burning by the Nazis, Lippmann wrote: "Only two things keep the Nazis in check: The French Army and the persecution of Jews." His implication was that the repression of Jews diverted the Nazis from conquering the rest of Europe. Lippmann was proven wrong both in his high estimate of the French army and in Hitler's inability to wage war and carry out pogroms at the same time. In a later column Lippmann said it was "as unfair to judge the German people by the Nazis as it was to judge Protestants by the behavior of the Ku Klux Klan or Jews based on the actions of the parvenues."

Lippmann, like many others, feared an influx of East European Jews who would not easily blend into the muted fabric of America's culture. American policy reflected this fear. During the crucial early years of Hitler's rule, American consular officials in Europe relentlessly pressed Jewish visa-applicants for proper documents. They could not have been ignorant of the fact that only Nazi authorities could provide these documents. In 1939 New York Senator Robert Wagner introduced a bill to allow 200,000 German Jewish children to enter above the immigration quota. President Roosevelt did not put the weight of his office behind the bill, which died in committee.

It is a matter of speculation as to how much of the Holocaust could have been averted had the rest of the world taken up the Nazis' early attempt to force the Jews to flee. The point is that the world did not respond. Wannsee succeeded; Bermuda failed.

Breckenridge Long's increasingly lame leadership finally brought Henry Morgenthau, Jr., into the refugee struggle. Morgenthau,

FDR's Treasury Secretary, was the son of a distinguished Jewish family. He was not normally interested in Jewish causes; religion was a private matter as far as he was concerned. By the end of 1943 he drafted a memo for his President. "The rescue of Jews," he wrote, "is a trust too great to remain in the hands of men indifferent, callous and, perhaps, hostile." Morgenthau offered to take over the job Long performed so indifferently.

At the same time Rabbi Stephen Wise, a shrewd politician and a practiced student of FDR's sometimes ambiguous motives, started his own campaign. For too long, Wise had missed an opportunity to exert pressure on Roosevelt by giving him and the New Deal almost unconditional support. Now he warned the President that American Jews could no longer abide the massacre of their fellow Jews while the White House ducked behind excuses.

Wise proposed a daring plan: bomb Auschwitz. Aerial reconnaissance photos showed clearly the location of the gas chambers. The low, flat building with the smoke stacks must be the crematoria. For the first time the Allies had air superiority. Their Flying Fortresses sat on Italian airstrips within easy distance of the gas chambers. Knock out the rail lines leading to the camp, the rabbi urged, and you can still save the last Jewish community left in Europe to save: the Jews of Hungary. The President listened intently but did not commit himself. He passed the proposal on to his War Department. The reply from Assistant Secretary of the Army John J. McCloy was swift:

> After a study it is clear that such an operation could be executed only by the diversion of considerable air support essential to the success of our forces now engaged in decisive operations elsewhere . . . there has been considerable opinion to the effect that such an effort, even if practicable, would provoke more vindictive action by the Germans.

One is hard pressed to fathom what the Army imagined could be "more vindictive" than Auschwitz. With that, the proposal died.

In London, Zionist representatives Dr. Chaim Weizmann and Moshe Shertok faced the same uphill struggle to get action through their Jewish Agency for Palestine. Dr. Weizmann called on Foreign Secretary Anthony Eden at Whitehall and presented him with a concise, six-paragraph proposal. The third paragraph recommended that "a stern warning to Hungarian officials, railwaymen and the population in general be published and broadcast, to the effect that anyone convicted of having taken part in the rounding up, deportation and extermination of Jews will be considered a war criminal and treated accordingly." The fourth was quite provocative: that Stalin should be approached to "issue a similar warning in Hungary on the part of the Soviet Union." But the final Jewish Agency suggestion was the crucial one: bomb the railway line from Budapest to Auschwitz.

Dr. Weizmann and Shertok were persuasive, and Eden was won over. After years of inertia he, too, felt that drastic measures were required. He quickly drafted a memo for Prime Minister Winston Churchill. Something must be done, he wrote, "to stop the operation of the death camps." He related to Churchill the proposal that both the railway lines to the camps and the camps themselves be bombed. "I am in favour," he added, "of acting on both suggestions."

No sooner did Churchill receive Eden's memo than he sent off one of his own. He added his support both for the bombing proposals and for the appeal to Stalin. He advised Eden not even to raise the matter with the rest of the Cabinet. "You and I are in agreement," Churchill wrote. "By all means bring it up if you wish to, but I do not think it necessary."

Eden sent a memo to the Secretary of State for Air, Sir Archibald Sinclair, outlining Dr. Weizmann's proposals for the bombing of Auschwitz. "Could you let me know," Eden asked Sinclair, "the feasibility of these proposals? I very much hope that it will be possible to do something. I have the authority of the Prime Minister to say that he agrees." It had taken Weizmann twenty-four hours to mobilize Eden and Churchill. But it was now July 1944, and 400,000 Hungarians had already been dispatched to the death camps.

One week later, on July 15, the Secretary of State for Air replied to Eden's inquiry:

> Bombing the plant [Auschwitz] is out of the bounds of possibility . . . because the distance is too great for the attack to be carried out at night. It might be carried out by the Americans by daylight, but it would be a costly and hazardous

operation. It might be ineffective and even if the plant were destroyed I am not sure that it would really help the victims.

Eden was disturbed by the reply. In his private papers he noted: "Characteristically unhelpful letter." Commenting on Sinclair's conclusion that even if Auschwitz was bombed, it might not help the victims, Eden added: "He wasn't asked his opinion of this. He was asked to act."

But the British, like the American military, did not seem to take kindly to civilian suggestions. The military's argument—that Auschwitz was too far away for the Allied bombers or represented too great a diversion of resource—proved to be patently untrue. In August, U.S. Air Force bombers left Britain on a special mission to Poland. They reported "good results and some losses" in their bombing mission of the Trzebinia oil refineries, some thirteen miles northeast of Auschwitz. Two days later, flying out of their base in Foggia, Italy, a cluster of U.S. aircraft passed even closer to Auschwitz. This time their mission was humanitarian. The planes, which dropped desperately needed supplies to the starving people of Warsaw, were manned by volunteers who had accepted the risk of flying beyond their normal range. Of a total of 181 aircraft, only 31 did not return safely.

Other such Anglo-American raids deep into the territory of the Reich followed. A synthetic oil and rubber plant at Monowitz, five miles east of Auschwitz, was the next target. The factory used 30,000 slave laborers from among the large pool available at Auschwitz-Birkenau. Among those trapped inside the Monowitz plant, when the Allied raid began, was Shalom Lindenbaum. "We ceased to work," Lindenbaum later recalled, "and the German soldiers and civilians ran to the shelters. Most of us didn't. So probably we expressed our superiority feeling, and a kind of revenge. This happy feeling didn't change after the Americans began to bomb, and obviously we had casualties, wounded and dead. How beautiful it was to see squadron after squadron burst from the sky, drop bombs, destroy the buildings and also kill members of the *Herrenvolk*."

This "happy feeling" was not shared by the inmates of Auschwitz. Allied bombers continued to pass over their heads, but they never released their cargo on the gas chambers or the crematoria.

The planes were always due for other destinations. Hugo Gryn was a fifteen-year-old Hungarian boy who kept his eyes on the blue summer sky waiting for the bombers. "One of the most painful aspects of being in the camp," he said, "was the sensation of being totally abandoned."

But Roosevelt, suffering from a long list of maladies, from high blood pressure to congestive heart failure, had been mobilized. He gave Morgenthau's War Refugee Board the go-ahead. It was, of course, much too late. Morgenthau's effort did manage to blot a portion of the shame from Washington's war record toward the Jews.

Morgenthau chose John W. Pehle, director of the Treasury Department's Division of Foreign Funds Control, as the board's overseer. Pehle was a brilliant choice. Young, unintimidated by titled bureaucrats, he attacked the job with the appetite of a starving man faced with his first real meal. Roosevelt had originally sought a better known figure for such a key position. But Pehle's quick grasp of the problem and his organizing flair made the President forget to look elsewhere. With thirty-five bright, committed, unconventional civil servants under him, and practically unlimited funding behind him, Pehle shaped an intelligent response to the Final Solution.

Typically, Pehle was once called by the head of the State Department's Passport Division. Ruth Shipley wondered if all the people on the War Refugee Board were Americans. "Yes, of course," Pehle replied. "Why wouldn't they be?"

"Well," came her sheepish reply, "it's just that I've never read diplomatic cables like the ones your people send."

It was true. The War Refugee Board had a mandate to move fast, even at the risk of stepping on diplomatic toes. The keystone of the eleventh-hour rescue was the neutrals. Sweden, Switzerland, Turkey and Portugal still had diplomatic relations with the Nazi-occupied lands. They were now enlisted to help Washington's effort to save Jews. It was time for unorthodox measures to prolong lives until the Axis was defeated.

Among the board's first aims was to put pressure on the International Red Cross to make its own stand for captive Jews. They urged the Red Cross to demand the same rights for Jews in camps as those guaranteed POWs or interned civilians. The Red Cross had in effect accepted the Germans' own classification of Jews as "stateless," and thus without rights. Spurred on by the War Refugee Board, the performance of the International Red Cross improved immeasurably in 1944.

Europe's third largest and last surviving Jewish community was the primary target of the board's effort. The Jews of Hungary were next on the schedule for extermination. As part of Washington's new strategy, FDR personally began broadcasting special messages to the people of Hungary. The American President urged them to record evidence of Nazi atrocities. He threatened those who participated in crimes against Jews with postwar retribution. "The United States," FDR promised in the final year of the war, "would somehow find the means of support for the Jews, until the tyrant is driven from their homelands." It would be a major tragedy, FDR warned, "if these innocent people who have already survived a decade of Hitler's fury, should perish on the very eve of the triumph over the barbarians."

This spirited, if belated, message went unheard by most Hungarian Jews. By 1944 Jews no longer had the right to own radios. As for the Christian population of this demoralized country, Washington seemed extremely remote to them. Berlin drew closer every day.

4   The Right Man

I ver Olsen, the War Refugee Board's newly appointed representative in Stockholm, was a man in a hurry, but after
several weeks in the Swedish capital he had still not found
his man. The job he was trying to fill was not an easy one. By this
time, June 1944, the Wehrmacht had taken over Hungary three
months before. Eichmann and his *Einsatzkommando* were well on
their way to sweeping the countryside clear of Jews. Since the
middle of May, each day 12,000 men, women and children had
been packed into airless trains, their death sentences sealed in
with them. Rudolf Höss, commandant of Auschwitz, traveled to
Budapest to complain to Eichmann. He was threatening the
smooth-functioning crematoria with overload. Twelve thousand a
day was too great a burden. But Eichmann was also in a hurry.

Olsen, an easygoing man of Swedish background, kept running
into brick walls. There were not many Swedes interested in walking
right into the jaws of the Nazi death machine. Nor would many
suggest friends or acquaintances for the job. Olsen was too
straightforward to brighten the job description.

It was in the elevator of the eight-story building on Strandvägen
that housed both the American legation, to which he reported, and
the export-import firm known as Meropa, that Olsen first heard the
name. A short, square man in a dapper pin-striped summer suit
greeted the American with an unmistakably East European–
accented Swedish.

"Hungarian?" Olsen ventured.

"Yes, I'm Kálmán Lauer," the man answered, extending his hand.

Olsen did not let an opportunity escape. He engaged Lauer in
rapid conversation and got to the point quickly. "I am looking for a
Swede," he told Lauer. "Someone with good nerves, good language

ability. He'll have to speak both German and some Hungarian. Someone who would be willing to go to Budapest and spend the next two months trying to save Jews from the Nazis. An independent spirit who does not need much direction. It's a big order," Olsen concluded. Lauer got off the elevator and wiped his brow; it was a hot day in June. "You probably don't know anyone who fits this bill . . ." Olsen's voice trailed off.

On the contrary. Lauer had just the candidate. He himself had been talking to Raoul Wallenberg about going to Budapest. His wife Marika's parents lived in the town of Kecskemét, in central Hungary, and lately their news had not been good. Maybe Raoul could do something for them. "Yes," Lauer told Olsen. "I know the man for the job. His name is Wallenberg."

This was the second time Lauer had proposed Wallenberg for such a mission. One month before, Lauer had suggested him to Stockholm's Chief Rabbi, Dr. Marcus Ehrenpreis. The rabbi was also anxious to mobilize some kind of Swedish rescue of Hungarian Jews. The stern former Chief Rabbi of Sofia, with his biblical beard and bushy white brows, was skeptical about Wallenberg. Raoul struck the rabbi as too young, too brash, too ready to talk about bribes and payoffs, whatever it took to save lives. That was not what the slow-moving, taciturn rabbi had in mind. A month went by. The trains had already pulled out of the northern and eastern provincial railway stations of Hungary. By the end of May, 116,000 Hungarian Jews had become part of the soil and sky of the Polish countryside near Auschwitz-Birkenau.

Olsen pushed ahead. He wanted to meet the young man with the famous name. While two men discussed his fate in a Stockholm elevator, Raoul Wallenberg was sliding on his belly over a grassy field in the Stockholm suburb of Drottningholm. Wallenberg was leading a score of men through war maneuvers that warm summer afternoon. He had for some time served as a volunteer instructor in the National Guard. Unlike a great many of his countrymen, he did not feel that Sweden's security was inviolable. Since the outbreak of the war he had spent much of his free time leading these war games. He learned to be a fair marksman, and had built up stamina from long workouts in the fresh air. It was during a cigarette break from these exercises that Raoul received a twenty-four-hour pass to return to Stockholm. It was more a command

than an option. Iver Olsen, the American War Refugee Board's
special representative in Stockholm, was summoning him to dinner.

The great rambling summer resort of Saltsjöbaden was where
the rich and well-born went to swim and sail in warm weather.
Fifty years earlier it had been developed by the Wallenberg family,
a tiny jewel in their richly encrusted crown. Three men—a tall
spare American diplomat; a short, neatly dressed Hungarian businessman; and a Swede, distinguished primarily by an expression of
great intensity—sat down to dinner in the hotel's ornate Victorian
dining room. It was seven o'clock on a gentle summer's evening.
At ten o'clock it was still light out, but the three diners were too
absorbed to appreciate the spectacular scenery. They finally left
the hotel, three lone figures, at first sunlight the next morning.

Olsen, unlike the old rabbi, did not need time to ponder the
young man's suitability for the assignment. He was struck by the
man's passion, a quality he did not frequently encounter in the
country of his ancestors. He liked the way Wallenberg's mind
worked, his unusual grasp of human nature. Olsen was not at all
put off by the young man's undisguised desire to prove himself.

Olsen had originally wanted Count Folke Bernadotte, related
to the King and President of the Swedish Red Cross, for the job.
But though he had the backing of the Swedes, the Hungarians
objected to the choice. Budapest ultimately accepted Wallenberg
because they had no alternative: accepting his appointment was the
price for the continued presence of a Hungarian chargé d'affaires
in Stockholm.

The American arranged to extend Wallenberg's twenty-four-hour
leave from the National Guard. Wallenberg, fired up by the prospect of the Budapest mission, still had to jump another hurdle. The
American minister to Sweden had to give the choice his blessings.
In the course of another long evening the portly, bow-tied Herschel
V. Johnson was also convinced. The three men spent hours discussing the war, Hungary's precarious situation as the Nazis' reluctant ally, and the plight of her Jews, more critical each day.
The Americans did not give their new recruit precise instructions
on how to proceed with his assignment. They were all on uncharted
waters. Ultimately the enterprise would have to be shaped by
Wallenberg's own instincts. For Johnson, Olsen and their Presi-

dent, the main thing was that they had found the right man. To this end, the American minister in Stockholm cabled Washington:

There is no doubt in my mind as to the sincerity of Wallenberg's purpose because I've talked to him myself. I was told by Wallenberg he wants to be able to help effectively save lives and that he was not interested in going to Budapest merely to write reports to be sent to the Foreign Office. He himself is half Jewish, incidentally.

Wallenberg, proud of his ancestry, had probably exaggerated his Jewishness. He was, in fact, only about one-sixteenth Jewish.

The President, who was finally listening to both the smooth Rabbi Wise and the War Refugee Board, told them to go ahead. Roosevelt and Pehle continued their broadcasts to German-occupied Hungary. "The Jewish community must destroy all membership lists," radios crackled over the countryside. "Avoid registering Jews. Do not keep records, addresses, baptismal papers. Jews must not agree to wearing the yellow star." These were the lessons passed on by Dutch, Polish and French Jewish communities. They were the required steps toward the Final Solution. The warning came too late.

5   The Journey Starts

R aoul Wallenberg was elated. The mission entrusted him was worthy of one of the "Big Men." This assignment was perhaps beyond even the realm of those steely-eyed elders. An ambassador, two foreign ministries and, somewhere far off, an ailing but still supremely powerful man were all confident he could do the job. It was an opportunity to break out of a routine that no longer challenged him. It was also a chance to show others what he already knew about himself: that he had energy to spare, that he had an uncanny way of sizing up a man's motives. And perhaps, just perhaps, he could save Jews from Nazis.

His adrenalin must have been racing too fast for fear to have a chance to settle in. His youth and relative inexperience were like protective shields, guarding him from an older man's sense of his own fallibility. He was a smart man who had seen slices of the globe not normally on anybody's Grand Tour—his grandfather had seen to that. He had, somehow, communicated with Serbs in Belgrade, with Turks in Istanbul, with Mexicans in Tijuana, and with Jews, reeling from their brush with the master race, in Palestine.

Wallenberg combined two qualities that often fight each other: he was a man of passionate conviction and at the same time a very practical organizer. He was enthusiastic but not wide-eyed as he approached his mission. He had some very specific views on how to pull it off. He would need diplomatic cover if he was going to be something more than another expendable do-gooder. He also needed money if he was going to bend the weak-willed and make brave men out of the meek. He did not want a bunch of pin-striped diplomats telling him he was stepping on their toes and not playing by the rules.

Wallenberg insisted on being his own man, to call his own shots and make up his own rules to a game no one had played before. Washington and the Swedish Foreign Office agreed to the young man's long list of conditions. They even agreed that it was all right for this low-ranking "diplomat" to seek an audience with the Regent of Hungary. They did not have much choice; there just weren't any others willing to walk into the Nazis' final thrust.

His last forty-eight hours in Stockholm were spent behind the closed doors of his two-room apartment on Bragevägen. He devoured all the diplomatic cable traffic between Budapest, Stockholm and Washington. He read confidential reports detailing the grim ritual of the rounding up, walling in, and the final train trip of Hungary's Jews. Not trusting the Swedish Foreign Office's diplomatic code, which he assumed the Gestapo had already cracked, Wallenberg fabricated his own. He was given copies of an exchange of telegrams between the two aging figureheads, the Regent of Hungary, Admiral Miklós Horthy, and King Gustav V of Sweden. King Gustav's, dated June 30, 1944, stated:

> Having learned of the extremely harsh measures Your Government is applying against the Jewish population of Hungary, I take the liberty of intervening personally with your Serene Highness, in beseeching you to take steps to spare the surviving members of that population. This appeal to Your Generosity of spirit is dictated by my long-held feeling of friendship toward your country and my sincere wish that her good reputation in the community of nations be preserved.

The royal plea obviously touched a chord in the frightened old Admiral. He replied immediately:

> I have received Your Majesty's appeal in the greatest spirit of understanding. I pray that Your Majesty be assured that I am doing everything in my power in the present circumstances to maintain respect for justice and humanity. Greatly sensitive to the feelings of friendship Your Majesty holds toward my country, I pray that those feelings are held for the Hungarian people during the grave trial which we are experiencing.

For all its artificial language, there was a forlorn and plaintive tone in this note. Horthy, Wallenberg surmised, was a man who badly wanted respect. The Regent was someone who may well be open to manipulation and pressure.

Dr. Ehrenpreis asked him to call. His voice deeper than his usual rich baritone, the old rabbi delivered the traditional Hebrew blessing for those about to embark on a dangerous journey. This man, who had at first been skeptical about the decision to send this privileged son of neutral Protestant Sweden, now wept. "You are in the hands of God," the rabbi told Wallenberg.

Before leaving, Wallenberg went shopping for a weapon and ended up with a secondhand turn-of-the-century model. The revolver, two knapsacks, a sport suit and a dinner suit, plus a large trench coat that was beyond repair, made up his diplomatic trunk. He also deposited the first installment of $100,000 from the American Jewish Joint Distribution Committee in his special Swedish bank account. With his pockets stuffed full of letters from members of the Swedish-Hungarian community to their relatives in Budapest, wearing hiking shoes and a windbreaker, with two bulging knapsacks, Wallenberg looked more like a Boy Scout than a diplomat. Buried deep in his rucksack was a list of corrupt Hungarian passport officials and another one of underground anti-Nazis who might prove helpful. He also had the name of a lawyer who, for many years, had very skillfully been playing the part of an ardent Nazi and anti-Semite, with the aim of helping Jews.

Wallenberg was relieved that no one from the Foreign Office was there at Bromma Airport to see him off on the first leg of the journey. He had already taken a calm, restrained leave of his mother. Neither mother nor son needed to articulate deeply felt emotions. She would have been the last to dampen his enthusiasm for this uncertain undertaking. Maj von Dardel knew her son too well.

Raoul Wallenberg's plane took him only as far as Berlin; there were no direct flights to Budapest. The Reich's capital was also where Nina lived. He wanted to say goodbye to her. He felt close to this lanky, strong-featured young woman with her lively, wide blue eyes. Six years his junior, Nina worshiped him. No one could make her laugh the way Raoul did, with his wide repertoire of imitations, his ability to see something absurd in the most serious situations. She and her tall, elegant young husband, Gunnar Lagergren, picked Raoul up at Berlin's Tempelhof Airfield. Red-and-black-emblazoned Luftwaffe aircraft were buzzing overhead; camouflage netting covered the fighters on the ground. Raoul's brother-in-law, a lawyer, was on special assignment representing the interests of those countries which had broken diplomatic relations with Germany.

Nina, six months pregnant, had booked Raoul on a sleeping car to Budapest. The train was scheduled to leave the next morning. Raoul was delighted to see his sister but he did not want to wait until the next day to travel. He told the Lagergrens he intended to continue his journey the same day. Once the three were in their car, he told them what his Budapest mission was really about.

They were barely out of Tempelhof when air-raid sirens shattered the calm Berlin afternoon. Lagergren pulled off the road, and all three ran for a nearby air-raid shelter. It was Wallenberg's first real taste of the war. He was visibly shaken by the ear-splitting explosions of Allied bombs. In a few months' time he would no longer look up to check whose bombs were blasting life around him to little bits.

At Berlin's Anhalter Bahnhof, Wallenberg discovered there were no seats left on the Budapest express. He managed to squeeze on board and settled on one of his knapsacks in the train's corridor. An endless stream of uniforms walked by. It must have looked as if all of Europe were migrating, from east to west, and west to east, some by choice, fleeing bombs; others, by the hundreds of thousands, had no say in their destination. They were not travelers but cargo.

For hours Wallenberg stood in the passageway of the tightly packed express, looking through the dirty window at the flashes of ravaged countryside. The carpet bombing had done its job. Skeletons of yesterday's prosperous towns tore by, some still smoldering. Wallenberg passed the time committing to memory the list of Jews who needed saving right away: outspoken well-known men and women, leaders in all fields—industry, the press and theater. They were the easiest prey for Eichmann and his *Einsatzkommando*.

The steaming train finally snaked across the Austro-Hungarian frontier and pulled into the Hegyeshalom station. Here, black-uniformed, jackbooted SS climbed aboard. "Papers!" they shouted in German. Welcome to Reich-occupied Hungary. Wallenberg had no trouble making out the freight train a small distance away, sitting on a siding. Hungarian soldiers, their kepis trimmed with cockfeathers, the anachronistic uniform of the feared Gendarmerie, paced up and down. There was nothing old-fashioned about their Mauser automatic rifles. Others stood atop the freight train, their eyes skimming the barren, scrubby landscape.

Hegyeshalom was the end of Hungarian responsibility for the freight train's cargo. This was the switching station for the human delivery. The smartly uniformed Hungarian guards would shortly hand over to the SS those still able to walk after several days without much food, water or air. The last leg of their journey between Hegyeshalom and Auschwitz-Birkenau was the responsibility of the Germans.

Wallenberg was too far from the freight train to hear the deep groans which did not much resemble human sounds. Nor could he see the thin arms that were barely able to squeeze through the tiny crack that was the cattle car's window. An occasional hastily scribbled message to anyone who still cared was pushed out. Raoul Wallenberg was not yet in a position to pick up the calls for help.

Several hours later the Berlin-Budapest express pulled into the Nyugati Pályaudvar, the city's western terminal. Wallenberg was familiar with the cavernous glass-and-steel-domed Art Deco railway station. He recognized the signs of occupation. Swastikas blurred the city's well-known landmarks. Somewhere a loudspeaker blared the martial tune of the "Horst Wessel Song": *"Wenn das Judenblut vom Messer spritzt, dann geht's nochmal so gut . . ."* "Let Jewish blood squirt from your knife and see how good it feels . . ." Wallenberg was tired, hot and thirsty. He also wanted to get to work.

6 An Admiral Without a Fleet

ust before dawn on April 2, 1941, a shot echoed through the vast chambers of Budapest's Royal Palace, the home of Hungarian monarchs since the thirteenth century. The Vár, as this rambling, Baroque edifice is called, housed the Regent of Hungary, Admiral Miklós Horthy, as well as his Prime Minister, Count Paul Teleki. Teleki had just put a bullet through his own head. Hours before the count's suicide, some officers of the Wehrmacht, under General Friedrich von Paulus, had arrived at the palace. They intended to make the Vár their temporary headquarters. Several German divisions were on their way south to occupy Yugoslavia. Hungary had been promised a part of the spoils in exchange for her cooperation in her neighbor's rape.

Count Teleki, possessed of an old-fashioned code of conduct, did not wish to be associated with the joint German-Hungarian occupation. Only a few months before, he had signed a Treaty of Eternal Friendship with the country his own army was helping to slice up. "We betrayed our words," the count wrote in his suicide note, "out of cowardice. . . . the nation is aware of it and we disregard our honor. We have sided with the scoundrels. We will become despoilers of corpses. The lowliest of nations. I am guilty." The bullet he fired preserved the nobleman's most prized possession, his honor. His suicide did not do much for his country. Hungary's slide into an abyss, only partly of her own making, had begun.

In many ways Count Teleki embodied all that was wrong with this traumatized country, and the few things that were still right. Like the kingdom, which no longer had a king but only a regent without a crown, Teleki was narrow-minded, intolerant, chivalrous and extremely proud. He sprang from one of the noble families that still held the land and continued to live their feudal lifestyle.

Three hundred aristocratic families owned one third of the country's fertile plains. It was planted and tilled for them by the vast majority of the country's population, the peasants. They owned only the soil that stuck to their boots when they returned to their thatched-roofed, whitewashed huts at the day's end. A country of one million beggars, it was called. The aftermath of the Great War, which Woodrow Wilson said would put an end to feudalism and oppression, to all that was degrading and undemocratic, achieved the opposite for the Hungarian peasant. Overnight the wise men of Versailles—Wilson, Lloyd George and Clemenceau—decided to punish Hungary for being on the losing side. In 1920, in the Paris suburb of Trianon, they decided to strip her of two thirds of her territory and one third of her population, which were awarded to Rumania, Yugoslavia and Czechoslovakia.

Not that the ramshackle Austro-Hungarian Empire had done much for the population it was now losing to the so-called successor states. But what the statesmen of the victorious Allies did not consider was the impact this carving up would have on the masses, on the landless peasants and the middle class; the Allies meant only to punish the ruling class, who lived like monarchs on their estates.

If the peasant had had trouble finding work before the Great War, now, with much of the land gone, work became the exception rather than the rule. One third of the peasant population was regularly employed at any given time after the war. Hundreds of thousands of the rest headed for tiny red-brick rail depots in Kecskemét, Miskolc and Mohács. They boarded the trains for Budapest.

For many, it was an overwhelming experience. They were seeing their first electric light bulbs, their first tram and underground. On the surface, the city on the Danube had all the hallmarks of the sophisticated urban center it had fashioned itself into in the nineteenth century. It was all quite new, this sleek, modern look. Less than fifty years before, the two banks of the Danube, Buda and Pest, had merged and decided that henceforth Vienna would have a rival.

Cities tend to reflect the character of their residents. Budapest is a dramatic, theatrical kind of place. More than anything else it resembles a stage set. Buda, perched on steep hills, her sprawling Royal Palace, and her Citadel carved into jagged cliffs which plunge into the river, craves the attention of the visitor arriving down the Danube from Vienna. Pest, on the flat plain that is the continuation of the Puszta, is all business, commerce and intellect, all conversation and art. Fantastic amalgams of Romanesque, Gothic and Byzantine straining to find their Magyar soul face the boulevards, which are unabashed imitations of both Paris and Vienna. The Parliament, ostentatiously outdoing Westminster, spire for spire, Gothic arch for Gothic arch, faces the dirty, gray Danube, the heart of the city.

All of this, washed in the ochre light that is characteristic of Central European cities, made a stunning impression on the newly arriving migrants from the countryside. But beneath the worldly surface they found a city in shock. Magyar nationalism, which in the nineteenth century spawned the Revolution of 1848 and a literary, artistic and musical flowering, now had only one outlet. Revanchism, getting back the lost land and the dispersed Magyar population, became the national religion. Two million Magyars were living as second-class citizens under Rumanian rule. Schoolchildren began each day pledging to the God of the Magyars to right this injustice.

As a last resort Hungary turned to her traditional enemy: Russia. An unassuming insurance clerk named Béla Kun came home from a Soviet prisoner-of-war camp, freshly indoctrinated and burning to spread the gospel of Bolshevism to his fellow Hungarians. "The Russians will help us," Kun promised his countrymen. And the people of Budapest, with very few options, listened.

But Kun had not paid very close attention to what they pined for. When he and his Moscow-inspired commissars achieved power, in 1920, they succeeded in making almost no one happy. Instead of giving the peasants their long-dreamed-of land, they forced them to collectivize. Rather than restore the lively spirit of the capital, they hung signs saying "Requisitioned" on the city's cherished cafés and restaurants. They arrested anyone who voiced his displeasure too loudly.

In precisely one hundred and thirty days, Red Terror was replaced by White Terror. The city and the countryside had had its fill of Bolshevism. Besides, Béla Kun was Jewish and so were many of his commissars. Kun escaped to Vienna and from there found

asylum in Moscow. The memory of Kun and the national humiliation caused by the Allies at Trianon proved to be the greatest
burden the unfortunate Jews of Hungary had to bear.

Miklós Horthy, the former Admiral of the Imperial Navy of his
Apostolic Majesty Emperor Francis Joseph I of Austria-Hungary,
was picked by the nobility to restore order. Mounted on a white
stallion, dressed in his beautifully braided naval uniform, Horthy
unleashed a wave of terror on the Jews and on the urban proletariat,
both of whom he blamed for the Communist experiment. His
commandos arrested thousands, dragged them before hastily rigged
military tribunals, and generally finished them off in front of firing
squads. It was a squalid chapter that did not augur well for a
society with liberal, democratic pretensions.

But the venom of anti-Semitism soon petered out, and the country settled into a period of relatively contained frustration. Only
one anti-Jewish law emerged from Horthy's fury: in 1920 Hungary
became the first country to pass the so-called numerus clausus law,
limiting the number of Jews who could be admitted to universities.

The flirtation with the left was over, but irredentism was still
alive. It was the one aspiration that linked the nobility, the middle
class and the latest arrivals of Budapest, Hungary's proletariat.
They had all been reared on the intoxicating epic of their legendary
forefather, Árpád. Árpád had led his twenty thousand fierce tribes-
men all the way from the Urals across the Carpathians to settle in
the gentle mid-Danubian valley, one thousand years ago. The
Slovaks, the Slovenes, the Rumanians and the Croats, all subju-
gated at one time by Árpád's successors, did not share in this romantic vision of the Magyar's inherent right to rule.

Humbled Magyar chauvinism was a powerful force among all
segments of the population. In the late 1930s it seemed to have
only one sympathetic ear, Adolf Hitler's. Neither Horthy nor
Teleki had much respect for the Führer. In the old days of the
Empire they would almost certainly never have taken notice of
such an Austrian lowlife. Horthy found him to be entirely lacking
in "humor and tact." Not a gentleman. His hysterical outpourings
of anti-Semitism embarrassed the Hungarian gentry. Their own
brand of anti-Semitism was much more refined.

In 1938 Hungary joined in dismembering Czechoslovakia. It
was the first of the Reich's many gifts and it worked wonders for

bruised Magyar pride. Within three years the gifts from Berlin became increasingly more lavish. By 1941 she was no longer *"csonka Magyarország"*—"barebones Hungary." She had nearly doubled her territory. And she was still a sovereign state. The Wehrmacht had already crossed into Austria, Czechoslovakia, and Poland, but no swastikas flew in Hungary. Life in Budapest was good again. The dues for the little pieces of land tacked onto the humiliated country in the last three years had not yet been paid.

Teleki, the small owlish-looking man who was known for his iron devotion to principle, would pay the first bill. The count was more than a politician; he was a world-renowned scholar of geography. The Allies had asked him to help redraw the borders between various French- and British-held territories in the Middle East, after World War I. (No simple matter even then, as oil fields had recently been discovered around Mosul, in northern Iraq.) Teleki bristled with integrity and dignity. If one of his students addressed him as "Excellency," the title of Hungarian Cabinet ministers, he risked a public humiliation. A simple "Professor" sufficed, Teleki would inform the youth.

Like all the politicians who served Horthy, Teleki was an arch-conservative. He despised Bolshevism even more than Nazism. He was spared the spectacle of Hungary in the grip of the "tactless and humorless" Führer of the Third Reich. Nor did he live to see the grotesque offspring of the polite anti-Semitism he helped to nurture among his countrymen. Teleki earnestly believed, as he wrote to an English friend, that "the expansion of Jews is as detrimental to the nation as it is dangerous. We must take steps to defend ourselves against their propagation. Their relegation to the background is a national duty." But, he added, Hungary's anti-Semitism "would never reach the brutal methods of Germany."

The suicide of this prominent Roman Catholic momentarily shocked the country. Horthy had used Hitler for the purpose of retrieving territory to appease the population's feverish nationalism. By 1942 Hungary found herself at war with three of the greatest military powers on earth: the United States, Great Britain and the Soviet Union. She had joined the Axis powers, merging her own fate with that of the Reich, Italy and Japan. It was partial payment for Berlin's bounty.

When the Reich's armies unleashed Operation Barbarossa in June 1941, they expected the Hungarian army to march along. The Hungarians, ill-equipped and unmotorized, did not distinguish themselves in the Russian campaign; in fact, in March 1943 their army was pathetically routed. Thirty-five thousand of their troops were killed on the banks of the frozen Don. Twenty-six thousand more were missing or taken prisoner. Not only had the Hungarians been ridiculously outnumbered, but their morale was low. The Germans had already lost the Battle of Stalingrad, the turning point of the war in the East. The soldiers' dispirited performance reflected their view that theirs was a lost cause.

The Hungarian government had already begun to take hesitant steps toward extricating itself from this doomed alliance. Prime Minister Miklós Kállay sent a message to the American ambassador to Turkey in early 1943, through the Hungarian Nobel Prize-winning biologist Albert Szent Györgyi. Through Szent Györgyi, he wanted to make the Allies understand that Hungary's anti-Jewish behavior was a "practical façade" meant only to appease the Germans. But Kállay was too late, and the Abwehr, the German military counterintelligence, was too efficient.

By 1943, in the wake of its battlefield losses, Berlin had a single measuring rod for a friendly nation's loyalty: how resolutely it dealt with its own Jewish Problem. The presence of one million Jews in Hungary, in the very heart of a nearly *judenfrei* Reich, began to rankle. Not that anti-Semitism was not a more or less constant presence in Hungary. University quotas and laws barring Jews from government and military posts had already encouraged the emigration of such talented young Jews as Edward Teller, Leo Szilard, John von Neumann and Eugene Ormandy. But the majority of Jews found positions in banking, commerce and the arts. In fact, thousands of Jews flooded across the Polish and Rumanian borders to Hungary, where it was still possible for them to live something like normal lives.

Hungary's own fledgling Nazi party, the Arrow Cross, remained insignificant through the early forties. It was, in many ways, a genuinely proletarian movement which attracted the newly arrived provincial migrants. They had left behind them roots, traditions, family and friends. The Arrow Cross offered them instant accept-

ance and a form of family life. The shiny boots and crisp green
shirt were an added bonus, compliments of the Third Reich.

As late as March 1942, the official Hungarian Nazi paper was
banned, and the party itself did poorly during elections held the
same year. Until the fall of 1944, few of Hungary's ruling class
took this "rabble" seriously. They were too crude, too uneducated,
too obviously carbon copies of the German original to represent a
threat to Hungary.

Throughout 1942, Berlin continued to insist that Hungary take
more decisive steps to deal with the Jews. Prime Minister Kállay,
like Teleki, a member of the landed nobility and an Anglophile,
resisted the pressure to deport the Jews. The Reich, Kállay insisted, had not provided adequate information regarding what happened to those Jews resettled in the East. In January 1943 Kállay
disbanded the agency of the Hungarian government in charge of
finding a solution to the Jewish Problem.

One year later the Führer decided that Hungary could no
longer be trusted to solve her own "problems." On a crisp spring
day in 1944, the seventy-six-year-old Regent received his summons
to Hitler's Salzburg retreat. The Admiral remembered Schloss
Klessheim from another time. Emperor Francis Joseph had once
used the Baroque castle to house his aristocratic guests. And in
1908 the stern Hapsburg ruler had banished his younger brother,
Archduke Ludwig Victor, to Klessheim—the archduke had in-
curred his brother's displeasure by appearing in a bathing costume
on a public beach. In 1944 the serene hideaway was the scene of
the humiliation of one of the last surviving officers of the Austro-
Hungarian Empire.

Twice the old Admiral returned from the castle, where he was
virtually kept captive overnight, to the handsome oak-paneled
coach that had brought him from Budapest to the Salzburg station.
Twice he hesitated about pocketing his small pearl-handled revolver. He knew that unlike Hitler's generals, he would not be
searched. But decisions, great or small, had become painful for him.

When he finally decided against taking the revolver and descended to the train's platform, he found Adolf Hitler pacing the
ramp. The ramrod-straight Hungarian towered over the Führer,
whom he found embarrassingly stooped, pale and awkward. Hitler

seemed unable to control several nervous tics that contorted his drawn features. Eisenhower's troops, the Führer had been informed, were swarming on the English coast, awaiting good weather to mount the Normandy invasion. Stalingrad, the year before, had broken the back of the invincible Eastern Army of the Reich. The Red Army was now on the offensive.

"Hungary is betraying the Reich!" he thundered. Horthy's prime minister was making secret deals with the Anglo-Americans, Hitler charged. But his most poisonous rage he saved for Hungary's lax attitude toward her Jews. Two "full Jews," he bellowed, had just been elected to the upper house of the Hungarian Parliament. Horthy had only enough time to splutter something about the Hungarian constitution. There wasn't much he could do about that, could he?

"I have taken their jobs. I have taken their property," Horthy replied in defense of his Jewish policy. "I cannot, after all, just murder them. Or let them die. Can I?" he asked.

"No," Hitler said, suddenly calm. "That is not necessary. You must place them in concentration camps. Like the Slovakian Jews." It is possible that Horthy was not aware there were very few Slovakian Jews left in concentration camps. Most of them had completed their journey east.

Then the Führer, excited again, launched into his set speech on the benevolent course of the Final Solution. "There is no cruelty in killing innocent animals by the thousands," he told his astonished guest, "in order to satisfy the hunger of man. Why should we suffer these Jewish brutes to live if they wish to infest Germany with Bolshevism?"

Horthy, squirming and afraid to hear any more of this crazed tirade, promised that he would review his Jewish policy. He then began to take his courtly leave. Suddenly, in an elaborately orchestrated performance befitting a Viennese operetta, sirens began to wail and an artificial fog descended on the castle grounds. Telephone lines were mysteriously cut. The Admiral, like his friend the archduke long ago, was a temporary prisoner of the lovely old castle.

Hitler proceeded with his script for the charade and claimed an air raid was under way. "There is no way," his Führer told the Hungarian, "you can return to Budapest this evening." Horthy, tired and drained of all fight, was forced to share a silent meal with Hitler. By the evening's end, the Regent agreed to remove his Prime Minister and install a government more to Berlin's liking. Horthy still thought he was stalling for time.

By the time he boarded his royal coach to return to Budapest the following morning, he was told the truth. Wehrmacht divisions and airborne troops of the Luftwaffe were entering his country from all points of the compass. As his train pulled slowly out of Salzburg, SS motorized units were roaring up the steep hills of Buda to the Vár. Operation Margarethe was under way.

7 The Nazification of Hungary

BUDAPEST HAD BEEN CAUGHT SLEEPING. The Regent, accompanied by his two top military advisers, was on a train somewhere between Vienna and his capital while Operation Margarethe, carefully planned since the fall of 1943, was set in motion. It was a bloodless blitz, borne with remarkable meekness by the population. Twenty-one of the country's twenty-nine top military officers were of German origin. They did not issue orders for their troops to resist.

Only one shot was fired. Endre Bajcsi-Zsilinsky, a member of Parliament, the last of the great romantic Magyar patriots, greeted the Gestapo with gunshots. Along with scores of others, he was arrested that morning, tortured and finally murdered by the Nazis. His reward, despite his right-wing politics, is a major boulevard in central Budapest that still bears his name.

Left-wing politicians, Social Democrats, men and women of all political stripes, united only by their loathing of National Socialism—and, of course, Jews, the most prominent and potentially troublesome—were all rounded up well before the city understood that it was now the capital of a puppet state.

By the time the city began to come to life in the early-morning hours, small yellow cars with the license plate POL, signifying the Gestapo, were parked in front of all government buildings. The red-and-black swastika of the Reich flapped in the breeze from the arched windows of the Vár. Within a matter of hours the vitality, grace and swagger of Budapest were replaced by fear, and something even stronger, the stirring of pure survival instincts.

Upon his return from Salzburg, the Regent, still going through the motions of being the helmsman of this sinking ship, called a Cabinet meeting. "We are accused," he told his ministers, "of the

crime of not having dealt with our Jewish question." His Prime
Minister, Kállay, the chief target of Hitler's fury, still insisted that
the solution to their "problem" was emigration of the Jews. Not
now, but after the war. Horthy told Kállay it was too late. The
Prime Minister was out of a job, and Horthy advised him to go underground. His Interior Minister did not wait to be told. "I will not
allow one single Jew to be taken out of town," Ferenc Keresztes-
Fisher declared and resigned on the spot. He, too, joined those in
hiding.

Horthy, reduced to a papier-mâché façade of respectability behind which Berlin hoped to conduct its business, appointed Döme
Sztojay as the new Prime Minister. Sztojay, Budapest's minister in
Berlin, had for years served the Reich more zealously than he had
his own government.

Horthy's own bodyguard, the quiet, tall man who always stood
just behind the resplendent Regent, was also rewarded. During
one of the Admiral's agonizing meetings with Hitler at Klessheim
Castle, Peter Hain was enlisted into the service of the Gestapo.
Hain served well, provided Berlin with crucial information about
Horthy's lame efforts at reaching the Allies, just in time. His
compensation was the job of heading Hungary's own little Gestapo.

The Regent closed his Cabinet meeting with his characteristic
absence of realism. "We will," he told his shattered ministers, "by
the grace of God, be able to survive the present critical times."

On the promontory of one of the many hills that jut out of the
Buda landscape, Karl Adolf Eichmann, the thirty-eight-year-old
chief of the Gestapo's Jewish Office, had already set up his own
operations. Seven days before Operation Margarethe, Eichmann
had summoned his three most trusted SS officers to Linz, his birth-
place and war-time hideaway.

Dieter Wisliceny, justly proud of his record in Slovakia and
Greece, both now *judenfrei*, was to be Eichmann's deputy in Budapest. Wisliceny, protruding jaw notwithstanding, was a man known
for a certain softness—not for human beings, but for gold cigarette
cases and chocolates, preferably enclosing small but valuable jewels.
This little weak spot the Jews of Budapest soon discovered and
used to their own advantage.

Hermann Krumey, overweight and bespectacled, had a different
vulnerability. Known as the "Bloodhound of Vienna," he could

also claim Warsaw, Paris and Amsterdam as trophies in his collection. His weakness was women, and he quickly found one in
Budapest. Éva Kosytorz, a perfumed beauty of the least subtle kind,
soon became as feared by the Jews as her lover. Kosytorz's whim
became Krumey's command, and Kosytorz did not think Jews contributed much to her beautiful city.

Theodor Dannecker, the exterminating angel of the French
countryside, completed Eichmann's inner circle of men with proven
records in the service of genocide. They were ready to serve again
in Budapest.

The *Einsatzkommando* chose the elegant Hotel Majestic, on
Buda's Sváb Hill for its headquarters. The apartment hotel's residents were unceremoniously ordered to find other lodgings. The
Majestic and its spectacular view of the Danube would henceforth
be the exclusive domain of Obersturmbannführer Adolf Eichmann
and his extermination squad. Peter Hain, their loyal Hungarian
ally, set up his operations in the cellar of the hotel. Cases of wine
were removed to make way for various instruments Hain used to
speed confessions from his endless supply of "enemies of the
Reich." The Majestic and its new residents became two more symbols of despair for the city on the brink of a nervous breakdown.

Eichmann, impeccably tailored in his silver-gray SS-officer's
uniform, with its dramatic double-lightning-flash insignia, had hit
his stride. At the peak of his personal ambition, with the full confidence of the Führer, he had decided that the destruction of Hungary's Jews would be his crowning achievement. He was a socially
awkward man, agonizingly aware of his lower-middle-class origins
and scant education. In the other occupied lands of Europe, Eichmann had preferred to let his lieutenants confront Jewish leaders.
This time it would be different. He knew his name meant terror
for Jews and he wanted to make a strong impression on Europe's
last surviving Jewish community. To do that, he needed their help.

Eichmann invited the Jewish Council of Budapest to his headquarters. He faced eight frightened old men—bankers, lawyers and
industrialists who had been stripped overnight of whatever position
they had still retained in Hungarian society. They were now beggars. Eichmann made an attempt at humor. "You know who I am,
don't you? I am the one known as the bloodhound!" He roared
with laughter, but it was not picked up by anyone else in the ornate

lobby of the Majestic. He tried another approach. With his narrow, angular face, which was itself a broken promise, he leaned toward his "guests" and in low, confidential tones reassured them that all new measures would be temporary: "When the war is over, you can go back to your normal lives. Help me, and you can avoid a lot of trouble." He told the old men what they wanted to hear: "I am a reasonable man. Trust me, and keep your people calm." It was all very genial, very lulling. They were to print their own newspaper, but it had to be drafted first in German, for the SS censors. Actually the paper, like the Jewish Council he had just summoned, was to be a vital link between the death squad and its quarry.

But the old men heard just enough to maintain their illusions. One of them called his wife from the Majestic itself. "Everything is all right," he whispered. "They only want us to cooperate." The next day the council received its first set of demands: six hundred mattresses, and the evacuation within quarter of an hour of all Jewish buildings, schools and places of worship, henceforth to be Gestapo property. All was delivered, all was accomplished in the allotted time. Within days the Orthodox Synagogue on Kazincky Street was turned into a stable. The Rabbinical Seminary of Rök Szilard Street became the most dreaded prison in a city that now boasted more jails than hotels.

In the first issue of the council's German-censored newspaper, the country's Jews were told: "The commercial and cultural life of the Jewish community is to continue undisturbed . . . No one will be arrested because of his Jewish origin. Should arrests take place, these will be for entirely different reasons." The same issue warned fellow Jews that they could no longer "leave the precincts of the capital, nor may they change their address." Provincial Jews were not allowed to travel to Budapest. The issue closed with this warning: "The attention of all concerned is drawn to the necessity for the strictest and most conscientious observance of all these regulations. Only if they are observed carefully can it be guaranteed that everyone will be able to live a normal life." By now "normal" life included wearing a prominently displayed canary-yellow star at all times. It also meant riding only in the last car of trolleys and not attending theaters and movies or using public swimming pools. Park benches were also off-limits to Jews. Still, the council's house organ warned: "Wear the star! It will safeguard you!"

Every day their status as outcasts became more sharply defined. But the Jews made do. Their expectations diminished along with their possibilities. Self-preservation became their abiding impulse, an impulse they shared with their fellow Hungarians, who allowed all of this to happen to them.

Eichmann carefully reinforced the optical illusion that resulted in just enough confidence to keep them going. Though he set up an internment camp at Kistarcsa, a short trolley ride from central Budapest, he agreed to exempt from it men over sixty and women over fifty. It was a temporary and minor concession, but it did the trick. It showed the Jews there was a grain of humanity in the man who now controlled their fate.

Eichmann's requests of the Jewish Council became daily more outrageous; field glasses by the score, a set of crystal champagne glasses, ladies' lingerie and quantities of silver cutlery. When Hauptsturmführer Franz Novak, Eichmann's transportation expert, expressed a longing for a piano, the Jewish Council produced six baby grands. "Gentlemen," Novak protested, laughing, "I do not wish to open a music shop. Only to play a little music!" Samu Stern, the council's president, was asked to find a Watteau land-scape for another officer with a keen appreciation of art. It was de-livered within twenty-four hours.

Eichmann found the time for even more grandiose schemes. He summoned Joel Brand, an influential member of Budapest's embry-onic Zionist underground, to the Majestic. Brand was puzzled by the degree of freedom the Gestapo had allowed him. Since the German occupation he had been busy organizing some sort of re-sistance, a different sort of Jewish Council from Eichmann's. Now he was about to find out why he was still a free man.

Eichmann and Brand were a study in contrasts. Eichmann was narrowly built, his movements were all close to the body, guarded. All the features of his bony face seemed to meet somewhere in the center. Brand was a square-faced, genial man who under normal circumstances might have been either a grocer or a lumberjack, not an organizer of political resistance. He seemed incapable of subterfuge. His broad-nosed, wide-open face perfectly reflected his character. Brand was a man trusted by nearly everybody, including, now, Eichmann.

"I have a deal to propose," Eichmann began. "Let's call it blood for money, money for blood." In exchange for 2 million cakes of soap, 800 tons of coffee and tea, and 10,000 trucks, Eichmann would agree to stop deporting Jews. All Brand had to do was come up with the goods. "I will allow you to go abroad," Eichmann offered. "Meet with Jewish groups. Tell them I mean business. If they accept the offer, I'll close down Auschwitz and bring one hundred thousand Jews to the frontier. Nine hundred thousand more on delivery." Eichmann even agreed not to use the trucks against the Anglo-Americans. They would be sent to the Eastern Front, to be used against the Russians.

Brand, ready to try anything to stall for time, agreed. He had the support of Budapest's Jewish Council to travel to Turkey and talk to American Jewish leaders.

There was, of course, a catch: Brand would not be traveling alone. Accompanying him was Bandi Grosz. Grosz, a totally charming and witty scoundrel, was known to be in the employ of whoever could afford his services. At the moment it was the Gestapo. His presence beside Brand did not lend the mission badly needed credibility.

Brand's conversations with the Anglo-Americans in Istanbul led nowhere. The Jewish agencies were interested, but they lacked the authority to carry out a deal of this magnitude. The Western Allies were alarmed at this attempt to drive a wedge between them and the Russians. They fell back on their well-rehearsed reason for inaction. London cabled Washington:

> Assuming suggestion was put forward by Gestapo in form conveyed to us, then it seems to be sheer case of blackmail that we should accept responsibility for maintenance of additional million persons is equivalent to asking Allies to suspend essential military operations.

Meanwhile, the American embassy in Moscow informed the Soviets of a proposed plan to negotiate with Eichmann to stall extermination. The Kremlin's veto was swift and blunt. Joel Brand missed the deadline Eichmann had set for the deal, but he was spared the Gestapo's wrath. He was arrested by British agents on his roundabout way home through Syria. He spent the next few months, a forgotten man, in British prisons. Brand finally met Adolf Eichmann again, fifteen years later, in a Jerusalem courtroom.

The trucks-for-lives deal failed. The Allies never found out if Eichmann's offer had been serious.

The Nazification of Budapest proceeded apace. Not far from the Jewish Council's Sip Street headquarters in central Pest, the lobby of still another graceful old hotel became a busy branch of the Gestapo. The Astoria, on Louis Kossuth Street, long a favored meeting place of the capital's literati, was now crowded with those residents of the city seeking to improve their lot in life. The Astoria housed the Wehrmacht, and a special branch charged with receiving public denunciations. Citizens could come here to inform the authorities of Jews not wearing the yellow star, or those in hiding in Christian homes, or still holding down jobs they were officially barred from. These bits of information were generally rewarded with either the apartment of the lawbreaker, or his job. The lobby of the Astoria was nearly always crowded that spring and summer.

Later, when the sweltering summer gave way to fall, and illusions turned to terror, the Jewish Council was often blamed for not standing up to Eichmann, for serving him instead of sabotaging his efforts. The members of the council were in the unenviable position of being held personally responsible for the behavior of the country's Jewish population, and they were too old to fight, too wary to be imaginative, too stubborn to change. There were no energetic potential urban guerrillas or zealous pioneers among these men. They had made their reputation and fortune in another, more comfortable age. That is why Eichmann picked them for the job. Like much of the Budapest Jewish community, they hung on to the conviction that *"Extra Hungarian non es Vita"*—"Outside Hungary there is no Life." They continued to insist that Hungary would not sell them down the river.

The council did learn in small ways to outfox the killers. They learned the fine art of prevarication, the techniques of stalling. When Eichmann delivered a list of Jewish lawyers to be collected for deportation, compiled by the Hungarian Bar Association, the council did not immediately produce the victims. Young boys and girls, children and grandchildren of the council members and their friends, were dispatched with warning messages to the lawyers in question. "Disappear," the children told the marked men. "You have two hours before they come for you. Check into a hospital or an insane asylum. Find a friendly Christian. But move!"

Very often these Hungarian patriots waited in disbelief for the Gestapo to deliver the invitation personally. When young Elizabeth Eppler, active in the fledgling Budapest Zionist underground, came rushing with such a warning to a lawyer who was both color-blind and near-sighted, he wouldn't listen to her. "Why should they take me?" he asked her. "I am of no use to them. I can't do much work anymore." She tried to alert another Jew, an albino, to no avail. He insisted that his paleness would exempt him from forced labor. They simply refused to accept reality.

The council also secretly pumped money into the Jewish underground and sheltered its members. As the decrees became plainer day by day, when Jews lost not only their civil rights, their right to make a living, their right to look and feel Hungarian, but their right to exist at all, the council kept the country's nearly one million Jews calm. Ultimately, as it turned out, that was not in their best interest.

8 Hungary's Jews: Down the Slippery Slope

I t had all happened so gradually, almost imperceptibly, like a car moving from second to third and then finally fourth gear before the passenger realizes he is doing well over one hundred miles an hour. That is how smoothly the Jews' slide from being a vital part in the Magyar landscape to becoming the internal enemy was accomplished.

Every day the Jews lost a bit more of their foothold in Hungarian society, a tiny bit of their self-respect. They could not fathom that it was really happening to them. When they boarded the trains—an event whose message should have been unmistakable—they were still pushing pieces of paper through the cracks saying things like: "Dear children, it isn't so bad. The important thing is that you are well. I was able to take a bit of sausage along for the trip. Love, Mother."

In the end the Nazis and their Hungarian puppets even managed to pull off their ultimate, extraordinary feat of witchcraft: they convinced a large proportion of the Jews that they were guilty of some unspecified crime. If no one in the world was doing anything to haul them from certain death, there must be something wrong with them! The Nazis succeeded in this, since all newspapers and radio broadcasts were carefully censored by the German army of occupation. They repeated the same monotonous message of Jewish inferiority and Jewish duplicity. Listening to the BBC or any foreign broadcast was an act of treason, so no words of hope or encouragement were permitted to reach these people.

Through their despair they were sustained by the declining fortunes of the Third Reich. Only the most fanatic of their countrymen still believed in an Axis victory by March of 1944. It was just a question of holding out a little bit longer. Hungary has always been a paradoxical kind of place, this parliamentary system with its mystical attachment to an ancient crown. So now, again, Hungary would not follow the pattern of her neighbors. She would not allow her Jews to be taken from her. Weren't there even now Jewish members of Parliament? And didn't the Regent play bridge every Thursday with Leo Goldberger, the country's most successful textile magnate?

They clung fiercely to these signs, lifeboats in a rough sea. And they ignored many others. True, the Hungarian Jews were the most assimilated in Europe. They had settled in the country as early as the twelfth century. More arrived later fleeing the Spanish Inquisition. Some had come in the nineteenth century, one step ahead of the pogroms of Poland and Russia. In the relatively liberal climate of this picturesque, semifeudal monarchy, they found a home. The majority settled in Budapest and played a crucial part in the transformation of a pair of sleepy Danubian villages into a vibrant city. In a great release of energy, long repressed in the East European *shtetl* they had fled, the Jews became Hungary's middle class. They performed all the functions the landed gentry was uninterested in and the peasants were not qualified to do.

Another important segment of Hungary's Jewish population was made up of Jewish capitalists migrating from west to east as the more developed capitalist societies squeezed them out and replaced them with their own "native" bourgeoisie. In Hungary these Jewish entrepreneurs found an unrivaled opportunity to exploit an embryonic capitalist state. Not surprisingly, all the abuses of capitalism and its political representatives seemed to the masses to be "Jewish" problems.

In the capital, and in the small towns, they were the bankers, the doctors, the journalists and the lawyers. In the eyes of the barely literate peasants, "Jew" meant commerce and capital. A turn-of-the-century Hungarian laborer answered a survey about Jews this way: "In my village, there are two Jews. One of them is a Jew by profession only. He manages the bank."

They were conspicuously successful, these new arrivals, with their remarkable ability to absorb new habits, customs and culture. Historians sometimes call this flexibility "the psychology of the renegade." The Hungarian artisan and peasant saw only that he was clumsy and slow in comparison to the Jews.

The Jews were grateful to the country. In their first census they pronounced themselves Magyar. Thousands took the ultimate step of assimilation and had themselves baptized. Given two or three more generations, they may have achieved their dream of full assimilation. But they were not given one more generation of stability. World War I, the wound of Trianon, and the Depression, slammed the door shut on the Jews' future.

It should not have been a total shock. There had been signposts along the way, alerting the Jews to the fragile hold they had on the country. Although, by the end of the last century, they owned a quarter of the largest estates in the country, they were barred from such traditional "country gentry" positions as justice of the peace or county prosecutor. An unwritten law discouraged them from seeking state administration posts at all levels. A Magyar could be the wealthiest and most learned man in the kingdom, but if he had Jewish blood he could not gamble at the gaming tables of Budapest's most exclusive clubs. And yet Jews, as much as any single group, made their mark on the capital. It fairly hummed with their humor, intellect and vivacity.

The collapse of the Austro-Hungarian Empire shattered the unwritten pact between Jews and the rest of society. Suddenly Jews discovered that they were tolerated as the guests of the chivalrous Magyar people. And guests can overstay their welcome. This became plain as Hungarian society, a tiny bruised stump of its former splendor, turned on any element it regarded as a threat to its once exalted and now frustrated nationalism.

Jews now found no segment of society that would defend them or guarantee their precarious assimilated status. The problem was aggravated by hundreds of country squires, who had formerly held undemanding but prestigious positions at the royal court. The court gone, they were now looking for gentlemanly occupations. In Budapest, where one quarter of the population was Jewish, most of these "gentlemanly" positions were filled by Jews.

On the other end of the social scale, the Jews lost the tacit support of the peasants. With the Depression, the price of everything skyrocketed, and the "town Jew," the merchant or the banker, was forced to inflate his prices to stay afloat. Biblical images of the usurer were revived. As the Depression spun out and provoked a general disenchantment with capitalism, the Jews, the country's capitalist class, were blamed for both the unemployment and the hard times.

All the pieces started conveniently fitting the puzzle. The biggest piece by far was Béla Kun's abortive, predominantly Jewish stab at a Soviet Hungary. Kun's experiment would give Hitler's monotonous tirade about a Bolshevik-Jewish world conspiracy a certain edge of reality for Hungarians. But though tacit anti-Semitism became increasingly acceptable and even fashionable, Hungarian politicians, who like to boast that they invented anti-Semitism, did not appreciate having their well-bred version compared to that of the Germans. A well-known Hungarian wit defined this open anti-Semitism as "hating Jews even more than is necessary."

Until the mid-forties, Hungarian anti-Semitism retained this well-defined, almost polite quality. It was as much a part of the Hungarian gentleman's wardrobe as the starched white shirtfront he wore to the première of the Vienna Opera season. But by 1944 he was no longer in control of what constituted the acceptable level of Jew-hating. The polite pronouncements of Count Teleki and Regent Horthy had done the spade work for a much more savage flowering.

Until 1944, Regent Horthy clung to the view that Hungary's Jews were Hungary's problem. In contrast to the rest of occupied Europe, Hungarian Jews had not yet become total outcasts. When they were banned from universities, high school teachers would often "flunk" bright Jewish pupils and give them an advanced extra year of secondary school. When, one by one, the professions were closed to them, lawyers became accountants and engineers became chauffeurs. Many Jews to whom the Talmud was foreign literature now started attending synagogue, their last refuge in an increasingly hostile environment. Budapest opened its first Jewish theater, and in the grimmest times, they found the biting satire of the city's new Jewish cabaret a reviving tonic.

As the atmosphere became electric with hate, a kind of Jewish consciousness forced its way into cosmopolitan Budapest. But Zionism was still regarded as far too extreme for the Jews of Hungary. A Jew risked getting expelled from his synagogue if he voiced

Zionist views. Budapest Jews continued to look down on the un-assimilated, unsophisticated Ostjuden, the dark, exotic-looking Orthodox Jews who had streamed into a still relatively tolerant Hungary when the Nazis marched into Poland.

There were glimmers, isolated moments, that threw a beam of light on the darker corners of the national psyche. In August 1941 the Hungarian army herded together about 20,000 Jews without Hungarian citizenship in the eastern province of Ruthenia. They were pushed over the border into German-held Ukraine and certain massacre. The following year a zealous contingent of German and Hungarian troops lined up 2,000 Jews against the Danube's embankment near the Yugoslav border and conducted a mass execution by firing squad. The Hungarian soldiers who had a hand in the butchery escaped across the border to German-occupied Austria. They were given a hero's welcome.

To the Jews of Budapest, this was all so remote. There were worlds between them and their provincial cousins. Their own view of the unassimilated country Jew was something very akin to anti-Semitism. The Nazis, already preparing their full-scale occupation of Hungary, would make no distinction between the two groups.

Like the mists that hug the Danube each morning, and lift to reveal her dirty, viscous surface by midday, so, bit by bit, reality pushed its way into the consciousness of the Budapest Jews. But like the rest of this city of dreamers, they pretended that the war—not their war, after all—would be over before it ravaged their world. The capital had actually rejoiced at the humiliation of the Hungarian army on the Eastern Front. Most Hungarians just wanted the war to end before the Führer realized what a half-hearted ally he had in the Magyars.

Meanwhile the dancing bars on the Margit Island, a strip of green between Buda and Pest, were overflowing. The English waltz and the tango were still popular in Budapest. And along the Korso, in front of the elegant hotels facing the Danube, after-dinner strollers hummed "Stormy Weather," the latest tune from across the Atlantic. For a while Count Teleki's suicide had shaken the country out of its hazy optimism. But even that was soon forgotten. Humor, the mainstay of Budapest life, second only to paprika as the national staple, thrived. The riddle that was making the rounds was: "What is the difference between Hitler and Chamberlain?

Answer: Chamberlain takes his weekend in the country. Hitler takes his country in the weekend."

And so he did. One early spring Sunday, when the chestnut and plane trees on Margit Island were starting to show off their first greenery, the Reich's army marched in and the music died.

9 The Provinces Are Purified

B y the time Raoul Wallenberg's train pulled into Budapest in early July, nearly half a million Jews were beyond saving. There was no one to protest the rounding up of Jews in the Carpatho-Ukraine, in Transylvania or in Transdanubia. The rounding up, entraining and final westbound transporting of Hungary's provincial Jews had been accomplished in record time. The smoothness and speed of the operation was a credit to its ambitious overseer, Karl Adolf Eichmann.

On the first day of the Jewish Passover, Hungarian gendarmes in their Beau Brummel hats, lists in hand, had begun a house-to-house rounding up of Jews in Eastern Hungary. The startled Jews were given a few minutes to collect a parcel of clothing and food for several days. They were driven in trucks to the courtyards of local synagogues or brickyards. They spent the next week in the open air, fed a thin soup brought them once a day in bath tubs by the local members of the Jewish Council. All their valuables were stripped from them. Their houses were left open and were quickly vandalized. German troops retreating from the Eastern Front often used them as their quarters. On their way home to the Reich they took what was left: furniture, carpets, paintings were all packed into freight trains marked "Gift of the Hungarian Nation to Germans Bombed Out of Their Homes."

The Budapest Jewish Council, hearing word of the brutal treatment of provincial Jews, protested to Eichmann about this "lack of good faith." There was not one word of truth in it, Eichmann calmly replied. "I know personally," he told the elders, "having just returned from a tour of the provinces. The situation of the Jews there is no worse than that of German soldiers during maneuvers.

The fresh air is only doing them good." A tour of the provinces was beyond the power of the Jewish Council.

One of the Budapest Jewish Council's final letters to its country brethren exhorted them: "Brothers! The organization of Hungarian Jews is under an obligation to execute the official instructions; this means that the Central Council is not an authority, but is simply carrying out the orders of the authorities. It cannot permit orders to be disregarded on account of lack of discipline. The Jewish Council cannot tolerate the nonobservance of instructions by individuals, as this would lead to a disaster of unprecedented magnitude for the whole Jewish population." This was the council's final communication to the countryside. After this note there was no one there to receive further messages. A "disaster of unprecedented magnitude" had swept away the entire Jewish population of the countryside. It was not the result of the "nonobservance of instructions." Quite the reverse.

How explicitly the Jews observed the new instructions presented them each day is described in the diary of a thirteen-year-old girl. Éva Heyman had an adolescent's passion for recording her own reactions to the days' events. She and her family of middle-class Jews lived in Nagyvárad, near the Hungarian-Rumanian border.

> March 31   Today an order was issued that from now on Jews had to wear a yellow star-shaped patch. . . . When Grandma heard this she started acting up again and we called the doctor. He gave her an injection and she is asleep now. Agi [Éva's mother] again wanted to telephone the doctor but couldn't. Then Grandpa told her that the telephones had been taken away from the Jews. . . . They also take the shops away from the Jews. I don't know who will feed the children if the grownups aren't allowed to work. . . .
>
> April 20   . . . Today they took all our appliances away from us: the sewing machine, the radio, the telephone, the vacuum cleaner, the electric fryer and my camera. . . . Agi said we should be happy they're taking things and not people.

But very soon the gendarmes ran out of "things" to take away. Then they took people. The thirteen-year-old continued to fill in her diary from the ghetto.

May 10   Every time I think: this is the end, things couldn't
possibly get worse, and then I find out that it's always possible
for everything to get worse and even much, much worse.
Until now, we had food, and now there won't be anything to
eat. At least we were able to walk around inside the ghetto,
and now we won't even be able to leave our house.
May 14   . . . We can't look out the window because even for
that we can be killed. . . .
May 18   . . . I couldn't sleep so I overheard the adults talking . . . They said that the people aren't only beaten but also
get electric shocks . . . The gendarmes don't believe that the
Jews don't have anything left of their valuables. For example,
we deposited Grandma's jewelry for safekeeping with Juszti,
that's true. Agi said people are brought to the hospital bleeding at the mouth and ears and some of them also with teeth
missing and the soles of their feet swollen so they can't
stand. . . . In the ghetto pharmacy there is enough poison and
Grandpa gives poison to the older people who ask for it.
Grandpa also said it would be better if he took cyanide and
also gave some to Grandma. . . .

The gendarmes finally came for Éva Heyman and her family
on June 2, 1944. At Auschwitz she was allowed to live for four
months before she was sent to the gas chamber on October 17. Her
diary was kept by the family's Christian housekeeper.

Until early April the Jewish Council of Budapest was under
Eichmann's spell. The council's legal staff was busy drafting plans
for the organization and administration of Hungarian Jews. Simultaneously, the *Einsatzkommando* and the Hungarian Ministry of
the Interior were circulating internal memos on the systematic
elimination of Jews from the provinces.

Eichmann had set a four-week deadline for the rounding up of
nearly half a million provincial Jews so he could get the trains to
Auschwitz rolling. The two possible escape routes for Jews, the
Slovak and Rumanian borders, were now sealed. Budapest itself
was surrounded by a police cordon to check, as far as possible, any
hemorrhaging of the provincial Jewish population into the more-
difficult-to-control city. Despite repeated warnings broadcast from

abroad, all Jews had by now been carefully catalogued and accounted for.

On May 14, the trains were ready. At first the gendarmes charged with rounding up their fellow Hungarians still worried about the rest of the population's reaction to the "deportations." It was still dark when the gendarmes in their picturesque uniforms surrounded the ghetto at Sátoraljaujhely in the northeast. Men, women and children, the old and the young, the sick and the fit, had been huddled in the town brickyard for two weeks. Their weakened condition made the guards' job easier than anticipated. Still, they did not hesitate to use their rifle butts and whips on the laggards. By the time eighty or ninety of them were packed into a cattle car, they had assumed the posture of the doomed.

Those Christians who hurried to the trains with loaves of bread or warm clothing were often rewarded with a place on the train. Mothers who tried hiding their infants under the car had their babies snatched up by the guards, who then hurled them by one leg into the train. By the time the *Einsatzkommando* slammed the heavy wooden door of the train and lowered the outside bolt shut, there was only enough room inside to stand. One pail of water and one loaf of bread in each car were the travelers' ration for the five-day journey. When they reached their destination, about 10 percent were deemed fit to work. They were the ones who were spared.

The grim ritual was repeated daily throughout those fine spring weeks of May and June. In Budapest, relatives sometimes received postcards marked "Waldsee." "I have arrived," the message always read. "I am safe." There was never any word of husbands or wives or children. But the relative from Sátoraljaujhely or Debrecen was safe. Somewhere. The Budapest Jew could continue to nurse whatever skimpy bit of fantasy he could still conjure up.

People in the capital could have no illusions about the Royal Hungarian Government's official views on the subject of Jews. Not after they read an interview in a national paper with László Endre, an Undersecretary of State at the Ministry of the Interior charged with the Jewish Problem:

> Today, in the glorious May sunshine, I have seen a new Nagyvárad come to life. A Nagyvárad devoid of Jews, a truly nationalist town. I have convinced myself that the Jews have

become effectively separated. Nagyvárad has solved this problem and I know that this solution answers the requirements
of our epoch. But with this, the Jewish problem is not yet
solved. All contagious matter and all possibility of infection
must be removed from the blood circulation of the nation.
In this respect the Hungarian government advances step by
step. I do not wish to make a detailed declaration now, but
please watch events carefully.

The vocabulary of *Mein Kampf* had been fused into the new
Hungarian policy. Regent Horthy, the much tarnished but still
vaguely respectable face of the old order, complained to his Prime
Minister of rumors about "his" Jews. Undersecretary Endre was
dispatched on a tour of the provinces. "Everything is in perfect
order," he reported to the Regent upon returning to the capital.
"The provincial ghettos have the character of sanatoria," he claimed,
when there were very few ghettos left in the country. "At last,
the Jews have taken up an open-air life and exchanged their former
mode of living for a healthier one." Eichmann and Endre both
showed a keen interest in the "health" of the Jewish population.
    But Horthy could no longer muffle the truth about what the
"fresh-air ghettos" and the freight trains really meant. When his
Prime Minister told him the wives and children of Jewish men
sent to join "work brigades," accompany them to "uplift their
morale," he finally had heard enough. The Regent was under
mounting pressure from abroad to do something. The Papal
Nuncio, Angelo Rotta, paid several calls and urged him to save
those Jews who could still be saved, and along with them the
reputation of his country. Through the Swiss envoy in Budapest,
President Roosevelt also sent Horthy a warning. Hungarian towns
would be bombed into the Dark Ages if the deportations did not
stop. And on the first of July, King Gustav V of Sweden—like the
Regent a member of the *ancien régime*—whose words carried the
greatest weight of all for Horthy, dispatched his courtly message.
    Hungary's own Roman Catholic Primate, Justin Cardinal Seredi,
also abhorred what was happening to the Jews. His Excellency's
concern was primarily for the fate of Jewish converts to Christianity. "I herewith insistently request the Royal Hungarian Government of Christian Hungary," he wrote, "to consider the baptized

Christians even though they be of Jewish origin, and distinguish them from the Jews, as by the act of baptism they have already distinguished themselves." As a concession to the cardinal and the Roman Catholic Church, the Royal Hungarian Government granted baptized Jews the right to wear a cross next to their yellow star.

Slowly, the nearly extinguished spirit of the once proud Admiral was stirred. He was worried about posterity and his ancient title. He was also bolstered by reports from the Western Front of the early success of the Allied invasion. The massive Soviet summer offensive was already under way in the region of Tarnopol and Lutsk. Red Army artillery reverberated through the Hungarian Carpathian mountains.

To Eichmann's amazement, Hungary suddenly started behaving as though she still ran her own affairs and was not simply the well-behaved lap dog of a demanding master. The Regent put his signature on an order ending deportations.

Only days before, Eichmann had sent word to Himmler that "the complete liquidation of the Hungarian Jews is an accomplished fact. Technical details will only take a few more days in Budapest." Horthy's unexpected assertion of power was a slap in the Austrian's face and a stinging blow to his prestige. Furious, but for the moment helpless, Eichmann withdrew from Budapest to receive his new instructions from Himmler. The dreaded gendarmerie, tireless helpers of the *Einsatzkommando*, were marched back to their barracks outside Budapest. László Endre, who had publicly rhapsodized about the purity of the countryside, unpolluted by Jews, was given a leave of absence.

It was too late for half a million Hungarian Jews. But for the four hundred thousand Jews of Budapest, it was a stay of execution. Raoul Wallenberg had gained precious time.

10 The Summer Before the Fall

I t was not the same city Wallenberg remembered. The lively
irreverence that used to vibrate in the cafés along Váci Street
was gone. So were the lissome women who used to parade
their finery along the Korso. The elegant hotels had all been requisitioned by the city's only flourishing business: the trade in human
lives. The Astoria, the Royal, the Ritz and the Majestic all served
the Gestapo, the *Einsatzkommando* and the Hungarian National
Guard, efficient drill teams come to solve Budapest's Jewish Problem.

The city that once lived on wit and charm now lived on rumors.
Rumors of how soon the Red Army would roll back the demoralized
army of the Reich and liberate the capital. Rumors of the Allies'
progress in France. Rumors of when the Jews of the city would be
herded on freight trains bound north and west. And the Jews,
400,000 of them, lived mostly on fear. They had already been
packed into 1,900 houses marked with the yellow star. Even those
who had managed to hang on to their jobs despite government bans,
whose employers needed them too badly to obey the law of the day,
even these privileged doctors and craftsmen had joined the rest of
their people as pariahs.

Now they were only allowed to leave their homes between
11 A.M. and 5 P.M. and not many employers would put up with
those hours. Up to 50,000 of the city's Jews defied the authorities
and hid in the homes of Christians, who acted either out of courage or were well rewarded for their decency.

Wallenberg found the once lovely city with only scraps of its
former self-respect and dignity. Major street traffic consisted of
people pushing wooden carts holding the remnants of their worldly
goods: a city of migrants. Jews were migrating from unmarked to

marked houses. Christians were moving from smaller to larger apartments.

The smartest shops in Pest were boarded up and smeared with stars of yellow paint. Women, no longer concerned about their reputation as among Europe's most fashionable, stopped dressing to please. There were very few young men left—they were either at the front or in forced-labor battalions. It was a city of the old, of women and children.

Several times a week Budapest's lunch hour was shattered by the roar of U.S. Air Force Liberator bombers, cutting a white streak through the perfect, cornflower-blue summer sky, before the city shuddered from their freshly released cargos. The residents had strangely mixed feelings as they scattered to air-raid shelters. The Jews had a vague affection for these impersonal carriers of destruction. The bombs they emptied on the city's industrial sites and railway lines did not bear anyone's name, or care about anyone's race or religion. For a few moments the Allied bombers made equals of Jew and Christian alike. It made the Jews feel as though perhaps the world had not entirely forgotten this dreary corner of Central Europe.

In the turreted mansion atop Buda's Gellért Hill, Wallenberg found a Swedish legation under a different sort of siege. Scores of impatient, desperate Jews lined up in front of the mansion as rumors of magic Swedish passports spread quickly through town. For several weeks prior to Wallenberg's arrival, Swedish Minister Ivan Danielsson had been putting his signature on documents attesting to a family or business connection between the passport holder and Sweden. Thousands more wanted them. The legation was reluctant to endanger its own credibility, as well as that of the document, by continuing to issue any more. Danielsson was concerned about Stockholm's reaction, and its effect on his own career, if he continued to meet the demand for ever more passports.

By July, 700 Budapest Jews held these so-called provisional passports. They had been exempted from wearing the humiliating yellow star. They had suddenly been given the rights of Swedish citizens, whose eventual intention was to be "repatriated" to Sweden. For the rest, this was a heady vision in the middle of their nightmare. They were willing to fight for more.

Already a number of Swedish-passport holders had successfully extricated themselves from Gestapo raids by showing their Swedish papers. A precedent was in the early stages of being established. But the legation did not know how to cope with this snowballing demand for more.

Raoul Wallenberg was not accustomed to the languid pace of diplomacy. He had come to do a job: to save as many lives as possible from the Nazi exterminating machine. He knew there was no red tape to tie Eichmann's hands. There were no quotas on admission to Auschwitz. Wallenberg did not see why his cause, the rescue of human beings, should be any more hamstrung than that of his enemies.

Wallenberg was imbued with a conviction that anything was within reach, any goal could be met if one just applied oneself, and all of one's God-given gifts to its fulfillment. To the professionals at the legation, the young man with his boundless enthusiasm for the job, decked out with the rucksack he always carried, a second-hand revolver he hoped he would never need to use ("It's to give me courage," he told them) tucked inside his sport coat, did not fit their image of a Swedish diplomat. He looked different from the tall, fair-haired Swedes, with their rather diffident air, who peopled the legation. Wallenberg, of unexceptional physique, looked older than he was. His dark hair had been thinning for some time. His nose and lower lip were prominent, his chin was not. His penetrating brown eyes, eyes that did not miss very much, and his very direct, communicative way with people, were the things one remembered about Wallenberg. Not his looks.

He did not wish to alienate Danielsson or his junior diplomats, Per Anger, Dénes von Mezey and Lars Berg. He wanted to win them over by persuasion and conviction. So he listened to their assessment of the current situation in Budapest. And he immediately set to work on his own solution to their impasse.

Wallenberg cared little about who had Swedish connections and who did not. A life in danger was the only qualification that interested him. Unlike his colleagues, he seldom referred to these people in trouble as Jews; they were simply the people he came to help. And the people immediately perceived the difference between Wallenberg's large vision of his mission and the others' more circumscribed approach.

Wallenberg's first call after presenting himself to the Swedish mission was on the headquarters of the Jewish Council in central Pest. This was another world. The council's Sip Street office was the last refuge of a sea of lost, disowned people. In the bare-walled, heavily curtained room the air was stale from too many people and windows bolted tight, despite the summer temperature. Wallenberg was immediately struck by how defeated these people appeared. They sat there with the vacant expressions of those with no plans, no place to go.

The Swede in his well-cut dark-blue suit, unmarked by a yellow star, with his purposeful gait and the determined air of a young man on his first day on the job, stood out like a bright flash in the gloomy room. Speaking his nearly flawless German, he asked to see Samu Stern, the head of the Jewish Council. The weary Jews around him could only assume he was yet another agent of the Gestapo. Who else would penetrate this obscure bureau for the hopeless?

A Hungarian named László Petö—a childhood acquaintance of Wallenberg's, a ghost from another life when both Petö and Wallenberg summered in a youth hostel on Lake Geneva—spotted him. Petö pushed through the crowd and whispered in Stern's ear, "Tell the others to leave. This man may have something important for all of us." Wallenberg, confident and smiling, produced a letter addressed to Stern by Rabbi Ehrenpreis. Stern quickly skimmed the recommendation that he assist this young man in his rescue mission. When he looked up, skepticism was written all over his tired, lined face. The Swede looked too callow, too freshly minted, too Christian to be of much use. Still, Stern promised he would cooperate in whatever way he could. There weren't that many people holding out a hand.

With his precious list of important contacts already committed to memory, Wallenberg then began calling on people he hoped he could persuade to join his mission either out of conviction or for money. This was how he spent his first two weeks in the capital. He built contacts for future use, entertained them, diverted them with his vast range of stories of other lives, other worlds. He'd dine with the Devil himself, he said, if he would cooperate. He was lavish with money.

Wallenberg's arrival coincided with a strange period of uncertainty for the capital. The first wave of Nazi terror, which followed the spring invasion, had subsided. The most outspoken critics of the new ultra-right-wing regime had been rounded up. Many were already in concentration camps. No soldiers of the Wehrmacht patrolled the city's streets. Their symbols, their swastikas, music and slogans, were there to remind the residents they were the weak link in the Axis. The SS and Eichmann were somewhere in the capital, no one doubted that. But they stayed largely in the background.

Berlin's greatest fear, that Hungary would jump ship and achieve a separate peace, had been pacified. Hitler now considered Hungary more or less under control.

But the country was still in the hands of non-Nazis. Horthy, the figurehead, was first and foremost a Hungarian patriot. There were Nazi elements in his Cabinet, but Horthy increasingly tried to hang on to a remnant of sovereignty.

This period of ambiguity, when Hungary straddled between subservience and independence, was opportune for Wallenberg. He used his status as a neutral diplomat to open doors in the Hungarian Foreign Ministry. There were only a handful of countries left who had not yet broken relations with Hungary, and they were prized by the leadership, which badly wanted respectability.

Wallenberg stated his mission—to save Jews—to Hungarian officials. He found many, frightened of Berlin's answer to the problem, willing to negotiate with him. He did not reveal the original sponsor of his rescue plan. Officially Washington was the enemy, and he could not have gained public support for saving Jews if people had known that Roosevelt was behind it. However, Wallenberg's colleagues at the legation were aware of his dual portfolio, as envoy of both Washington and Stockholm. Thus Minister Danielsson accorded him far greater freedom of movement than any other diplomat.

Among his first communications home was a telegram to Kálmán Lauer, then acting as go-between for Wallenberg and the War Refugee Board. "Send money," Wallenberg wired. The example of Hungary's richest Jewish dynasty, the Manfred Weiss family, which bought themselves a train to neutral Portugal by leaving the Gestapo their vast steel works, was vivid proof of the power of the Nazis' greed in their most desperate hour.

Two weeks after his arrival he wrote home: "I am distributing money to supply Jews with baptismal papers and personal identification. This is money better spent than trying to get them out of the country. I have to pursue the possibility of using German or Hungarian officials. Very often these people try to use blackmail." The thirty-one-year-old neophyte was learning fast.

Wallenberg used this period of relative calm to prepare for the future. He did not believe that the executioners could be held at bay for long. He knew the Regent was indecisive, a vain man who had been cajoled into decency under pressure by the King of Sweden and world opinion. But Wallenberg doubted that Horthy could stick to his decisions, so he went about devising some "passports" of his own. His was a more sweeping approach to distributing protective cover than anything previously attempted. These were identification papers of Wallenberg's own design, bearing the impressive triple crown of the Swedish monarchy and the signature of the minister. Within weeks, thousands of Jews possessed them, and within a few months they owed their lives to the documents and, especially, to the man who stood behind them.

Wallenberg formed a special section within the legation, and quickly built a staff of his own. He recruited four hundred Jews to work in his Section C. They occupied offices in three different buildings. For his co-workers, the reward for long hours and the total dedication Wallenberg expected was exemption from wearing the yellow star, and the right to stay in their own lodgings rather than move into the specially marked houses. These concessions Wallenberg wrung from the Foreign and Interior ministries after many hours of persistent negotiations.

Once Wallenberg's operation was functioning smoothly there was nothing he considered beneath him, no job too menial if it would help somebody. If a mother needed baby formula, he would research available milk powders. When an old people's home complained of not having adequate footgear, he somehow, in war-ravaged Budapest, produced dozens of pairs of shoes. He never asked anyone to do anything he would not do. Nor was he concerned about his image if he was observed loading trucks with food or planning menus for the soup kitchens he would later set up. He had an unusually strong sense of himself and his identity. If he was trying to prove something, it had nothing to do with stature, dignity or presence. It had all to do with courage, energy, imagination and intelligence.

The moment was ripe for scoring points. The two most rabid Jew haters in the Sztójay regime, both undersecretaries of the Interior, László Baky and László Endre, had just been sacked by the Regent. They were caught planning a Nazi coup and were banished from the capital where they awaited a more propitious moment to strike. Endre, a close friend of Eichmann's, offered his country estate for the SS lieutenant colonel's use while he, too, was biding his time.

Wallenberg, perceiving a wider crack in the door, doubled his already feverish pace.

For a Jew to qualify for a Wallenberg protective passport, all he needed was to establish a link, however thin, between himself and a Swede. Jews stormed Budapest's Central Post Office and copied the names and addresses of unknown Swedes from the Stockholm telephone directory. They wrote pleading letters to strangers requesting some proof of familiarity. The government soon caught on to this ruse, and the Stockholm directory vanished from the post office.

But Wallenberg had already managed to have 4,500 of these passports, entitling the bearer to a trip to Sweden, recognized by the authorities. The Swiss legation picked up the cue and began issuing its own "Palestine passes," documents even more fictitious, since Great Britain, and not Switzerland, held the mandate to Palestine. The idea was always to stall for time.

In the diplomatic pouch of July 18 Wallenberg sent one of his rare letters to his mother. As usual, he was surrounded by people with favors and requests to ask of him as he dictated his message home. It is in German, as his Hungarian secretary spoke no Swedish. "Please invite the Lauers to the house," he asked his mother. "I don't dare tell them that Marika's parents and a small child in the family have certainly died during one of the deportations." Wallenberg failed to accomplish one of the early goals of his mission: the rescue of his former partner's relatives.

The discovery of a death or a disappearance touching one of his colleagues was almost a daily routine for him by now. Nearly all of his staff had already lost a family member to either the deportations or the forced-labor battalions, which amounted to extermination squads.

By the end of July, less than one month after his arrival, Wallenberg succeeded in getting the government to approve the repatriation of "his" protected Jews to Sweden. Though none of them ever made it to their new country, this was a crucial step. It showed the Hungarian government that unlike the British in Palestine, the Swedes were committed to assuming responsibility for however many Jews could be rescued. This later added weight to Wallenberg's efforts on behalf of the Jews, and for the moment it gave Hungarian officials the impression that they could not act with total impunity toward a class of people they had assumed the world was not much interested in.

Wallenberg launched the idea of separate housing for "international" Jews, those with protective papers. He started renting and buying apartments, houses, villas, entire buildings in the heart of Pest, in the former Jewish quarter. These buildings were immediately decked out with the blue-and-yellow flag of Sweden and were regarded as diplomatic property. They thus benefited, for as long as that mattered, from extraterritoriality. As was often the case, Wallenberg's idea spread to the other neutral diplomats, who joined him in creating a veritable international ghetto. By the end of the war, 30,000 people were thus sheltered, 20,000 of them in buildings flying the Swedish flag.

Raoul Wallenberg's most significant achievement during this period of calm was to establish his own credibility in the eyes of the authorities. He was the most tireless, persistent and stubborn diplomat any of them had ever encountered. He was not shy about flooding officials with telephone calls and memos until he got what he was after. Without his Swedish diplomatic credentials, these qualities would not have cut very deeply into Hungarian officialdom. What opened doors for Wallenberg was his single-minded dedication to his mission, combined with his privileged status.

Equally important, he instilled in thousands of Jews some kind of confidence in a future they had stopped believing in. "The attitude of the Jewish population," Wallenberg wrote home in July, "has evolved a great deal since my last report. We must get rid of their feeling that they have been abandoned." The involvement of the other neutrals in Budapest, the Swiss, the Portuguese and the

Vatican, all spurred on by Wallenberg, was a tremendous morale booster. Wallenberg proved that intelligence and courage can be as contagious as apathy and fear.

His own self-confidence marched in step with the results he achieved. By summer's end he was giving advice to his own Foreign Office, and the world beyond. He was not happy with the tone of the Allies' broadcasts to Hungary. He felt they were misusing the potentially powerful propaganda tool. "They only threaten those responsible for complicity in anti-Semitic actions with harsh judgment for war crimes," he cabled his Foreign Office. "They should also speak of clemency and encourage a change in the present attitude." Wallenberg concluded: "Russian propaganda is superior because it speaks of appeasement. It would be better to promise help for those who protect Jews." Rather sophisticated advice from a diplomat of less than a month's standing.

There is no record of how his seasoned superiors took such unsolicited words of wisdom. Wallenberg, with the unimposing title of First Secretary of the Swedish Legation, seemed undaunted. The point was to get the message across, no matter how many eyebrows shot up at his unorthodox behavior. He was getting the job done. He was also earning the respect of people who had stopped paying attention to the rest of the world, both the hunters and the hunted.

Early in August the Swede climbed the steep Buda hill to the sprawling Royal Palace. He had requested and been granted an audience with His Excellency, the Regent of the Kingdom, Miklós Horthy. The tall, erect old man greeted his guest in one of the mirrored gilt reception rooms that had, for centuries, served to shrink the guests of Hungarian monarchs down to size.

The simply dressed, unassuming Swede was intimidated neither by the size of the room nor by the towering, bemedaled figure who received him. Speaking to Horthy in the German which they both held in full command, he was courteous but unambiguous. Hungary's treatment of her Jews would be used against her after the war, he told the Regent. The example of Rumania, which had refused to turn her back on her Jewish population, Wallenberg pointed out, would not help Hungary's case. The audience was brief, the Admiral mostly listening in gruff silence. Wallenberg felt he had made his point. It was perhaps not too late to inject a shot of moral outrage and a bit of fear about history's judgment in this essentially chivalrous but spineless man. "He is an imposing figure," Wallenberg later said of the Regent, "but during my audience, I felt morally taller than him."

The same day, Wallenberg turned thirty-two years old. His secretary surprised him with an attaché case, flowers and champagne. He was in high spirits when he wrote his mother that he had just rented an eighteenth-century villa with a superb view.

Wallenberg's spirits were not the only ones to rise in the late summer of 1944. The Jews of the city, encouraged by the proximity of both the Russians and the Allies, received yet another shot of confidence. Horthy, shaking off the somnolence which had engulfed him since his elder son and chosen heir, István, a pilot, was shot down by the Russians, decided to make another move. Without further ado, he dumped the man Berlin had forced him to take on as his Prime Minister. Sztójay, the puppet, was replaced by General Géza Lakatos, a man of moderate views on most issues, including the Jews. Though the new Prime Minister paid the obligatory lip service to the "pernicious hold" the Jews of Budapest still had on the heart and soul of the country, he announced that Hungary's Jews were Hungary's problem.

The news was intoxicating, but the country was still Hitler's ally. So the lines continued to twist around the Swedish legation. Wallenberg no longer had time to examine each passport application personally. There were too many, and he wanted each one to be processed without delay. He was equally concerned about the passport's validity in the eyes of the authorities. Fakes had begun appearing all over town. Swedish passports were big business for black marketeers preying on the fears of the desperate.

One day there was a summons from SS headquarters—always a terrifying moment for a member of Wallenberg's staff. Though these Jewish employees were exempt from wearing the yellow star, the Germans could still impose their will on Hungary.

Attempting to control his nerves, Lászlo Hegedüs strode through the arched entryway of the massive gray structure that held SS headquarters in Pest. Dr. Theodore Grell, counselor in charge of Jewish affairs, known for his undisguised impatience to start the deportation trains rolling again, ushered Hegedüs into his office. Leaning back in his chair, with an outsized portrait of the Führer behind him, Grell pushed a document in front of the Hungarian. It bore the Swedish crown and Danielsson's signature. It was plainly a crude fake. Hegedüs had processed thousands of lifesaving documents. He tried now to recall the name of Dr. Arthur Kende, the owner of this particular passport. Had it ever crossed his desk? His memory drew a blank. Grell waited for a reaction. Was this document a fake or was it real?

Hegedüs sensed a trap. If he answered it was a fake, he would be sealing the fate of a Jewish doctor, guilty only of trying to buy himself an illegal protective passport. If, on the other hand, he insisted on the document's authenticity, he would risk damaging the credibility of the entire operation. Nervously, he asked Grell to allow Wallenberg to inspect the passport and make a final decision. Grell let him go.

Presented with the forgery, Wallenberg immediately sent his team on a search for its owner, Dr. Kende, and to alert him to possible danger. Then he told Hegedüs to go back to the Germans and tell them that the document was a fake. The Swede refused to risk his whole operation for the sake of a single individual. "This is a collective action," he told his staff. "We have to look out for the greatest number possible, not for single cases." Dr. Kende was never found. The passports' authority had been preserved.

But it wasn't only the Germans who threatened the passports' credibility. Wallenberg's own staff would often ask him to make shortcuts on behalf of friends and family members, and to do away with the required proof of a Swedish connection. In the early days he would deny these requests. He wanted the Jews as well as the authorities to take the passports seriously. But he would always find his own way of getting passports to the people who needed them. Ultimately, no one was turned away.

The advance of the Red Army and the Regent's new show of independence clearly made the Germans uneasy. In early August the SS staged one of its periodic parades to remind the residents just who was in charge. Green Tiger tanks and dark-blue armored personnel carriers rolled down the deserted tree-lined boulevards of the capital. The SS goose-stepped to a small but enthusiastic group of onlookers. Hungary's own clones of the original cheered them on, and waited for their time.

There were still sporadic attempts to arrest Jews and pump up

Eichmann's body count. Twelve hundred Jews interned at a camp not far from the capital were rounded up by the SS and pushed on freight trains. The Hungarian authorities got wind of the plan and stopped the trains from pulling out of the Kistarcsa station. But Eichmann's henchmen did not give up easily. Under cover of night they forced the Jews to march to another station, farther from Budapest. Unobserved by Hungarian officials, they drove the Jews into box cars, whose doors were only unlocked one week later in Auschwitz.

By mid-September there were only 450 Hungarian Jews still interned. But the internment camps were now in Hungarian, not German hands. More and more Jews in Budapest were removing their yellow stars. No one was stopping them.

Wallenberg wrote home that he envisaged the liquidation of his special Section C. He would first complete the processing of 8,000 current passport applications. He had already cut his staff back to one hundred people.

In a letter to the War Refugee Board's Iver Olsen, Wallenberg sounded very much like a man winding up a fairly successful operation.

When I look back on the three months I have spent here I can only say that it has been a most interesting experience, and I believe, not without results. When I arrived the situation of the Jews was very bad indeed. The development of military events and a natural psychological reaction among the Hungarian people have changed many things. We, at the Swedish Legation, have perhaps only been an instrument to convert this outside influence into action in the various government offices. I have taken quite a strong line in this respect, although, of course, I have had to keep within the limits assigned to me as a neutral.

It has been my object all the time to try to help all Jews. This, however, could only be achieved by helping a whole group of Jews to get rid of their stars. I have worked on the hypothesis that those who were no longer under the obligation to wear the star would help their fellow sufferers. Also I have carried out a great deal of "enlightenment" work among the key men in charge of the Government's Jewish question here.

I am quite sure our activity . . . and that means in the last
instance yours . . . is responsible for the freeing of the interned
Jews. These numbered many hundreds. . . .

Mr. Olsen, believe me, your donation on behalf of the Hungarian Jews has done an enormous amount of good. I think
that they will have every reason to thank you for having
initiated the Swedish Jewish action in the way you have in
such a splendid manner.

This is a characteristically understated rendering by Wallenberg
of his own achievements.

"I'll try to be home several days before the Russians arrive in
Budapest," he wrote his family. Wallenberg did not have high
expectations of the Russians. He was not enamored of Communism
or of the methods the Soviet leaders used to secure control. But
like many people, he was of the view that anything would be an
improvement over the Nazis. Hungary, at any rate, had no choice
in the matter of who "liberated" her. Wallenberg did not expect
liberation to turn into occupation.

He also wrote a letter to Kálmán Lauer, asking him to use his
contacts with Raoul's godfather and cousin, Jacob Wallenberg, to
make sure a position would be waiting for him somewhere in the
Wallenberg empire. Wallenberg could take justified pride in the
efficiency, energy and imagination he had exhibited in his most
challenging assignment to date. His achievement in Budapest had
already far surpassed anyone's expectations of a rescue mission. It
could not but impress his powerful Wallenberg cousins.

He had certainly not been ignored by the Foreign Office. On
August 10 Iver Olsen wrote to John Pehle in Washington:

I get the impression indirectly that the Swedish Foreign
Office is somewhat uneasy about Wallenberg's activities in
Budapest and perhaps feel that he has jumped in with too big
a splash. They would prefer, of course, to approach the Jewish
problem in the finest tradition of European diplomacy, which
wouldn't help too much. On the other hand, there is much to
be said for moving around quietly on this type of work. In
any case, I feel that Wallenberg is working like hell and doing
some good, which is the measure.

In fact, Raoul Wallenberg's real testing was just about to begin. By the time it was over, the young man had stopped worrying about his future in the dynasty. He was no longer obsessed by what this demanding family thought of him. He did not have time to ponder anything but his own survival and that of a growing number of people whose last hope he had become.

11   October 15

T he Regent's surviving son, Miklós Horthy Jr., had plenty of reason to feel optimistic on the morning of October 15, 1944. It was a fine Indian-summer day. The morning mist had already lifted off the Danube when young Horthy requested an armed escort to take him from the Royal Castle across the river to Pest. Miki Horthy, whose distaste for the Nazis was as well advertised as his father's loathing of the Bolsheviks, had finally prevailed on the old man. The Regent was about to break with the Reich, officially and irrevocably. After months of clandestine negotiations in various neutral capitals, Hungary was going to sign an armistice with the Soviets. It was late in the day. Hungary's much-vaunted national honor was in shreds: she had allowed 600,000 of her Jews to suffer Nazi justice, 600,000 loyal Hungarian citizens who had been deemed expendable by their own state.

But there were still lives to save. The Regent's son was convinced that it was not too late for the old man, who had averted his eyes from reality so many times, to redeem himself. If the Jews of Budapest were saved, young Horthy felt the Allies would be willing to forgive his country's remarkable lack of resistance to the Nazis. A passionate Anglophile, Miki Horthy was anxious to have Hungary figure on the Western Allies' liberation agenda.

The young man had no way of knowing that only the week before, Winston Churchill had casually scribbled "50-50" on a piece of paper marked "Hungary" before sliding it across a Kremlin conference table to the man with the thick mustache sitting across from him. He was even less likely to know that Churchill's interest in Hungary was to prove to be as substantial as his cigar's smoke. The Soviet "50," both the British and Communist leader tacitly understood, would shortly be rounded off to 100. No Western forces intended to moderate the harsh occupation the Red Army had planned for Hungary.

Miki Horthy was too preoccupied with his morning rendezvous with agents of Marshal Tito to worry about the unpredictable future. He was excited by the prospect of linking Hungary's fate with that of the legendary Yugoslav partisans, who had successfully driven the Germans back from their own country. It was only when his car hit a roadblock a few blocks from the Castle and he was suddenly surrounded by hooded men in trenchcoats bearing the yellow star that he stirred from his reveries of what might have been. It was too late by then.

He drew his pistol, but before he could take aim he was overpowered, knocked unconscious, wrapped in a Persian carpet and tossed in the back of a truck. His bodyguards lay bleeding on the ground. Later that day, not the Yugoslavs, but the gatekeepers of Mauthausen received Miklós Horthy Jr.

The Regent's last surviving son had fallen into a brilliantly staged assault by one of the Nazis' master kidnappers. Otto Skorzeny, an Austrian and one of Hitler's known favorites, was still flushed from his daring rescue of Mussolini from his mountaintop fortress, at Gran Sasso. This time the aristocratic roughneck had disguised himself and his cohorts as Jews, for the benefit of potential eyewitnesses. By abducting the Regent's well-loved son, Skorzeny finally crippled the old man, who had been on the brink of making his long, desultory political career's most decisive move.

Word of his son's kidnapping reached Horthy within minutes. The Gestapo's message momentarily cleared the thick fog of self-delusion with which he had, for so long, surrounded himself. The operation had been instigated by Hitler after he learned of Horthy's planned cease-fire; the German master strategist was not about to let his last ally go. The Admiral had waited too long, talked too much and failed to count heads carefully before letting out word of the rapprochement with the enemy.

Now the silver-gray-uniformed figure of Edmund Veesenmayer, the Reich's envoy in Budapest, stood before the Regent, who sat slumped behind his ornate desk. "We have your son," Veesenmayer said, telling the Regent what he already knew. "Call off this armistice and you can see him again." The old man was completely shaken. All resolve, all will power, had slipped away in the last few moments. He no longer cared much about his country's future or about history's judgment. Horthy did not even care much about his cherished honor anymore. He was a father who wanted to see his son again.

But though the Regent had abandoned any thought of a separate peace, the machinery of the long-planned armistice had already been set in motion. Horthy's prerecorded broadcast to the Hungarian people was being beamed across the country. Military trucks with loudspeakers had been circulating through Budapest. "Citizens of Hungary! This is Admiral Horthy. Please go to your radios." Buses and streetcars disgorged passengers who raced anxiously toward their homes and their radios. "We shall not become the scene of the Reich's rear-guard combat zone," the Regent told his countrymen. "We have agreed to abandon further participation in the fight against the Soviet Union." Hungary was out of the war.

Or so hundreds of thousands of Hungarians, half-crazed with joy, thought. Jews spilled out of their marked houses and began ripping off their yellow stars. Bonfires were started with scraps of the hated piece of cloth. At the front, units of Hungarian soldiers started distributing arms to unarmed Jewish forced-laborers. "We're on the same side now," the amazed Jews were told.

While the street celebrations were still under way, four German divisions moved on the capital. Tiger tanks surrounded the Royal Palace. By the end of the second broadcast of Horthy's peace declaration, the familiar martial strains of the "Horst Wessel Song" brought the capital back to reality.

Horthy's cease-fire never had a chance. His order to lay down weapons was sabotaged by pro-German elements inside his own army. As before in recent history, the officer class was dominated by ethnic Germans. The Regent was convinced his officers would follow their Supreme Warlord down any path he chose. They were not ready to stop fighting the Russians. They had stopped believing in their own leader.

The Nazis captured the capital's strategic points after the most cursory struggle. Only Horthy's personal bodyguard of two hundred men put up anything like a real battle, and that only lasted for two hours.

At the Buda headquarters of the Arrow Cross, the SS were busily arming young men as bright-eyed and eager as children on

Christmas morning. Their moment had come. From now on, the city belonged to them. In a nearby house under the protection of the SS, Ferenc Szálasi, leader of the Arrow Cross, the most extreme and least subtle party in the national landscape, waited for his signal to march on the Royal Castle and claim his victory.

That Szálasi should occupy the traditional home of Hungarian monarchs was a prospect too absurd for members of the ruling class to contemplate. Considered the rabble-rouser of the lowest common denominator, this former army captain had never been taken seriously by anyone except the street gangs that he fused into his Arrow Cross. Though he shamelessly mimicked Hitler, he had neither the charisma nor the perverse vision that catapulted Hitler to power.

A man with a forgettable face, he was absolutely sure of what he opposed, but vague as to what he stood for. He was opposed to Jews, socialists and liberals, and to middle-class values. Mostly he hated Jews, and this, despite his mixed Armenian-Slav origins, endeared him to Hitler. He was Berlin's last card in Hungary. Szálasi, overwhelmed by gratitude for the Reich's sudden blessing, for the lavish supplies of uniforms and arms and, above all, for the keys to the kingdom, if not the power, was prepared to do all that Berlin required.

For Regent Horthy, handing over the trappings of power to this common street brawler was the final and most bitter pill to swallow. By now he had no choice. The Admiral did not have the stomach for martyrdom. He could not, like Count Teleki, three long years before, take his own life to salvage a scrap of honor. So he signed the piece of paper Veesenmayer pushed in front of him, giving the Szálasi government, still calling itself the "Royal Hungarian Kingdom," all power. Or whatever power was left when the Germans, now finally in total command, were done.

Horthy stirred long enough to make two requests of his captors. He asked that his "good name" not be maligned on radio or in the press. He also requested that he be allowed to claim his personal possessions, the last reminders of over thirty years of rule, to take with him to exile in Germany. He was granted both. In return he signed a statement that was his final and total capitulation. "Only the misuse of my name," he declared, "made it possible for a proclamation of the nature of that of October 15 to be published."

So much for the Admiral's armistice. By the time the broken man in the splendid Admiral's uniform, which now hung from his spent frame, left the palace, the Gestapo was in full control. They were already loading priceless Hungarian antiques into trucks bound for the Reich. The Regent had given away his kingdom, but he did not get his son back. Young Horthy would have to wait for Allied troops to liberate him from his concentration camp.

Hitler did keep his word and treated his aristocratic prisoner "in accordance with his rank." Horthy was given a small castle in southern Germany, where he could contemplate in comfort the dreary road he had paved for his kingdom.

12   The Crucible

T he carefully staged Nazi coup of October 15 signaled the end of more than just a ramshackle feudal monarchy. It was the end of rule by law. The most minimal respect for human life or property could no longer be assumed. It was the abrupt end of sanity for the people of Budapest. The new regime declared that all Jews were the same. There was no such thing as "protected" Jews. Swedish, Swiss, Vatican or Portuguese passes were not worth the paper they were printed on.

For Raoul Wallenberg it was the real beginning of his personal testing. It was only now that he would prove both to himself and to those who knew him what kind of man he had become. All of his special gifts, his uncanny ability to get a fix on people, to read quickly what motivated them, his self-discipline and his reserves of energy would now find their full flowering in an atmosphere of near-total anarchy.

Wallenberg would henceforth forge the various pieces of his privileged youth and early manhood into a substance of remarkable strength. He welcomed the challenge. He was pleased with what he was able to observe of his own behavior.

A week after the Hungarian Nazis grabbed power and began to unleash their special brand of horror on the city's Jews, Raoul wrote his mother: "I can assure you I am well. These are extraordinary and tense times but we are struggling, which is the main thing. I am sitting by candlelight with a dozen people around me, each with a request. I don't know who to deal with first. . . . The days and nights are so filled with work we can only have time to react now and then." The apprentice diplomat was clearly exhilarated by his work and by his ability to get things done, in spite of overwhelming odds.

The courage that Wallenberg displayed that fall and winter of 1944 was all the more startling because it was not based on a natural fearlessness. More than anything else, Wallenberg's bravery was a product of will. The calm he exhibited in the most unnerving situations did not come easily to him. This is what makes his behavior in those months remarkable. He was not by nature a man who embraced brinkmanship. On the contrary, he could be remarkably cautious. A small thing, like wearing the right shoes, he observed, could make a life or death difference if the Nazis decided to march you off. He had seen thousands collapse on their feet after a few miles as a result of wearing impractical, city shoes. From October he always wore hiking shoes, day and night. He insisted that his colleagues also do the same. His rucksack always held a change of clothes and some food. He was very young and had a healthy appetite for life.

Each day he also observed what a difference his own attitude and actions could make for the people around him. To a growing number of them he was the last remnant of decency and morality, the only one holding back the door against a tide of brutality and survival instincts. He was unwilling to disappoint either them or himself.

Washington, too, began to take notice of the performance of the War Refugee Board's Budapest representative. In a cable from the State Department to Iver Olsen in Stockholm, Acting Secretary of State Edward R. Stettinius, Jr. asked that he convey to Wallenberg the U.S. Government's "sincere appreciation of the humanitarian activities of the Swedish Government and the courage and ingenuity displayed by Mr. Wallenberg himself."

After the fall of Horthy, there were two kinds of terror at large in Budapest. There was the uncontrolled terror of the streets, the lawless rule of Szálasi's Arrow Cross—fascists and bullies who were motivated only by their own greed and the contagious bloodlust of the mob. And there was the carefully orchestrated, more articulate, strictly enforced terror of the men in Adolf Eichmann's *Einsatzkommando*, back now in their Hotel Majestic headquarters. They preferred to stay in the background, behind their Hungarian puppets, but there was little doubt who was pulling the strings. Eichmann had bided his time long enough. He came out of his retreat on the Austro-Hungarian border, and with him came his equally impatient hard core of henchmen. They did not have much time to waste. Russian artillery thundered louder each day. But, in fact, the advance of the Red Army proved to be agonizingly slow.

Wallenberg had to learn to deal with both sources of terror, the local and imported. His skill lay in his ability to devise different tactics for each situation. He quickly learned where to probe, where a man's vulnerability lay. He did not impose his own views. He always let others think they were doing themselves a favor by advancing Wallenberg's cause. He did not rely on anyone's innate goodness to surface; he played on whatever weakness he discovered.

With the Arrow Cross officials, he soon perceived a longing for respectability. These were the dregs of society who suddenly had more power than they had ever fantasized about. Though some of their leaders were members of the aristocracy, they had been largely disowned by their own class, for their radical views. They all yearned for international acceptance. Raoul Wallenberg, First Secretary of the Swedish Legation, held out the promise of diplomatic recognition. For a price.

If the promise of respectability didn't do the trick, money often did. Wallenberg nearly always carried large sums of money with him. That was his last resort. He was always prepared to deliver cash for services rendered. As the Russians tightened their noose around Budapest, and food became scarce, Wallenberg could somehow always get his hands on some. He had started stockpiling essential foodstuffs in October, when they were still available. He organized three secret warehouses in Pest and another three in Buda, piled them high with flour, milk powder, sugar and canned goods. Toward the end, he was feeding not only the ghetto but a portion of the city's uniformed terrorists as well. That was the price of getting them to help him save lives.

With the Nazis, natural authority often worked. He could do a startling imitation of German authority enraged. If his word was doubted, his signature on a passport questioned, he could fly into a fury. "*Aber das ist in meinem Ausweis geschrieben!* Those are my own initials!" he would scream. The SS, not accustomed to people talking back, were both startled and embarrassed. Thus he was able to pull a few more victims from the executioner's grasp.

As the Reich's fortunes declined from day to day, when it was clear no miracle weapons would descend like Lohengrin from the heavens, the Nazis' fear of the future was Wallenberg's best tool. He used it expertly. "I'll make a stand for you if you do this for me," he would cajole a wavering Nazi. "If you don't, I'll turn evidence against you." Roosevelt and Churchill had long since announced a future war-crimes tribunal. The criminals would be tried at the scene of their crimes, the Allies promised.

It was not always a straightforward exchange of one favor for another. To strike boldly, a person of great courage must still feel he is standing on solid ground, that his back is protected. Raoul Wallenberg's whole posture was a fiction. His position was based on nothing more substantial than his personal ability to convince, his growing reputation and his apparent self-confidence. That was all. No one was more aware of the thin ice he walked on than Wallenberg himself. There was nothing to prevent the roving bands of assassins who had free run of the city from taking his money and dumping one more body in the Danube. Life was very cheap in Budapest in those days. Wallenberg, perhaps better than anyone, understood this.

It started with a blood bath. Two hundred corpses, still wearing yellow stars, were left lying on the streets of Pest the morning after the Szálasi coup. Henceforth any Jew caught on the street risked getting hauled away to one of the Arrow Cross's improvised inquisition chambers, which sprang up overnight on both sides of the Danube. There the most sadistic parodies of justice were played out. Men and women alike were stripped of their clothes, beaten and left shivering in ice-cold cellars. They were either shot or dragged to the river, the city's most accommodating burial ground.

Jews no longer dared to leave their homes. They were rounded up at random. Even those not wearing their yellow stars—a crime punishable by death—were easily spotted now. Their clothes were in rags. They had been wearing the same suit or dress since they were given a few minutes to clear out of their homes and move into the specially designated ones. They lived like prisoners, twenty or thirty to a room. Washing, either themselves or their garments, had become a luxury.

On a woman's bike he found in the legation garage (for his own car had been vandalized), Wallenberg circulated through town. Thus he had to round up members of his own staff, who were afraid, like all Jews, to leave their homes. He persuaded them to take a chance and trust in his ability to protect them. With rare exceptions, they did. Most of them were sheltered in his offices during this period. His rescue operation had now become a twenty-four-hour service. His staff again swelled to nearly four hundred. His first concern was always for their safety. Without their help he could not have worked the miracles he did.

By now, Wallenberg had set himself apart from the Swedish legation, in its picturesque villa on the Gellért Hill. He moved to Pest, where his staff lived. It was more than a physical move. Henceforth he would operate as a separate entity, largely making his own decisions and reporting only to Stockholm. He took orders from no one.

In a memo to his staff he wrote: "This department must be in action day and night. There are no days off. If someone fails, he should not expect much help. If he performs well, he must not wait to be thanked." There were those among his fellow Swedish diplomats who were not enamored of his seeming arrogance and unorthodox methods. Was it proper, after all, for a first secretary to be Sweden's primary liaison with the Hungarian government? Minister Danielsson worried that Wallenberg was putting the entire legation staff in danger. But Danielsson resisted his Foreign Office's repeated calls that he and his diplomats return to Stockholm. Sweden had no intention of recognizing the Szálasi regime. It did not really see the point of maintaining a legation in Budapest. But Danielsson stayed on and thus enabled Wallenberg to perpetuate the fiction of eventual Swedish diplomatic recognition. Without the backing of the legation, Wallenberg would have cut an even lonelier figure in the lawless streets of Budapest.

Wallenberg was a driven man by now. He seemed to be everywhere. When he learned that an eighty-one-year-old man was being taken away to dig trenches at the front, he bombarded the Foreign Ministry with daily appeals for his safe conduct. With the help of his informers inside the Gendarmerie, he dogged the old man's steps through the countryside. After a half a dozen memos to the Foreign Ministry, the old man's tracks disappeared and Wallenberg gave up the battle to save him.

Every day rough placards pasted on trees announced the government's latest decree regarding the Jews. On October 20, all

Jewish males between the ages of fourteen and sixty-five were ordered to report to the city's largest sports stadium, to begin their forced-labor service. The following day's decree was for women between sixteen and sixty. They were to report to the same sports arena for the same purpose. These battalions consisted largely of trench diggers at the front. The laborers were equipped with neither uniforms, boots or helmets nor arms for protection. A yellow armband was their standard issue.

Panic was spreading like the plague through the city. People were looking for hiding places. Christians were implored or bribed to take in the persecuted. Thousands of Jews took on new identities. The fledgling Zionist underground had a printing press. Baptismal papers bearing such fine old Magyar names as Toth, Szabo and Kovács were turned out. The desperate even attempted to buy uniforms off the backs of the Nazis. Sometimes they succeeded.

Neither a new identity nor a new uniform guaranteed protection. In one incident, a Jew who managed to escape from his forced-labor battalion was provided with new identity papers by the Zionists, who worked under the protection of the International Red Cross. The young man was even provided with the uniform of a Hungarian National Guard. The Arrow Cross patrol that stopped him on the street spent long moments looking into the face of the Jew on the run, and down at the papers which said "Lászlo Toth." They let him go. "Toth" was only a few steps from the patrol when he heard his real name called out: "Tibor Szekacs!" He spun around automatically. The Arrow Cross bullet was well aimed. Szekacs-Toth never got up again. One of the patrol had recognized the Jew as a childhood playmate.

13   The Baroness

T he Baroness Elisabeth Kemény was not feeling well. The birth of the baby she was carrying was only a few months away, and on this late-October morning it seemed ready to fight its way into the world. The baroness, wife of Baron Gábor Kemény, Foreign Minister in the Arrow Cross government, went to the window for some fresh air. Three stories below, on Fö Street, which hugs the Danube beneath the Royal Palace, a familiar scene took place. A procession of scrawny kids, with hollow, old-men's faces, and bent, withered old people, eyes fixed on the ground beneath them, were advancing with slow, deliberate steps. The obscenities shouted by a truculent band of youths, armed with machine pistols, encouraged their progress. Although these parades had become a fixture of daily life in Budapest that fall, it was the first time the baroness had caught a glimpse of this ritual under the Arrow Cross.

For a moment the twenty-eight-year-old Austrian aristocrat forgot her swollen body and her discomfort. She rushed down the stairs to the front gate of the ministerial residence. "Who are these people?" she asked one of those green-uniformed Hungarian soldiers who stood constant guard over the building. "Where are they being led?"

The soldier's expression was mildly amused. "Oh, it's nothing to get excited about," he answered. "They're just going to do a little work. That's all."

The young woman was upset by the dismal scene and insulted by the soldier's clumsy lie. The group had disappeared toward the Danube. There was nothing more she could do but wait for her husband to come home that evening.

Baron Kemény claimed he did not know the meaning of the

procession. He was Foreign Minister, after all; these matters were
none of his business. He did promise his agitated wife he would
find out. He kept his word. He used the bland euphemism "deportation" to describe what both husband and wife realized meant
something else. The baroness could not forget the faces of the
people or the painfully slow shuffle as they were marched past her
window.

Elisabeth Fuchs Kemény was a product of the last century. She
was the daughter of a proud if somewhat faded aristocratic family,
left over from the dilapidated Hapsburg days. She was born and
bred in the picture-postcard town of Merano, tucked away in the
southern Tyrol, where the Italian and Austrian Alps are joined.
Merano is not a very serious place, and the blue-eyed baroness
was not a particularly serious person. Nor was she expected to be
one. Her mother's family tree claimed two popes. Her grandfather
had been the President of the Austrian Parliament. In nine years
spent in Sacred Heart convents in Italy, Austria and Great Britain,
she had acquired four languages, a sure grasp of bridge, and influential, titled friends across the European map. Until she met the
romantic, sad-eyed Baron Kemény, to ski in Cortina d'Ampezzo was
her chief passion.

It was almost inevitable that these two representatives of the
defunct Austro-Hungarian Empire, the Countess Fuchs and the
Baron Kemény, should meet. The setting was a shooting party in a
baronial hunting lodge. He was handsome in that peculiarly soulful,
Hungarian way, and would inherit three castles. His chief obsession was the country of his ancestors, the once proud Transylvanian
family of Kemény, feudal landowners who, even now, lived like
monarchs. Kemény did not share Elisabeth's internationalism. His
world began and ended with Hungary. To him there was no
greater evil, no greater danger for humanity, than Bolshevism. The
baron was willing to pay any price to keep the Russian menace,
which threatened to chew up his carefully constructed world, at
bay. To say he was an anti-Semite is to state the obvious. His was
the well-bred anti-Semitism of the Hungarian aristocracy, as solidly
fixed as its love of a sentimental *csárdás*.

The young baron had joined the predominantly under-class,
fanatically Jew-hating Arrow Cross because he saw it as Hungary's
last port in a hostile sea. The Arrow Cross was ready to fight all

odds to beat the Bolsheviks. Others of the baron's own class, like Regent Horthy, were ready to embrace the enemy. Kemény was also an ambitious man, and the Arrow Cross offered rapid advancement. The thirty-one-year-old former journalist, without any real government experience, was made Foreign Minister in the Szálasi regime. If their cause was doomed, Kemény would at least go down fighting for the vanished Hungary of his dreams. In his way, he was an idealist and a hopeless visionary. He would pay for his dreams with his life.

Kemény also had a domestic problem. His wife, the light-hearted, vivacious Austrian girl, carrying his first child, was angry and upset. The dismal parade in front of her window was only the beginning of her awakening. As the wife of the Foreign Minister, the baroness regularly entertained the diplomatic corps. During one such reception in their elegant, antique-filled apartment, the baroness met the First Secretary of the Swedish legation. The baroness and Wallenberg had a number of things in common. They quickly lapsed into English, the language they both loved to speak. In a room full of strident German accents and uniforms, she found him gentle, pleasant-looking and easy to talk to. They both liked music, art and the lovely city which was crumbling around them. The baroness liked his open, informal manner—unusual, she thought, in a diplomat.

It did not take Wallenberg long to tell his hostess that he needed her help. Talking fast, he told her about "his" Jews. The remnants of the city's Jewish population had nowhere else to turn but to Wallenberg, he explained. He told her about the new government's refusal to honor Swedish and other neutral protective passports. "Without those passports," Wallenberg told her, "I cannot save them. They will be marched to their deaths. I am a diplomat. I need some kind of legal basis under which to operate. I cannot conduct my business underground." She had seen the children and the old being marched away. His words penetrated.

Several days later Wallenberg called on the baroness. He was accompanied by a tall man of distinguished bearing in a dark-blue Savile Row suit—but with eyes like freshly sliced, overripe plums, and cheeks crisscrossed by unhealed scars. The tall man was the former director of one of Budapest's largest banks. He had been dragged from his house and worked over by the Arrow Cross. "But why?" asked the shocked baroness. "I am a Jew," he answered. They did not stay long, but Wallenberg had made another point.

Foreign Minister Kemény did not receive his wife's usual warm welcome that evening. When the servants had left the dining room, Elisabeth presented her ultimatum. "You must make the Arrow Cross respect the protective passports," she told him, "or I am going to leave you. I'll go back to Merano and never see you again."

Her husband flew into a cold rage. In one movement he sent much of their fine Meissen wedding china flying to the floor, splintering into hundreds of pieces. He pushed back the table, rose and declared, "You have betrayed me!" Out he went, slamming the door behind him.

It was midnight when the exhausted baroness flicked on the radio. "Attention! Attention!" the announcer began. "The following is a message from the Foreign Minister of the Royal Hungarian Government: As of today, members of the armed services, as well as Arrow Cross officers, are to regard passports as legal, that are issued by the neutral embassies. These passports are to be respected. In addition, the extraterritoriality of buildings flying neutral colors are to be observed. Those people possessing foreign passports are not to be deported for forced labor." The special announcement was repeated twice.

One hour later the baron returned to his wife. "Did you hear it?" he asked her. "Yes," she answered. And, yes, she would stay.

The radio message opened an important door for Wallenberg; though the government had decreed that only 4,500 of his passports were valid, about twice that number were in circulation. The renewed legal status of the documents enabled the Swede to operate in an atmosphere of near-anarchy. Wallenberg could use these passports to haul people from the brickworks, which were the reception halls for the death marches, from labor battalions that amounted to execution squads, and even from the death marches themselves. The passports and his constant presence were the Jews' chief weapons against terror.

From this moment on, Wallenberg's friendship with the baroness was cemented. They were in nearly daily contact. She was his conduit to her husband. And her husband listened to her. He respected her and, perhaps, realized she was the stronger of the two. Married only two years, he certainly did not want to lose her. Only once did he ask her to join the Arrow Cross, like all the other Cabinet wives. When she said no, he never asked again. "Had I met you sooner," he told her, "I never would have joined the Arrow Cross." Now it was too late. There was no place for him to go. He was permanently linked to the Nazis.

The baron agreed to help Wallenberg. But he would move cautiously. He did not wish to alienate the rest of the Cabinet. On many evenings Kemény would come home muttering, "Your friend Wallenberg, doesn't he think I have anything else to do but look after his Jews?" Wallenberg was bombarding Kemény's office with personal visits, followed by memoranda summing up their conversations. This was the Swede's way of letting the Foreign Minister know that his verbal commitments were on record. With his foot in the minister's door, Wallenberg was not about to withdraw. There was always someone missing, someone too old to work, who had been clapped into forced labor. No case was too small for Wallenberg's attention. Kemény was his link to authority.

The baron told his wife that the Swede was causing nearly as much discomfort in his own legation as in the Hungarian Foreign Ministry. "Danielsson is as bothered by his persistence as I am," Kemény claimed. "Wallenberg thinks only of his Jews. Danielsson is worried he'll get all the diplomats in trouble yet." Wallenberg was aware of the tension his zeal was creating. He told the baroness he would never be a diplomat. He knew he was not cut out for the precaution and protocol of that world.

Infected by Wallenberg's enthusiasm, the baroness began her own mission. Rumors about the wife of a high-ranking Nazi with Jewish sympathies spread quickly. Her apartment became a waiting room for people with favors to ask. Those who could were trying to flee the country, and visa requests were brought to her by the score. Liberals, Social Democrats, monarchists, half-Jews, nuns, all those with reason to fear the regime filled her apartment.

In her husband's chauffeur-driven official Mercedes, she delivered visa and passport applications to the desk of Dr. Edmund Veesenmayer, the Reich's envoy in Budapest. Veesenmayer could not easily decline such requests from the Foreign Minister's wife. But he complained heatedly to Kemény about his wife's meddling. Hearing for the first time of his wife's private campaign, the baron again lost his temper. But he was forced to calm down; he did not have much choice.

The baroness was mildly amused by the outrage she was creating. She felt safe behind her Austrian citizenship, her husband's protection and the impenetrable shield of lifelong privilege. When the wives of German or Hungarian Nazis cautioned her about pushing her luck, she would laugh. She was a baroness, by birth and marriage, she was young and pretty, and she could charm her way out of any situation.

She was also becoming bolder with her husband. She refused to attend official Nazi events. She would not have Eichmann in her house. She avoided Szálasi's invitations; he was a boring fanatic with whom she had nothing in common, she told her husband. She used her pregnancy as an excuse. Which is what she did when the German Foreign Minister, Joachim von Ribbentrop, invited the Keménys to Berchtesgaden.

In Raoul Wallenberg she had a friend. She liked to make him laugh, to distract him momentarily from his mission. Their backgrounds were not so very different. They might have met skiing or on the Riviera, or in one of the European capitals they both knew well. Under different circumstances they might have gone to the theater and the opera together. But now that was out of the question. What they now had was a genuine, mutual sympathy. She never felt he was using her; he was too forthright for that. They worked together. The only thing she ever asked of him was an occasional protective passport for a Jewish friend. She herself was a Roman Catholic and needed none. Nor, as the wife of the Foreign Minister, did she lack for food or anything else. It was a relationship based on good feelings and trust. For the Austrian baroness and the Swedish diplomat these were rare commodities in Nazi-occupied Budapest.

Commenting on her pregnancy, Wallenberg told her that someday he, too, would like to have a child. But not yet. There was no time really to think about such things now. As far as he was concerned, there was only time to think about saving thousands of people. The baroness thought he was very much like her own husband—passionate idealists, both of them, only for different causes. Her husband stayed on to fight for a Hungary everybody else thought was doomed; Wallenberg was a crusader for a people others had written off.

Their friendship lasted a very short time. Early in December her doctor advised her to leave the nightmare of the city for the quiet of her sleepy Alpine town. Her child was not expected for six more weeks, but, she was told, a short holiday would be good for the mother. Flanked by two armored Wehrmacht cars, she and her cook were packed into the Foreign Minister's Mercedes for their long journey across Hungary and Austria down the Dolomites to Merano. An enormous bouquet of yellow roses hid the face of the young man who had rushed over to say goodbye. Wallenberg looked sad, on that gray winter morning. He was losing a valued ally. He was also losing a friend. "I'll be back in three weeks," she told him.

She did not want to be away from her husband for her confinement. But the Red Army had reached Ujpest, not far from the city limits, and Raoul was not sure they would see each other for a long time. "You have been a great help," he told her. "I shall miss you." Then, as the convoy was starting to roll, he reached into the back of the Mercedes and held her hand for just a moment. "If anything should happen to you," he whispered, "I have told Kollontai about you and the child." The baroness had never heard the name before, so she did not know that Alexandra Kollontai, one of Lenin's vanguard during the Bolshevik Revolution, was the Soviet ambassador in Stockholm and a very influential figure in the Swedish capital. Her wide circle of friends included Wallenberg's mother. Later, when Wallenberg himself would need her help, she could do little for him. At any rate, the baroness was touched by his concern and waved him off with "See you soon." They would never see each other again.

Less than three weeks after Elisabeth Kemény's car pulled out of Budapest, she gave birth to her son, one month premature. By now, returning to Hungary was out of the question. The siege of Budapest was on. Her husband followed the rest of the Arrow Cross government to their exile in the western Hungarian town of Szombathely.

One of his final acts before leaving the capital was to make sure that the Crown of St. Stephen not fall into the hands of the Red

Army. This nine-hundred-year-old ornament has an almost mystical hold on Hungarian nationalists. It was from this crown that all Hungarian rulers drew their power and authority. For centuries they had passed laws, declared wars and let heads roll "in the name of the Hungarian Holy Crown." Baron Gábor Kemény packed the crown and its accompanying national treasures in a crate and sent it up the Danube on a barge to Austria. It eventually fell into the Allies' hands and was shipped to Fort Knox. There the treasures sat in a vault until 1978. That year, amid great pomp, the then Secretary of State Cyrus Vance personally delivered the historic jewels to Budapest. Despite Baron Kemény's best effort, St. Stephen's Crown now sits under a glass dome in the National Museum of the People's Republic of Hungary.

The Foreign Minister was less successful in saving himself. When the Nazis were finally routed, and the Russians in control of the ravaged country, Kemény escaped to Merano. Within a matter of weeks, Hungarian Jews turned him in to the United States Military Command, the local army of occupation. After brief periods in various Allied POW camps in Italy, tracked everywhere by his distraught wife, Kemény was finally escorted back to Budapest. There he was tried along with Szálasi and the other members of the Arrow Cross hierarchy. He was sentenced to death for collective guilt. His request that Hungary's new coalition government spare his life due to "mitigating circumstances" was rejected. The baroness heard the news of his public hanging on the BBC.

14 "I Want to Save a Nation"

C aptain Nándor Batizfalvy, a Hungarian army officer of the old school, did not have the stomach for the scene before him. He could not bear the sight of the endless column of pathetic humanity shuffling to keep up, on feet too swollen to carry them anymore. He turned away from the great-coated Hungarian gendarmes, who barely restrained their snarling Doberman pinschers on very short leashes. The people in the column resembled, more than anything else, the Nazis' own caricatures of the Jews. All flesh was gone from the death marchers' faces. They were all eyes and all noses.

Captain Batizfalvy called Raoul Wallenberg. The heavy-breathing, distraught Hungarian spilled out the entire repulsive picture for the Swede: 8,000 Hungarians had already been handed over to the Germans at Hegyeshalom near the Austrian border; 13,000 more were being marched toward the frontier.

Wallenberg did not wait for more details. He gathered what food he could, grabbed his typewriter, and accompanied by Per Anger and two aides, set off on the Hegyeshalom Road. He wanted to reach the border before the next group did.

When Wallenberg arrived at the barrier several hours later, he was an emotionally charged man. He had seen a picture of de-graded humanity even he was not prepared for. Eichmann and Wisliceny were standing in front of the border checkpoint, waiting.

It was Eichmann who had decided that if the trains could no longer be spared to transport the Jews to their deaths, then they should walk. Early in November he started the death marches, 125-mile hikes in the cold and rain of late fall. The distance had to be covered on foot without any real food or shelter along the way. For at least 10,000 people, who died of exhaustion or hunger or thirst, the march itself accomplished the job Eichmann was impatient to get on with.

The marches started whenever the Nazis could round up enough Jews to start them walking: on street corners, in shops, in their own homes. No Jew was completely safe from the fatal convoy. Soon the roadside from Budapest to Hegyeshalom was one long graveyard. Those who stumbled and fell were generally finished off with a single bullet. Others used the overnight rest in village squares or in open fields to end their own lives: bodies were often found hanging limply from trees the next morning.

In the village of Gönyü, on the Danube, where a number of marchers were stopped overnight, scores of them jumped into the icy black river. Others were driven in by Arrow Cross rifle butts. The endless columns snaked through the countryside, covering twenty miles a day.

The young were sometimes made to march longer distances. They never dared fall back or even lean against each other. The gendarmes competed with the Arrow Cross rifle butts to deal with stragglers. One such group of young people, having marched for three days without food or drink, was led to the attic of an abandoned farmhouse in the village of Szöny, for a night's rest. During the night the attic collapsed under the weight of the group. Seven of them were crushed to death, thirteen were critically wounded and seventy could not continue the march. They were all left in the deserted farmhouse, without medical attention or even food.

For those who had made it that far, Hegyeshalom was their final stop in Hungary. "*Fünf, sechs, sieben . . .*" Eichmann's lieutenant and Dieter Wisliceny started counting heads as soon as the marchers began to straggle into view. Wallenberg had only one chance. "In the name of the Szálasi government, I demand those with Swedish passports to raise them high!" A voice, unemotional, strong, with just a trace of an aggressive edge, a voice ready to do battle, had spoken. Eichmann and Wisliceny spun round. "I'm Wallenberg, Swedish Legation" was all the explanation he provided.

"You there!" The Swede pointed to an astonished man, waiting for his turn to be handed over to his executioner. "Give me your Swedish passport and get in that line," he barked. "And you, get behind him. I know I issued you a passport." Wallenberg continued, moving fast, talking loud, hoping the authority in his voice would somehow rub off on these defeated people. Eichmann did not relish public confrontations. He preferred a quiet, well-ordered passage from life to death. He would have to spare a few bodies for this strange, determined Swede.

The Jews finally caught on. They started groping in pockets for bits of identification. A driver's license or a birth certificate seemed to do the trick. The Swede was grabbing them so fast; the Nazis, who couldn't read Hungarian anyway, didn't seem to be checking. Faster, Wallenberg's eyes urged them, faster, before the game is up. In minutes he had several hundred people in his own convoy. International Red Cross trucks, there at Wallenberg's behest, arrived, and the Jews clambered on. Wisliceny resumed his interrupted head count. *"Fünf and vierzig, sechs und vierzig . . ."*

Wallenberg jumped into his own car. He leaned out of the car window and whispered, "I am sorry," to the people he was leaving behind. "I am trying to take the youngest ones first," he explained. "I want to save a nation."

Along the way back to Budapest, he and the Red Cross convoy stopped frequently. They set up first-aid stations and distributed food to the marchers. With the help of Per Anger, and his typewriter, Wallenberg filled out passport applications which they had brought along for the marchers. "I'll be back," he told the incredulous people. He handed mugs of cognac and cigarettes to the gendarmes as payment for tolerating his interference.

Wallenberg returned to the border the next day. Growing bolder, he mounted the train that already held Eichmann's body count. "Get off this train!" he ordered those who had the courage to move. "I issued you a passport. Your name is right there in my book!" Hundreds more were saved by this bluff. "I have the permission of the Foreign Ministry," he told the Nazis who stood in his way. "Didn't you hear Baron Kemény's announcement?" All the while the Jews were climbing off the train, and with sudden energy, sprinting toward the waiting trucks.

Wallenberg succeeded in snatching about 2,000 people from the Nazis before they decided he was more than a minor irritation. But by the second week in November they faced another problem.

The trains could no longer take their human sacrifices even as far as Strasshof, the nearby Austrian death camp. Russian and Allied bombs had finally knocked the rail lines out of commission.

Eichmann was still not ready to give up. "The main thing," he told Wisliceny, "is the statistics. Every Jew must be accounted for." Seventeen thousand of the capital's Jews were already on freight trains in Budapest's Jozsefvárosi railroad station. He had already marched 60,000 people to the Austrian border. Why stop there— why not make the remaining Jews walk all the way to the death camps? It would only mean a few extra days after they reached the border. Some of them might even make it.

But Szálasi, the nominal chief of state, had to face world opinion. A sharp note signed by all the neutral diplomats still in Budapest reminded him that they knew the precise horrors of the death marches. Szálasi answered that the deportations were over. He had Himmler's support. The Reichsführer was attempting to build his own credibility as a negotiator of a separate peace with the Allies. He put his signature on an order to end the extermination of Jews as official Nazi policy.

Eichmann, however, had a proprietary feeling about Budapest. He had spent more time there than any other high-ranking Nazi. He felt he had earned the right to dispose of its Jews as he saw fit. Himmler was much too far away and too busy attempting to construct his own future to enforce his order.

But by now Eichmann was forced to abandon his plans for further Jewish deportations. He had to settle for collecting those who until now had managed to escape each time the Nazis lowered their net, and move them into a central ghetto. These people were mostly the old and the disabled, and women and children. But they were statistics: 63,000 people nobody seemed to care about. They were without connections, without resources, without Christian friends to shelter them, or Swedish passports to protect them. They were certainly people without a future.

Eichmann relied on the highly successful model of the Warsaw ghetto in drawing up his plans for Budapest's. Six-foot-high planks were thrown up by Arrow Cross toughs, blocking off the streets that framed the three synagogues of the capital, the former Jewish quarter. And 12,000 Christians were moved out to make way for 63,000 Jews.

Eichmann's captives could not leave to obtain medicine or to take care of any other emergency. They were completely dependent on their guards to bring them food, which often meant long days without the necessities of life.

15   Playing for Time

With the majority of the Jewish population sealed in the ghetto, Wallenberg knew he had very little time left. Szálasi announced that, as of late November, the country's Jews would be separated into those holding foreign passports, who must leave the country by the first of December, those who were "on loan" to do work in the Reich, and the vast majority, who would only leave the ghetto when the authorities were ready for them to leave.

The last thing Wallenberg wanted was for "his" protected Jews to leave Hungary. They were his legal basis for continuing his rescue work for the rest of the community. So he stalled. He drafted memo after memo to the Arrow Cross Foreign Ministry, demanding to know how the Jews would be transported from war-torn Hungary, through the Reich, to Sweden. There was, of course, no way the Hungarian government could guarantee the safe conduct of Jews across Germany. "In that case Sweden," Wallenberg informed the Foreign Ministry, "cannot agree to their transport."

Wallenberg had an extremely supple mind. He could always spot an opportunity and seize it. This was one. If "his" Jews were to be a separate category, they should remain, outside the central ghetto, in houses under Swedish protection while they awaited their eventual "repatriation." He persuaded the Arrow Cross Foreign Ministry to accept his subtle conclusion. Wallenberg now fabricated a special passport for the use of the Jewish Council, to distribute to whomever it wished.

When San Salvador's minister in Geneva, George Mandel Mantello, offered his Caribbean island's "citizenship" to Jews still outside the ghetto who needed it, Wallenberg accepted the responsibility of protecting San Salvador's newest citizens. Wallenberg's name, his constant presence, his stubborn refusal to take no for an answer, all these things, not the pieces of paper or even the houses flying his country's flag made the life-or-death difference.

As much as Wallenberg needed the four hours of sleep he allowed himself on most nights, he gladly gave up his bed on a cold December night. The wife of one of his office workers had started her labor pains. Hospitals were barred to Jews, and Tibor Vándor and his young wife lived in a crammed, barely heated Swedish-protected house. So Wallenberg offered the couple his bedroom and even rounded up a Jewish doctor.*

While Wallenberg spent the night in his overcoat and hat shivering in the corridor outside his apartment, Ágnes Vándor was delivered of a healthy baby girl.

The Vándors insisted that Wallenberg be her godfather and that he help choose the baby's name. "She looks just like one of my grandmothers!" the new godfather exclaimed, "Nina Maria!" The couple were partial to Yvonne as a name for their newborn, so they compromised and named the baby Yvonne Maria.

Thirty-five years later Yvonne Maria Singer of Toronto, Canada, read an account of this birth in the Toronto *Star*. She recognized her own story. With one correction. Her parents, Mrs. Singer told the newspaper, were not Jewish. Actually, the Vándors had never told their daughter of her real background. They wanted to spare her what they regarded as an inevitable albatross. Yvonne Maria Singer did not wish to be spared. She had already married a Jew and had converted from Catholicism to Judaism, without ever knowing what her roots were.

There were times when Wallenberg's zeal got the better of him. He was so electric with energy and lack of sleep that he did not know when to stop. Spreading the rumor of a typhoid epidemic among the Jews was one of these cases of pushing too far. Wallenberg was getting tired of saving people from the Nazis or the Arrow Cross, only to have them fall right back into their hands. "If we let the word out," he proposed to one of the forty Jewish doctors he recruited to care for the sick, "that those who have returned from the death march brought with them a severe typhoid epi-

---

* The same doctor, the well-loved Béla Kende, also delivered the author, several years later.

demic, they would have to quarantine those people. They'd have to leave them alone." Wallenberg was a persuasive man, but the doctor was not enthusiastic about the idea. Still, he agreed to accompany Wallenberg to the improvised Swedish Hospital he had helped set up. They would see if any of the death-march survivors had anything like the symptoms of typhoid.

It was two in the morning, not an unusual time for Wallenberg to be circulating in the streets of Budapest. The hospital's gate-keeper had his own hours. He kept the Swede and the doctor wait-ing for fifteen minutes. Wallenberg, who had other visits still to make, berated the man for taking his time. The gatekeeper replied with a hard fist on Wallenberg's nose. "Don't you know who this man is?" the angry doctor shouted. "It's Wallenberg, you fool!" With blood trickling down his lips and chin, Wallenberg managed a half smile. "If this is how tough it is for me to get in this place," he said to the doctor, "imagine how tough it must be for the Arrow Cross." He told the man to forget it. The doctor saw the incident as an ill omen for their "epidemic." Wallenberg, who still thought it was not such a bad idea, agreed to call it off.

By the next morning he had other problems, which made him forget about the imaginary typhoid. A group of Arrow Cross thugs pulled several hundred Jews out of their "safe" houses. They marched them to the city's central synagogue, a Moorish-Byzantine structure in the heart of what was once the city's commercial dis-trict. Now there were very few people on the street to observe the uniformed hoods shove their quarry into the temple's courtyard. A cordon of regular police formed a protective shield around the synagogue to make sure no one interrupted the planned pogrom.

Wallenberg had been alerted. He showed his diplomatic papers to the police officer in charge and did not wait to be ushered in. "I'm Wallenberg!" he shouted to the assembled Jews before the Arrow Cross knew what was happening. "Some of you have my passports. I want you to step forward." The dazed group did not move. He had his massive book of names with him. "Mandl, Fried-man, Schwartz . . ." he began. He meant business. He looked much thinner now than when he had first arrived in the city. Yet he seemed totally unafraid of the mindless killers he was facing down. Like a balm, his courage spread among the people. If he can do this for us, they decided, we can do something for ourselves.

Thus he was able to save several hundred people from execution in the synagogue.

Incidents like this one boosted the Jews' morale. They began to have such faith in him that they stopped showing their special passes to the Arrow Cross—too often they would only get torn up in their faces. So they let themselves be taken to one of the Arrow Cross collection centers, and waited for Wallenberg to come.

Courage, of course, was not enough. Imagination and humanity were equally important. Wallenberg could play a great many roles, including matchmaker between an Arrow Cross guard and his Jewish captive.

The boy was called Junior by his pals. He had seen Wallenberg in action and looked on the older man with something like reverence in his eyes. Junior was supposed to be guarding a group of young Jewish girls in one of the Arrow Cross houses on Teleki Square. It was only a matter of days before the young women would be sent either marching or worse. Junior was smitten by one of these doomed creatures. She was about his age, very pretty, with fine blond hair and blue eyes. Only her yellow star and her clothes, which had turned to rags, gave her away. Junior had heard stories about the underground armaments factories of the Reich, needing women to do the work for which they could no longer spare men. Very few people were expected to walk out of those places alive.

Junior could not speak to his comrades about the girl. He talked to Wallenberg. The Swede saw his opportunity. He marched into the house where she was under guard and identified himself to the Arrow Cross. "Will those people who are Christian," he shouted, looking straight at the blond girl, "but who haven't got the papers to prove it, step forward." The girl picked up the signal and stepped forward. Wallenberg told the Arrow Cross to use her as kitchen help while he sorted out her papers. He slipped the girl some money and told her to make her escape from the kitchen. Junior made sure she got out.

16   The Photographer

I t was typical of Wallenberg that in the middle of the hell which was his daily life, he could concentrate on something as seemingly unimportant as engaging a photographer. He wanted a more permanent record of each day's horror than his own memories. Per Anger introduced him to Thomas Veres, the street-wise son of a well-known society photographer. Young Veres had taken pictures of children of the Swedish diplomats. A Jewish convert to Christianity, he signed on as Wallenberg's photographer, in exchange for Swedish protection. He did not really know what he was getting into.

Wallenberg wanted Veres to document the most telling moments in the Jews' debasement. Veres thought the idea far too risky. At first he accompanied Wallenberg on his rescue missions without taking out the camera he had hidden inside his jacket. Observing Wallenberg moving through the city, as though dealing with gangsters was the most natural of occupations, Veres soon forgot to be afraid. He devised a technique of shooting through a hole in his scarf, in which he had wrapped his camera. Soon he was recording, often hurriedly framed and out of focus, the most hair-raising incidents, without blinking. He would then develop the pictures in his own darkroom and Wallenberg would send them to Stockholm in the diplomatic pouch. For the Foreign Office, and later for the world at large, Veres' photographs proved to be an invaluable piece of historic evidence.

Wallenberg always behaved as though nothing was impossible. "Meet me at the Jozsefvárosi railroad station," the Swede scribbled in his nightly message to Veres, left at his Üllöi Street office. As simple as if the two men were seeing a favorite aunt off on her holiday. Before the Nazis found another use for it, the Jozsefvárosi station had been a freight loading yard. Grain and other foodstuffs from Budapest and the provinces were loaded onto freight trains, to be shipped to Vienna from this out-of-the-way station in eastern Pest. In the last few months, Jews on the way to forced labor in the Reich had replaced the cargo.

Veres was there the next morning. Wallenberg, flanked by heavily armed gendarmes, was waiting. The station itself was entirely ringed by gendarmes. Wallenberg's newly acquired Studebaker, driver behind the wheel, was parked a few feet from the platform.

An endless gray mass of men, some carrying bedrolls, others with suitcases, still wearing business suits and hats, stood waiting to be herded, sixty to eighty in each boxcar. Wallenberg and the head of the gendarmes, László Ferenczy, were bent over the Swede's ever-present black book behind a long table on the platform. "My people get in line here," Wallenberg called out. There were several hundred of "his" people. They were allowed to begin their walk home. There was no one at the yard to claim the Swiss or the Portuguese passport holders.

While Wallenberg engaged the gendarmes in animated conversation, Veres seized the momentary chaos caused by the crush of people flowing back toward the city and freedom. He slipped around to the other side of the packed trains, the side away from the gendarmes, facing the empty road. The photographer managed to slide open the bolt which had not yet been padlocked shut from the outside. Hundreds of startled people poured out, first walking, then running for their lives. A short distance from Wallenberg, a gray-uniformed SS officer who until that moment had stayed in the background now stepped forward. Hauptsturmführer Theodor Dannecker approached close enough for Wallenberg to see the skull and crossbones on his visored cap. "Nein!" Dannecker pronounced, raising one elegantly gloved hand.

A vigilant gendarme picked up the cue. He slowly lowered the barrel of his automatic rifle until the Swede was centered in his gun sight. Wallenberg was no longer behind the long table. Black book under his arm, he bounded across the platform to the other side of the train and into his waiting car. He pulled Veres in next to him while his driver barreled the Studebaker out of the station.

Dannecker, one of Eichmann's closest henchmen, was furious.

Henceforth he made no secret of his plan to even the score with
Wallenberg. Later, when diplomatic license plates became mean-
ingless, Dannecker ordered Wallenberg's car smashed by a German
armored personnel carrier. The Swede was not in it.

Veres' photographs served another purpose. They were additional
means of bolstering Wallenberg's Swedish passports. In the middle
of the death marches, Wallenberg paid a call on Ferenc Fiala,
spokesman for the Szálasi government. Wallenberg tossed a packet
of fifty Veres photographs on the desk of this former Hungarian
fencer of little note. The shots showed Hungarian Nazis rounding
up Jews from houses flying the Swedish colors. Wallenberg threatened to send them immediately to Stockholm, destroying the
Szálasi regime's chances of being recognized by Sweden. Fiala,
protesting vehemently against this piece of blackmail, said he would
give the Arrow Cross an unambiguous order: the Swedish houses
were to be off-limits. The problem, Wallenberg understood, was
that the Arrow Cross often did not pay much attention to their
own leaders. Nevertheless, he wanted some sort of commitment
from the top. That would give him at least a wobbly legal leg to
stand on. For the rest, he relied more and more on his own ability
to maneuver and manipulate. Wallenberg took back Veres' pictures
and told the Nazi they would stay with him, for now.

Veres was on his way home to his apartment on Vörösmarty
Square one evening, pockets bulging with a day's exposed film.
He was planning to develop the clandestine material in his darkroom overnight. Veres wore the long black boots and riding pants
favored by the Arrow Cross. Wallenberg thought this would be one
layer of protection for the young man who was taking far too many
risks. Veres felt a bright light stinging his eyes. For a split second
he could not see anything except a pair of black boots much like
his own in front of him. "Long live Szálasi!" Veres shouted automatically, flinging his right arm straight out, in his best imitation
Nazi salute. The Arrow Cross patrol lowered his searchlight and
returned the salute. Veres kept walking. That was the last night
Wallenberg allowed him to hand-carry the volatile material home.
After this incident the Swede shipped the undeveloped film straight
to Stockholm.

Veres' parents were Jews under the special protection of Regent
Horthy. As Horthy's one-time photographer, the elder Veres had

a special certificate exempting him from wearing the yellow star or living in the ghetto. Late one winter night, young Veres found his parents' apartment ransacked. There was no sign of the old couple. Neighbors told Veres they had been marched toward the Danube by a gang of Arrow Cross. Veres never saw his parents again. He stayed with Wallenberg until the very end.

17   The Reign of Terror

Wallenberg had now moved from the Swedish legation, in Buda, to Pest, where both the ghetto and the protected houses were located. One hundred thousand Jews continued to walk a thin line between life and death, and he could not on his own keep track of them all. He relied on his Humanitarian Action Group, as his special unit, staffed by Jews, was called. It was a well-oiled machinery, and indispensable for Wallenberg's mission. Wallenberg had a strong taste for order and precision, which he expected his staff of nearly four hundred to respect. (Only once did his colleagues see Wallenberg lose his habitual self-control. It was when an Arrow Cross mob ransacked his office. The sight of his neat files and his precious book of names of passport holders, strewn on the floor, shattered his composure.)

Wallenberg actually showed off his operation to members of the SS or the Arrow Cross leaders. It was his way of letting them know how carefully the Nazis' movements were observed and documented. Each human life was on the record, he showed them. Each missing person was noted. Even in the most anarchic times, he continued to compose elegantly phrased memos to the killers. He treated the Arrow Cross as a legitimate, dignified source of authority, worthy of the trust and recognition of the rest of the world. Sometimes the flattery worked, and the Arrow Cross behaved momentarily as though civilization had not sunk to one of its lower depths.

Wallenberg's spirit infected the Red Cross. The international body stopped cowering behind platitudes and red tape and moved to keep up with the Swedish effort. Like Wallenberg, it, too, received funding from the American Jewish Joint Distribution Committee based in Geneva. A massive rescue team was finally set up in the Hungarian capital. The Red Cross, like the Swede, recruited Jews to help their fellow Jews, and at the same time, protect themselves behind an international shield.

Frederick Born, the Red Cross representative in Budapest, picked George Wilhelm, a worldly, Cambridge-educated Hungarian Jew, to head up his clandestine rescue team. Wilhelm had already been caught once in a Nazi dragnet. He managed to escape from the Gestapo prison. Wilhelm's younger brother, Peter, had already abandoned any hope of seeing him again. He shot himself while Wilhelm was in prison. After that, George Wilhelm had little love left for life, and very little fear. The son of one of Hungary's most prominent lawyers, he inherited enough money to be able to buy uniforms off the backs of the Nazis, both German and Hungarian. In the end, it was primarily their disposition to accept bribes that made Hungary's various storm troopers reachable.

Clad in the somber black of the higher SS, and speaking the impeccable German natural to Hungary's educated class, Wilhelm brandished false documents and demanded the liberation of "mistakenly" held Jews. The Arrow Cross, barely literate at the street level, was impressed by both his appearance and his command of the language of the occupying army. Often they relented. Wilhelm was in daily contact with Wallenberg. With his unflappable calm and his quiet sense of humor in moments of sheer despair, the Swede spurred on the Hungarian. Like Wallenberg, Wilhelm was fueled by each perfectly executed bluff. The sight of the routine massacres on the city's streets only diminished his own survival fears. If Wallenberg can do it, Wilhelm told himself, with no real ties to this place, or to these people, then I can too. And so he did.

Wilhelm's old family connections helped. His twenty-five-man team was housed in the Baroque villa of a Hungarian army officer, an acquaintance from his past life. Colonel László Ocskay, out of step with the fanatical new order, had many friends in the German officer corps. Thus, in the bizarre twilight atmosphere of December 1944, it happened that a team of Hungarian Jews, under the shield of the Red Cross, was actually saving Jews from Eichmann under the aegis of the Wehrmacht. Through Colonel Ocskay, Wilhelm had the protection of SS Colonel Hans Weber, a splendid specimen of Hitler's tall blond Aryan ideals, who now toward the end of the war, did not share the Nazi vision of paradise.

Following Wallenberg's example, Wilhelm and his team had driven several Red Cross trucks to the notorious Óbuda brickworks. Wilhelm carried the signed, sealed order of Lászlo Ferenczy, head of the gendarmes, demanding the release of several hundred of the condemned. Both the uniformed impostor and the forgery he carried appeared beyond suspicion. Wilhelm drove off with three hundred astonished men, women and children.

Once these Jews had been driven to the safety of a former Jewish high school, they again became vulnerable to the next wave of thugs. It wasn't long before it arrived. They were all told to line up, and were relieved of their remaining money, jewelry and even their overcoats. A small child was pushed out of the line by her mother. What was there to lose? "Run for Wilhelm," she was told. When the Hungarian got word of the imminent deportation of the people he had just saved, he had only one recourse: Standarten-führer Hans Weber. He reached the colonel at Berchtesgaden, Hitler's Salzburg retreat. Weber, who had his own Luftwaffe two-seater plane, was back in Budapest the same night. By midnight he was at the high school. With five Tiger tanks to back up his words, he gave the Arrow Cross the command: "Give them back their clothes and their money. You are a bunch of common thieves. Get out of here." The SS took over guarding the high school. Eichmann and his Hungarian zealots lost a prize of several hundred Jews that night.

As the situation deteriorated, there were more and more confrontations between the German army, Eichmann and the Arrow Cross. The Arrow Cross's appetite for loot was more rapacious than their interest in defending the city. Wallenberg frequently turned this conflict between these forces to his own advantage.

The trouble was that as the end approached, the Nazis' regard for human life, including their own, diminished. "We shall die here," many of them now said quite openly. Wallenberg had to continually persuade the Arrow Cross that life would go on after the war. A halfway clean record was better than a soiled one, he kept telling them. There was still a chance for international recognition if Hungary started behaving like a civilized country. It was an uphill argument in that atmosphere, but it was the only one he could use.

Though it had been weeks since Himmler officially stopped the death marches, Eichmann was still in the city. He was still counting heads. Nearly 100,000 Jews were left, a blot on his record. He liked to boast that he went to sleep counting dead Jews. The survival of a large portion of Budapest's Jews could not have made his sleep easy.

Wallenberg was intrigued by this shadowy figure, who preferred to let others bask in the limelight while he got on with the job of extermination. He, like Wallenberg, was single-minded about his mission. Wallenberg, possessed of an intense curiosity and never one to avoid a potential challenge, wanted to meet Eichmann.

The Swede, who felt he lacked an appropriate setting for such an occasion, asked his colleague Lars Berg to arrange a dinner in Berg's more comfortable house. Eichmann, the son of an electric line worker from Upper Austria, a grade school dropout, did not like social situations. He seldom went to diplomatic receptions and kept to the company of only his closest lieutenants. In their company, he was not indifferent to the charms of Budapest women or the hearty Tokay wines. But this was a different sort of outing. Eichmann, too, was curious about this uncommon first secretary of the Swedish legation. He had seen him only twice before. The first time was in the dimly lit bar of Pest's Arizona night club. Wallenberg, on a rare evening out, struck him as soft, another decadent diplomat, Eichmann later commented. The months since had proved his first impression wrong. He remembered the momentary showdown at Hegyeshalom. The Swede was giving him too many headaches. He was turning up in too many places, getting in his way too often. Out of curiosity, perhaps, Adolf Eichmann accepted the dinner invitation.

Dressed in his immaculately tailored SS officer's uniform, Eichmann was driven from his handsome villa on Buda's Hill of Roses, to Berg's more modest Gellért Hill house. In Eichmann's car were two revolvers and a battery of hand grenades. His driver waited outside while Eichmann, his own miniature Walther pistol tucked neatly inside his jacket, entered the Swedish diplomat's house.

The thin, balding Swede with the prominent nose and straightforward gaze opened the door to greet him. Eichmann forced a smile, which was a grimace. Wallenberg, whose pulse quickened in challenging moments, enjoyed the evening. The Swede relaxed while the Nazi sat bolt upright, as if ready to spring to his feet. The windows trembled from the rolling thunder of Russian artillery. "Look," Wallenberg said, "the war is over. Why don't you call off your people? Why not leave now, while you still can?"

Eichmann replied that he would stay on the job until the end. "Budapest," he said, "will be held as though it were Berlin." Then he gave Wallenberg a warning: "Don't think that just because you are a diplomat, you are immune from danger."

Wallenberg could not resist a chance to lecture Eichmann on the preordained fall of the Nazis. "Your genocide plans were doomed from the start," he said in conclusion.

The Nazi shrugged. "When the Russians come, I know they'll shoot me. I'm ready." Eichmann would later exhibit far more enthusiasm for saving himself. For now, he still had his plans for the Jews of the city.

While the Hungarian Foreign Ministry was still engaged in an awkward dialogue with Wallenberg, the armed delinquents in the streets were behaving as though they were the only real order. They had guns, they had a seemingly boundless appetite for blood and for the remnants of Jewish property. There was nobody to stop them. Wallenberg, for all his backup, was still ridiculously outnumbered. His bluff became a high-risk game.

Those of Wallenberg's aides whose faces were not known to the Arrow Cross he supplied with SS or Hungarian gendarme uniforms and dispatched them daily to various collection places, to countermand orders and save at least a handful from extermination. That Wallenberg found the work, no matter how dangerous, exhilarating, is clear from the letter he wrote his mother in early December:

> Dearest Mother,
>   I don't know how to atone for my silence, and yet again today all you will receive from me are a few hurried lines via the diplomatic pouch.
>   The situation here is hectic, fraught with danger and I am

terribly snowed under with work. . . . Night and day we hear the thunder of approaching Russian guns. Since Szálasi came to power, diplomatic activity has been lively. I myself am almost the sole representative of our embassy in all government departments. So far I have been approximately ten times to the Ministry of Foreign Affairs, have seen the deputy premier twice, the Minister of Interior twice, the Minister of Supply once and the Minister of Finance once.

I was on pretty close terms with the wife of the Foreign Minister. Regrettably, she had to leave for Merano.

There is an acute lack of food supplies in Budapest, but we managed to stockpile a fair amount in advance. I have the feeling that after the Russian occupation, I will reach Stockholm only around Easter. But all that lies in the future. So far, nobody knows what the occupation will be like. In any event, I shall try to get home as soon as possible.

I had firmly believed I would spend Christmas with you. Now I am compelled to send you my Christmas greetings and New Year's wishes by this means. I hope that the longed-for peace is not too distant. . . . Love to Nina and her little one.

It was a rare night when Wallenberg, who now alternated between two apartments to evade his would-be assassins, did not receive a phone call for help. He was every Jew's last resort. Somehow they nearly always found him. The Swede had no time of his own.

The desperate late-night voice of an elderly Swedish legation employee stirred him from a light sleep one night. "It's my son, Mr. Wallenberg," the voice on the telephone whispered. "They've taken my son and his wife and their child. The whole family . . . pulled from their beds and gone." Wallenberg did not wait for details. He hung up and dialed a number he knew by heart: Peter Hain's mountaintop headquarters. Hain usually knew the location of the night's haul of Jews, and very few people passed through the Hungarian Gestapo's hands unscratched. "This is Wallenberg," he said when he had Hain on the other end. "The Semestyen family . . . Do I have to come and get them myself or will you release them? You know they have our passports." The family, Hain insisted, was already on their way home. "They should have vacated their apartment long ago and moved into the ghetto. That's why we had to bring them in." Wallenberg called the anxious father and went back to sleep.

Ten days later the three Semestyens had not yet turned up. By then Wallenberg had composed three of his firm but polite memos to the Foreign Ministry, demanding an explanation and, above all, the protected family's release. The ministry finally replied. Peter Hain had told the truth: he had, in fact, released the family. However, on their way home, late at night, the three were accosted by roving Arrow Cross thugs. The Jews were unarmed and still had a few valuables, plus their coats and hats and shoes. The three were stripped and robbed. And for ten days they endured the various tortures invented by the street marauders for their own amusement. The family was then dragged to Budapest's graceful Chainbridge and pushed into the frozen Danube. Only the mother was still alive when a boatman fished her out the next morning.

It was not the sight of the old ghetto, or the synagogue court-yard, the scene of countless executions, that evoked the most pain for the people who survived those months; it was the sight of the Danube, once the eternal symbol of beauty and harmony and Budapest itself, that later caused them to break down.

For Wallenberg, the useless, mindless extermination of one more family was a cause for impenetrable, dark hours. He became un-communicative, and would stir from his own thoughts only when another life was on the line.

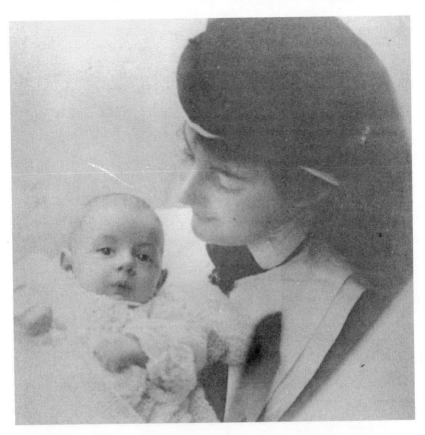

MOTHER AND CHILD. Raoul Wallenberg's mother Maj was still in mourning following the sudden death of her young husband when her son was born on August 4, 1912. (*Courtesy of The Raoul Wallenberg Committee of the United States*)

THE ADOLESCENT. Raoul already showed signs of the determined, purposeful air that was to distinguish him as an adult. *(Courtesy of The Raoul Wallenberg Committee of the United States)*

PORTRAIT. This is the photograph, carried by Swedish newspapers, that first brought Wallenberg to the attention of his countrymen. He was twenty-four and had just won second prize in a national architecture competition. *(Courtesy of The Raoul Wallenberg Committee of the United States)*

HOME GUARD. In 1943, Sweden was an island of neutrality in war-torn Europe. Wallenberg did not take that privileged status for granted, and became an active member of the Swedish Army Reserve. *(Courtesy of the Raoul Wallenberg Foundation, Stockholm)*

MICHIGAN. By the time Wallenberg arrived at the University of Michigan he had already seen parts of the globe not normally on any tourist's itinerary. *(Courtesy of Birgitte Wallenberg)*

THE BARON AND THE BARONESS GÁBOR KEMÉNY. He was the Foreign Minister of the Hungarian Nazi government. She befriended Wallenberg and coerced her husband into helping the Swede. The baron was later convicted as a war criminal and executed. *(Courtesy of Baroness Elisabeth Kemény)*

HUNGARIAN JEW. Shown wearing the star of David, reading public announcement in Budapest. *(Courtesy of The Raoul Wallenberg Committee of the United States)*

(Above) LAST-MINUTE RESCUE. Wallenberg, in a picture taken by his private photographer Thomas Veres, is shown here negotiating with German and Hungarian officials to win the release of a trainload of Jews bound for the death camps. He figures at right, his hands clasped behind his back. *(Used by permission)*

(Opposite top) JEWS RETURNING from the train station to the safe houses, their release having been negotiated by Wallenberg. *(Photograph by Thomas Veres. Used by permission)*

(Opposite bottom) WALLENBERG AND HIS COLLEAGUES. Wallenberg recruited once influential Jewish bankers, lawyers, and industrialists to help run his rescue operation. *(Photograph by Thomas Veres. Used by permission)*

LAST KNOWN PHOTOGRAPH.
Wallenberg in Budapest.
*(Photograph by Thomas Veres.
Used by permission)*

MONUMENT. A giant St. George
slaying the dragon was the
monument intended by the
people of Budapest to com-
memorate Wallenberg. The
Soviets removed it before it
was ever unveiled. *(Photograph
by Thomas Veres. Used by
permission)*

18   Eichmann's Final Days

T he Russian siege of Budapest began on December 8, 1944. With the entire city a battleground, the six-week struggle for the Hungarian capital became one of the war's bloodiest. To the residents, it also seemed agonizingly slow. The Red Army did not share the residents' impatience. The war had already cost the Russians six million soldiers, and they did not want any more casualties than absolutely necessary at this late hour. So they pounded away at the once beautiful city from a distance. Gradually, very gradually, they closed in on the battered remnants of the army of the Reich. The sky was a fireworks display of Soviet long-range artillery fire, Katusha rockets and Stalin organs. Soviet planes bombed Buda while German Messerschmitts and Focke-Wulfs released their deadly cargo on the outskirts of Pest.

For Wallenberg, it was a painful spectacle. From a small apartment near the Royal Palace, he could observe the town trembling beneath him. He loved her vaguely seedy grandeur. Now it was all crumbling in front of him. The river, which sliced the city in half, and never let you forget it was there, daily washed more and more corpses onto its banks. The ice floes that hugged its shores were bloodstained. Dark-green German tanks rolled through the snow-covered Buda streets, the only real street traffic left. At the major intersections, which once buzzed with life, with the gossip and humor that used to sustain the city, the Germans had set up antitank guns and machine-gun emplacements. Occasionally a creaky, overburdened wooden cart, carrying the dead of the night before and pushed by a ghostly figure, drifted across the deserted landscape. Mostly the bodies were left unburied in the streets. Sirens no longer bothered to warn residents of air raids that never ceased. Budapest had given up.

Eichmann and the Arrow Cross had not. Eichmann had succeeded in concentrating over 60,000 Jews in the Central Ghetto.
But there were still the 30,000 Jews, Wallenberg's Jews, living in
the so-called International Ghetto, whose freer and safer existence
rankled the Obersturmbannführer.

The Arrow Cross could make deals for their own purposes, for
the sake of some illusory future or money. Eichmann knew there
were people roaming the streets of Budapest who would have no
part of any deals between a stubborn diplomat and nervous, vulnerable rats looking to get off a sinking ship. Among the Arrow
Cross were a number of people that Eichmann could count on to
help him finish the job, although their motives were perhaps different from his. These people were mostly hoodlums, drunk on
their own power, with nobody around to say no. But the important
thing for Eichmann was that they would get the job done.

In one week in December 1944 the Budapest Ambulance Company, which, for some reason, still functioned, answered more
emergency calls than in all of the previous year. The sound of the
executioners' fusillade was as persistent as the bombers overhead.
Wallenberg's protected houses did not mean very much by mid-
December. Eichmann was still in town, but the Szálasi government had fled the city, to set up a hasty charade of a government in
the town of Szombathely, near the Austrian border. They had a
few weeks of life left. Interior Minister Gábor Vajna, in one of
his final pronouncements to Wallenberg before fleeing, told him,
"You'd better take your Jews, or you'll find them floating in the
Danube." Vajna knew there was no place Wallenberg could take
his Jews.

In late December two hundred Jews living in the Swedish protected house on Katona Jozsef Street were awakened by the relentless pounding on the door whose meaning was known to all of them.
There was no point in not opening. The idea was to open the door
and, at the same time, send someone to get Wallenberg. Which
is what these bone-weary, terrified people did. The eight Arrow
Cross brutes herded mothers, babies and the old into a neat convoy and briskly marched them off.

The messenger had reached Wallenberg. Before leaving his
apartment, Wallenberg called his Foreign Ministry contact to alert

him to what was taking place at a house flying the Swedish flag. He was told the people would be released immediately. Wallenberg jumped in his car, and despite the bombs, made it to Katona Jozsef Street in half an hour. Veres, and his new driver, Vilmos Langfelder, were with him.

When he pulled up, the street was as quiet as a morgue. He looked around at the sea of yellow-starred houses, incongruously flying the colors of his far-off kingdom. He knew it was too late. The door of the freshly raided house was still ajar. There was no one left except an Arrow Cross guard who was making sure no one had tried to outsmart them, by hiding in the rafters or the cellar.

"Where are my people?" Wallenberg demanded in his rough Hungarian.

"In the Danube" was the laconic answer.

"But why?" Wallenberg fought to stay calm.

"They were dirty Jews."

There was nothing more Wallenberg could do. There was no point in arguing or debating or wasting anything like reasonable words on this man. Wallenberg was silent in his failure.

Wallenberg had never witnessed an Arrow Cross ritual execution. He could not have stood by and watched. Either he would have stopped it somehow or he would himself have become one of the targets. But he knew the precise choreography. The Arrow Cross preferred the cover of night for their work. Toward the end of the siege they were no longer very particular. They would march their victims to an open area on the bank of the Danube. In the freezing cold of December and January, their captives were usually stripped of their clothing and huddled like shadows on a low hill. The favored number was three at a time, with their wrists wired together, facing the river. The rifleman would then fire into the back of the person standing in the middle. He would slump forward, dragging the other two into the Danube. This saved bullets and was just as effective as shooting all three. The freezing river and the weight of the corpse dragging them down would swiftly finish the job.

As the raids of the Swedish houses continued, Wallenberg turned from the powerless Hungarian authorities to what was left of German army headquarters. In a memorandum to the Wehrmacht Town Major's office, Wallenberg wrote as though law and order were still operative, as if diplomatic niceties were still worth the paper they were composed on:

> The Royal Swedish Legation of Budapest has been instructed by the Swedish Government to accord protection to several thousand inhabitants of Budapest, who have family or business ties with Sweden and to issue passports to these persons prior to their departure for Sweden. The Royal Swedish Legation has had evidence on several occasions that the above mentioned agreement has been interfered with by persons unacquainted with the facts, and therefore, takes the liberty of submitting the following request, pointing out its obligation as Protective Power, if it is given the necessary support by the responsible German and Hungarian authorities. . . . The expulsion of Swedish protected persons from the protected houses is not to take place, or if this should be necessary for strategic reasons, this is to be carried out and supervised by the Legation . . .

There is no record of an answer to Wallenberg's memo. Nor is there any record of any other neutral diplomat still corresponding and negotiating with both the Germans and the Hungarians during these final days. Wallenberg did not for a moment allow them to think they were free of the world's watchful eyes. In the name of the civilized world, he, Raoul Wallenberg, was there to hold them accountable until the last.

Thousands of Jewish children lived in special homes set up for the orphans of genocide by the International Red Cross, with the encouragement of the tireless Swede. Protecting them and keeping them out of that inevitable halfway house to death, the ghetto, became Wallenberg's obsession. His Humanitarian Action Group was able to keep them supplied with food. Keeping the Arrow Cross from massacring these children was less straightforward. Wallenberg darted between the Hungarian Foreign Ministry and Arrow Cross headquarters, reasoning, cajoling, pleading with whoever would listen, against the barbarity of moving these children into a ghetto that was not able to feed itself.

In the last week of December, Wallenberg drafted a letter to

Szálasi, who, though no longer in the capital, was still the nominal head of the country:

> Even in war, conscience and the law condemn hostile actions against children. Why, therefore, force these innocent creatures to live in places where the poor mites will see nothing but misery, pain and desperation? Every civilized nation respects children, and the whole world will be painfully surprised should traditionally Christian and gallant Hungary decide to institute steps against little ones.

As a last resort, Wallenberg marched into the office of Peter Hain. Hain's headquarters on the Sváb Hill was the most feared interrogation center of the Arrow Cross. It was known to be furnished with the most sophisticated electronic devices to make the most reluctant talk. Two children's homes, one run by Swedes and the other by the Scots, had already been raided by the Arrow Cross.

Even for Wallenberg, hardened after months of taking risks, calling on Hain amounted to crossing a heavily mined field.

There was no promise Wallenberg could hold out to Hain and his lieutenants of Swedish recognition or future redemption, to make them release the children. Wallenberg had run out of tricks. He was lucky to walk out of the interview alive. "I've never been closer to the end than in there," Wallenberg commented after he left the Sváb Hill.

Miklós Kalmár was a Budapest Jew who was trying to save himself and thirty Jewish orphans. He had passes from both the Red Cross and the Swiss, but they were not worth much by then. Kalmár did not even bother showing them to the teen-age brutes in uniform who came to take the children under his care "for a little walk." While they were shouting, "All right, you brats, line up over here like good boys and girls," Miklós Kalmár, who knew his own house, slipped down a trap door to the cellar. "He's in here someplace . . . he can't get away," Kalmár heard the executioners say while their flashlights scudded along the cellar walls and floor. Kalmár surfaced through a hidden shaft in his garden.

Kalmár had never met Wallenberg. Nor did he have one of the Swede's passes. But he knew the name and what it stood for. Even more important, he knew where Wallenberg's office was. With all the speed that only fear can inject into a man's legs, he tore through the deserted streets of Pest, to the only place where there was any hope left in the whole city. Wallenberg did not need to hear the breathless details of the man's story; he had heard others like it too often. He immediately dispatched two of his special rescue team and told them, "If it takes money, give it to them." Wallenberg himself picked up the phone and lodged his usual complaint with the authorities, mostly for the record, and for the sake of consistency. It was the money and the speed of the response that got the thirty infants and toddlers off the wooden cart that was already rumbling toward the Danube. Miklós Kalmár survived the siege, and so did his thirty infant charges.

Hundreds of other orphans fell victim to the Arrow Cross's random executions. The Russian advance, not Wallenberg or their own humanity, prevented the mass transfer of these children into the sealed ghetto.

The day before Christmas Eve, three Mercedes limousines with German plates pulled up in front of the walled-in ghetto. Three officers with pistols drawn entered the building that housed the members of the Jewish Council. An SS guard with a submachine gun followed closely behind them. They found only the cold silence of a place that has been hastily abandoned. The council had been warned by Wallenberg to vanish for the next few days. Eichmann, Wallenberg's informer had told him, was up to something. The Russians were in the eastern suburb of Budapest. A lone clerk was left to take the blows of the SS rifle butt. He did not reveal where the council members were hiding.

Eichmann, who sat waiting in one of the cars, left empty-handed. The next morning, with the eastern sky lit up by the Soviet artillery flashes, Lieutenant Colonel Adolf Eichmann and his cohorts turned their cars toward the Vienna road. The roadsides were scattered with the unburied corpses of death marchers. The Nazi's view was marred by the sight of the ragged columns of the army of the Reich, retreating, like Eichmann, toward Vienna. It may have been only then that it occurred to Eichmann that Raoul Wallenberg was, in his way, as skilled a technician of survival, as he, Adolf Eichmann, was of genocide.

19   The Siege

Wallenberg was exhausted, physically from lack of sleep, emotionally from the strain of having to maintain constant composure amid a daily nightmare. There were so many people leaning on him. He was much younger than most of them. He could not let them down. He could not show any weakness or temper or doubt or homesickness. They needed him too much, needed to feel that he seemed to need no one. He was really all they had. He, at least, thought he had a future.

That he was still keenly interested in his own future is made evident from his letter to Lauer in early December. He told his former partner he planned to stay on long past the Russian liberation "to organize the restoration of Jewish property." Then he again asked Lauer to "please speak to Jacob Wallenberg about my job prospects . . . if I stay away this long."

There were no days off and no really close friends with whom to share the revulsion he often felt. One source of support was Vilmos Langfelder, his chauffeur. Langfelder, like a great many people in those days, was a chauffeur by necessity. He came from a prominent family of Jewish industrialists. He had been an engineer when he was taken away for forced labor. Wallenberg freed him and gave him a job. They were roughly the same age, and alike in their reserve and closely checked emotions. Langfelder became Wallenberg's interpreter and companion. His calm, reassuring presence was exactly what Wallenberg needed. In the end, when Wallenberg was a hunted man, Langfelder stayed with him, prepared to share his fate.

Per Anger, the tall, fair Swede of easy charm, was also a diversion from despair. Anger had accompanied him on rescue missions along the road to Hegyeshalom, had helped him pull people out of the death march and from the brickworks. But Anger was cut from a different cloth. He was a cool, professional diplomat. He could never lose himself in a mission the way his friend Raoul did. He was, like the others at the legation, somewhat skeptical about Raoul's tactics and where they would lead.

Anger knew about Wallenberg's love of nature and his passion for endless hikes in the woods. He also knew the Swede had not had a break from his grueling routine since he arrived five months before. Anger persuaded Wallenberg to join him for a weekend at his retreat on the top of the Sváb Hill. "It will be so pleasant," Wallenberg told his secretary, "just to explore the forest for hours on end . . . not to hear the city." For once he did not want to tell her where he could be reached, so badly did he need the rest. But as he was leaving he called back from the door, "Take down this number, Mrs. Falk, just in case . . ." He had not yet unpacked his bag at the Angers' when the first emergency call reached him. It was the week before Christmas and Wallenberg would not have another chance to explore the woods of Budapest, or any other woods, again.

The next day the man who had been put in Baron Kemény's chair at the Foreign Ministry decided to even a score. Acting Foreign Minister Lászlo Vöcköndy, former Hungarian military attaché in Stockholm, had been given twenty-four hours to leave his former diplomatic post—the Swedish authorities objected to his avowed membership of the Arrow Cross. Vöcköndy summoned Wallenberg and Anger and informed them that their diplomatic status would no longer guarantee their safety. When the Swedes pressed him to answer if this meant that their lives were actually in danger, Vöcköndy simply told them to leave Budapest. "If not, who knows?"

Baron Kemény's once elegant offices now looked like they had been pillaged. Crates spilling documents and valuables stood on the parquet floors. The priceless Persian carpets of the Austro-Hungarian monarchs were rolled up in a corner. The formal Baroque chambers of the Royal Palace had the look of a theater on the night the closing of a show is unexpectedly announced.

It was dawn the next day when Vöcköndy proved he was a man of his word. Heavily armed Arrow Cross spilled from a bus onto the curved driveway of the Gellért Hill mansion of the Swedish legation. They rounded up whoever was in the house, including two women employees, and packed them into the bus. While one group drove the Swedes to the walled-in ghetto, another group finished the job of looting and ransacking the legation. Wallenberg had eluded them one more time: he was in Pest, with his own people. The Arrow Cross were clearly not interested in the other Swedes, and after some negotiation, released them.

By the first week of January 1945, the city was finally cut off from the world. The Russians closed it off from every direction. The Germans and the Arrow Cross were trapped inside their tightening hold. Their orders still were: "Fight to the last man!"

Now there was no authority left to whom Wallenberg could appeal. In the absence of an official chain of command he had to build new contacts, a new network of informers and supporters in a matter of days. The appetite of the street marauders was far from sated. Their looting and kidnapping, the spontaneous death sentences—which sometimes, when booty was in dispute, included one of their own—picked up in tempo. The inquisition chambers under Hain's headquarters were nearly always full of Jews dragged from either the Central or the International Ghetto. A defrocked Catholic priest named András Kun spurred on the crazed gangs. Father Kun liked to oversee the torture of Jews, and when the final moment arrived he held up his cross and cried, "In the holy name of Jesus, fire!"

The weary residents of Budapest waited in their cellars and air-raid shelters for the end to their own misery. They learned that a bomb preceded by a sharp, whistlelike noise was harmless; it was not about to fall on your head. It was when you did not hear anything beforehand that you were in trouble. Then there wasn't much you could do, anyway.

Six weeks of confinement in dark, airless underground holes had left their marks on the people. In the claustrophobic life of the cellar, women often preferred to sleep with their pot of reheated bean soup under their pillows rather than have to share it with the others in the shelter. The men bickered over whose turn it was to face the treacherous task of fetching the daily bucket of water from the Danube. Meat had become a dim memory. When a Russian shell hit a horse from the German garrison, several hundred

starving residents ignored the bombs overhead and carved its
carcass clean in minutes. No one understood why it was taking the
Russians so long. The hours passed with unbelievable languor,
broken only by the staccato rhythm of the falling bombs. It was
bread most people dreamed about, the rich, still-warm brown bread
of another lifetime, only six weeks before.

With his self-assurance and unconventional style, Wallenberg
was often able to turn his natural enemies into allies. Paul Szálai
was a veteran police officer and a member of the Arrow Cross.
Sporting the Tyrolean hat and black leather coat that were the
hallmark of Central European middle-class elegance of the time,
he turned up at Wallenberg's office near the International Ghetto.
The halls, the staircase and Wallenberg's own office were all teeming with "his" Jews, some of them holding candles, as electricity
could no longer be counted on. "I want you to think of me as a
friend," Szálai told the Swede. "I am only with 'them' officially."
Three months of Arrow Cross rule had cured him of his attachment to fanaticism.

Szálai warned Wallenberg that his life was in immediate danger.
He offered to put two of his most trusted policemen at the Swede's
disposal. The former Nazi proved to be not only a friend to Wallenberg but an invaluable eleventh-hour ally for the Jews. Through
Szálai, Wallenberg learned precise details of the comings and
goings of various Arrow Cross and German factions. Most significantly, he was able to offer the International Ghetto Jews some sort
of protection. Szálai arranged for one hundred policemen to mount
guard over the ghetto. The order he gave them was simply: Shoot
to kill anyone who tries to enter the ghetto by force. "This is my
diplomatic career's greatest achievement," Wallenberg told Szálai
as he watched the ghetto police guard take up its post.

The Red Army was still ten long terror-filled days from sweeping
the city clear of the Nazis. For Wallenberg, that meant ten days
of constant struggle for lives that still hung by the thinnest thread.
He had already succeeded in keeping 30,000 Jews from the walled-
in ghetto. But nearly 70,000 more captives still sat huddled together,
waiting for their nightmare to end somehow.

In the cellar of the city's massive Town Hall, Wallenberg con-
ferred with the remnants of the Hungarian government. The first
secretary of the Swedish legation still addressed these underworld

figures as though they were the respectable representatives of a legitimate government. As long as the Red Army was only skirting the city they remained the only people Wallenberg could try to deal with. The German army headquarters had turned a deaf ear to his entreaties.

In exchange for the Arrow Cross agreement to stop raiding the ghetto, Wallenberg promised them food. He had his secret warehouses, and until recently, had been receiving food parcels from the Red Cross in Switzerland. When you sit across a bargaining table from hungry men, food is a potent weapon. So Ernö Vajna, the head of the Arrow Cross, a rabid anti-Semite who stayed on to oversee the extermination of the city's Jews, agreed to leave the ghetto alone. Wallenberg, who was still devoted to his habit of backing verbal agreement with written confirmation, sent one off to the Hungarian Nazi.

> I wish to confirm the agreements entered into between ourselves yesterday. At the same time, I would like to take this opportunity to inform you that I have acquainted His Excellency the Swedish Minister with your very friendly remarks concerning Sweden. His Excellency has asked me to voice his deep gratitude and would like to assure you that the Swedish Legation will do everything in its power during these difficult days as well as in the future to help the needy and war-afflicted population of Hungary.
>
> May I take this opportunity of expressing my best wishes for the besieged capital and for yourself.
>
> I remain, with the highest esteem,
>
> Raoul Wallenberg

The tone of the note is pure Wallenberg: diplomatic, flattering, still holding out the vague promise of some brighter future. It is a brilliant piece of fantasy in the apocalyptic atmosphere of January 1945.

But not all members of the Arrow Cross responded to Wallenberg's Machiavellian charms. Through Szálai, he learned of yet another plot to do away with him. Kurt Rettman, a shadowy Arrow Cross figure, hoped to succeed where Eichmann's faithful

Dannecker had failed. "I'm not going to take any more care of my person," Wallenberg replied to Szálai's warning, "than I do of my signatures." He was now signing protective passports for whoever requested them. "The more people can get protection from them both, the better," he said.

So, despite Szálai's cautionary words, he returned to the Arrow Cross cellar for another round of negotiations. Vajna was still pushing for the transfer of all Jews from the International Ghetto to the closed one. One of the men sitting around the candlelit table, a man known to have particularly close ties to the SS, told the Swede, "You'd be doing yourself a favor if you just moved into a cellar yourself. Instead of risking your neck for a bunch of Jews."

Wallenberg pushed back his chair and stood up. "There is no point in trying to deal with someone who holds those views," he said and walked out of the meeting.

Szálai was still there when the same man whispered to Vajna, "We've got to deal with him on very short order."

The meaning of the move of 30,000 Jews from the relative safety of the International Ghetto to the walled-in one was unmistakable. Wallenberg would not stand for it. In desperation, he went back to the Germans one more time. In a memo to their army headquarters he gave a graphic picture of life in the ghetto:

> Some 53,000 persons inhabit the Budapest Ghetto. . . . of these, several thousand suffer from under-nourishment and are lying in the tenement houses used as hospitals. Most of these people have no mattresses and many lack even blankets. The Ghetto is not heated. Originally, the area now serving as a ghetto was inhabited by 15,000 people, and under these conditions the Jews are living at a scale worse than any Hungarian refugee. Naturally, they have no soap and very little water and but a few candles. As it is impossible to accommodate the whole of the population in the air-raid shelters during the attacks, the death rate in the ghetto is higher than anywhere else in the capital.
>
> On paper, the authorities of the capital have made a food allotment of 900 calories per head a day. Even today, the members of the Armed Forces receive 3,600 calories per man per day and the lowest ration in prisons amounts to 1,500 calories.

Here it must be mentioned that the Jews have to carry out all the necessary work to maintain the ghetto themselves, including clearing up after air raids and extinguishing fires started by incendiaries.

The authorities have provided only a small portion of the supply promised. For instance, there has been no issue of salt, vegetables or flour. Cooking oil was the only commodity of which the greater part was delivered.

In order to keep alive Jews living in the ghetto, the International Red Cross found it necessary to intervene and to send a certain amount of food to the ghetto. Today, transport facilities have ceased to exist, as the contractors, since yesterday, have refused to carry out transports. Furthermore, as a result of military and other official and unofficial requisitioning, the supplies of the International Red Cross have been diminished to such an extent that it has become impossible to solve the food problem of the ghetto from this source, even if transport were available.

As there are no quantities of food worth mentioning in the ghetto, it is a fact that the ghetto will be starving within three days, that is, January 5. It is impossible for the Jewish population to obtain food by their own efforts, as Jews are not permitted to leave the ghetto. This was the position when the Legation was told that it was intended to march the occupants of the Foreigners [International] Ghetto into the Central Ghetto. In the Foreigners Ghetto, in which some 35,000 persons are held, the food positions are similar as that in the Central Ghetto.

It would be absolutely impossible for the inhabitants of the Foreigners Ghetto to take even the minutest quantity of food with them on such a foot march.

For humane reasons this plan must be described as utterly crazy and inhuman. *The Royal Swedish Legation is not aware of any similar plan ever having been carried out by any other civilized government.*

As the Royal Swedish Legation is of the opinion that the circumstances described in this memorandum must lead to the intervention of the highest responsible authority in Budapest, that is, the General Commanding Officer, the Royal Swedish

Legation has considered it necessary to submit all facts of the case to this officer.

Raoul Wallenberg

The letter's message was straightforward: The world will hold German Army headquarters responsible for this "crazy and inhuman" act.

But the Germans could no longer be touched by even the shrewdest diplomatic poker playing. The authorities gave as their reason for the dissolution of the International Ghetto the fact that Sweden and the other neutrals had failed to deliver their promised diplomatic recognition of the Arrow Cross regime. Thus, they announced, they were no longer bound by their own agreements with the neutrals.

Early on the bitterly cold morning of January 5, under the relentless pounding of Russian bombers, 5,000 Swedish-protected Jews were marched out of their relatively safe houses. They were led into the nightmare world of the ghetto, squeezed in among people even less well nourished, and closer to despair, than themselves.

No others would follow them. Wallenberg, using his least subtle diplomacy, informed Vajna that he could no longer count on even the meager food parcels that he had made available for the Arrow Cross's consumption. The Hungarian was running out of appetite for combat, but not for food. He canceled any further transfer of Jews into the walled-in ghetto. But the Jews trapped inside were about to face their greatest danger.

Szálai was the first to pick up the scent of something new in the offing. A Hungarian policeman in a hurry jostled him in the lobby of the now deserted Town Hall. Szálai stopped the officer. "What's the rush?" he asked. "Where are you off to?"

"Five hundred soldiers of the Reich, and twenty-two Arrow Cross are standing on alert at the Royal Hotel, across town," the gendarme answered. "They've requested two hundred of our men to help finish off the ghetto. In fact, if we don't help them, they say they'll go ahead and start the firing squads without us."

Szálai and Wallenberg had arranged for a go-between, Károly Szabo, a mutual acquaintance and a Christian who could still circulate freely. It was to this man, who would create less suspicion crossing the city than Szálai, that he turned. "Get to Wallenberg," Szálai told Szabo. "Tell him the pogrom is about to start." Szálai himself headed for Ernö Vajna's shelter. The man charged with the defense of the city showed not the slightest surprise or outrage hearing the report of the planned massacre. Nor was he willing to lift a finger to stop it.

As Szálai slumped out of Vajna's office, his messenger had just returned from Wallenberg. "You must tell Schmidthuber," his friend told him. "Wallenberg says to tell the German general that if he doesn't stop this, the Swede will personally see to it he is charged with murder and genocide by the War Crimes Tribunal."

SS General August Schmidthuber was also headquartered in the Town Hall. Szálai had nothing to lose by turning to the German. With five hundred SS men on alert a few blocks away, ready to perform their final service for the Fatherland, there was little time left.

The middle-aged, tired SS general had only a grain of devotion left for the Reich. He was seriously concerned about his own future. He was not prepared to go down with Budapest, or to defend it as though it were Berlin. Szálai's words got through. Schmidthuber picked up his telephone and ordered Vilmos Lucska, assistant barber, Arrow Cross member and eager organizer of the too long postponed slaughter, to report immediately to his office. Next, he sent for the commander of the German garrison, who had put his men on alert. Vajna, representing the Hungarian government, was summoned.

"Call off your men," Schmidthuber ordered both the German and the Hungarian. "There will be no pogrom." He did not explain or reason with the astonished, disappointed men. He placed the German commander under military arrest. He asked Vajna to do the same with Lucska, the Arrow Cross barber. Vajna refused, and the two Hungarians walked out together.

Wallenberg did not participate in this abrupt, unceremonious gathering. His name, however, and what it stood for, was entirely responsible for the countermanding of the orders.

20   Wallenberg on the Run

"Big Danube" was the code word that opened the massive wooden door of the cellar of Wallenberg's Üllöi Street office. On the night of January 8 the Jews huddling behind the door heard the code and cautiously opened up. The only light touch on the dark uniforms of the half-dozen men who faced them was provided by the white death's-heads on their armbands. The Jews lying on bags filled with hay stirred out of their trance and staggered to their feet. The impossible had happened. The sanctuary of Wallenberg's office had been violated. The Swede was not there. There was no one to stop the Arrow Cross execution squad. The police guard at the door, Szálai's man, did nothing to prevent the assassins from leaving undisturbed with their victims.

First they were marched to one of the Arrow Cross's underground shelters. They were pushed down dark stairs, through black, rat-infested corridors, until they reached the damp cellar that served as an inquisition chamber. As they stumbled in the dimly lit, cavelike place, they jostled other Arrow Cross men in various stages of drunkenness. Stirred from their stupor, the thugs cursed and jumped to their feet. They joined the others in stripping the new arrivals of their money, coats, hats and shoes. The group was taken to yet another hiding place. "You've still got valuables you haven't told us about," the leader of the group barked. "You'd better tell us before the fish in the Danube get them." The group obliged meekly with wedding bands, watches and loose change.

Outside, besides the routine nightly bombing, it was snowing hard. The lawless mob, happy with its new plunder, was unexcited by the prospect of finishing off the Jews by the Danube. It was a long hike from the warm, safe cellar. Drunk and listless, the thugs started quarreling over whose turn it was to lead the victims to their end. One claimed he had just returned from a similar mission. "See, there's still snow on my boots," he said. His comrades were not moved.

One of the captives saw this as a moment to seize. "I am not a Jew," protested a woman holding a small child in her arms. "We just haven't got our papers with us."

"Okay," the leader of the death squad agreed. "Give me the kid."

The mother, paralyzed with fear, handed over her child. "If you're Christian," he told the child, "let me hear the Our Father."

The child, frozen with terror, was incapable of uttering a single word. The angry mob relieved its frustration by beating up both the mother and child.

There was a new shadow in the cellar. "What do you think you're doing with these people?" a voice roared from the corner. "Don't you fools know the Swedes are feeding you and half the city?" The brash voice was that of Károly Szabo, Wallenberg's liaison with the faithful Szálai. "I've got police orders right here"— he flashed some snow-wet documents—"and there are policemen outside to make sure you do it." Szálai had been alerted by a Wallenberg employee, overlooked by the Arrow Cross raid. The thugs had no choice but to release their catch, who were led back to their Üllöi Street shelter by Szabo. Szálai had already dispatched a new police guard for Wallenberg's office.

But Wallenberg realized that his amazing luck, which for six months had bordered on the mystical, was running out. His enemies were having too many near-misses. He was clearly no longer off-limits to marauding street gangs. Wallenberg decided it was time to save himself. Dead, he would not be of much use to anybody. There was much to live for.

Giorgio Perlasca, a colleague from the Spanish embassy, offered him the safety of his air-raid shelter, not far from the ghetto. He ruled out joining the other Swedes in Buda, where he would have been cut off from "his" people. He finally decided to go into hiding with the men and women who had worked alongside him since he arrived in Budapest. His aides Hugo Wohl, a former industrialist (with wife, daughter and son-in-law), and Vilmos Forgács, along with Vilmos Langfelder and Thomas Veres, all sustained by Wallenberg's spirit, decided to weather the last days together. They moved into the place they thought would be safe from the armed gangs: the vault of the Hazai Bank, not far from the International Ghetto.

For now there was nothing more Wallenberg could do. But he was no good at playing refugee, he was restless. He called Szálai and asked him to join him. "Have you ever seen a vault that held greater treasure than this one?" Wallenberg asked the Hungarian. "Human lives, not money." He told Szálai and Szabo he wanted to go over to the Russians as soon as possible. The new army of occupation must be alerted to the terrible suffering of the capital. They must be told that the population was on the brink of famine. They must speed up the liberation of the city.

This was not the first time the Swede had spoken of seeking contact with the Russians. Already, late in December, he and the few other diplomats still left during the siege held a candlelit meeting in the Town Hall air-raid shelter. Wallenberg and the Swiss diplomat Harald Feller volunteered to try and make contact with the Russians. But Feller had since been picked up by the Arrow Cross and Wallenberg had lost touch with him.

His friends inside the bank vault tried to dissuade him from his plan. "It's too uncertain," they told him. "Why not wait for a while?" Szabo said he'd take him if he still wanted to go.

The siege was taking much too long. Wallenberg followed it with the same obsession he used to pursue the movements of Eichmann's *Einsatzkommando*. Like a general poring over his map before the battle, Wallenberg followed the progress of the Red Army as it circled the capital. Each day he moved his pins and arrows, tracing the Russians' sluggish advance toward Budapest.

But he wasn't content to listen to the BBC's nightly reports of the Red Army's progress. He wanted to see it for himself. He talked Szálai into taking him up the Gellért Hill, to the Citadel, the highest peak overlooking the Danube. With Langfelder behind the wheel of his Studebaker, Wallenberg and Veres squeezed into the car, which already held three armed policemen, Szálai's guards. It was a long and jagged road up the Gellért, full of hairpin curves, made more dangerous by the shells flying overhead. "I haven't felt this way since I was in the company of a bunch of robbers, long ago, in America," Wallenberg commented, laughing. "Only I was in much less danger then."

The Danube beneath them reflected the smoking carnage of the ghost town. The Russians had blown up all the grand old hotels along the Korso. All the symbols of the bourgeois good life were gone: the Ritz, the Duna and the Royal, and the Vigado, the garish music hall where Budapest used to see reproductions of the latest burlesque shows from Paris and Vienna. Only the beautiful bridges that spanned the two banks of the city and made her one, had not yet been blasted by the retreating Germans. They too were soon to be slumped into the gray river, like the carcasses of pre-historic creatures.

From the Gellért, Wallenberg could see the German troops still firing from the Royal Palace, desperately, suicidally hanging on. But the Russians were visibly closing in on them. Despite the destruction around him and the deadly fireworks blasting the night sky, Wallenberg was in good spirits. "It's almost over," he told Veres and Langfelder. "Thank God."

On the way down from the hill, Wallenberg noticed unburied bodies everywhere, their stench overpowering the smell of gunfire and burning buildings. He had no illusions about the new army of occupation. "They have to be better than the last." That was all he could say about them.

His sense of humor was still intact. His car was equipped with several license plates, "Diplomatic" for the Nazis, "First Aid" for the Arrow Cross. "What I really need," he told his companions, "is an automatic plate changer. So I don't have to get out of the car before every roadblock."

On January 11 Wallenberg said goodbye to his friends at the Hazai Bank. "I don't feel secure here," he told them. "I must keep moving." He was restless and nervous. Inaction did not suit him. He asked them if there was anything more he could be doing for them, or the city, or the Jews still living in the unrelieved torment of the ghetto. No, they assured him, there was nothing to do but wait.

For six months they had worked alongside this man, in the most consuming of all jobs. And yet none of them really knew him. They knew his courage, his remarkable poise under pressure. They knew he came from a blessed, gilded background. They did not really know the man. His personal life he did not share with any of them, not with the Hungarian Jews he worked with, not with the Swedish diplomats whose background more closely resembled his own. There was, it is true, precious little time for him to have a private life. He was a very young man, with barely a trace of emotional baggage. There would be time for all that later, he thought.

Now, when Wallenberg was saying goodbye, and looking for asylum himself, they still did not worry about him. They were too accustomed to him worrying about them. Wallenberg was shielded by a magic armor, and it would protect him. He was a Swede, and a diplomat, and the son of a tremendously influential family. Nothing could touch Raoul Wallenberg. So they said goodbye and resumed worrying about their own uncertain futures.

Wallenberg now had only one place where he knew he would be both welcome and safe: the headquarters of the Red Cross, on Benczur Street. The gates of the stately villa were guarded by a pair of German soldiers, thanks to the owner's friendship with SS Colonel Weber. Wallenberg now asked George Wilhelm for refuge. The location of the villa was another advantage. It was near the City Park, which was already under Russian control. Thus Wallenberg would be among the first to be "liberated."

Wallenberg spent the next three days in the company of this group of once eminent Hungarian Jews, who had themselves survived the year by saving others, less privileged, from extermination. Wallenberg slept more than he had in months. Since the former chef of the Astoria Hotel was cooking for the group, he also ate well. He was quiet and reflective. But his mood was basically optimistic. Nearly 100,000 Jews were alive largely as a result of his efforts. His own survival bordered on the miraculous. He was not prepared to move on and close this chapter of his life. He wanted to do more for them.

Since November, when the end of the Nazis had appeared much closer, Wallenberg had actually begun organizing for the future. He wanted to help the community, stripped not only of its property but of position and self-esteem as well, to get on its feet again. He charged a group of his most trusted colleagues, including Wohl and Forgács, with drawing up the paperwork for the restoration of Jewish property. He knew he could count on the American Jewish Joint Distribution Committee to continue to pump money into war-ravaged Hungary. He wanted to help thousands of Magyars who had been forced to flee their homeland to return and rebuild their lives. It was an ambitious plan, and it had nothing to do with his original mandate. Nor did it involve the Swedish Foreign Office or his position as a member of the legation. He had, in effect, severed his ties with the legation when he decided not to follow Danielsson, Anger and the others to the safety of the Buda Hills, but to weather the siege in Pest. He was now operating on his own, no longer representing anyone but the interests of the people he had brought this far.

Wallenberg again left the relative safety of his shelter, to call on some friends. At the Swedish offices on Üllöi Street, he was greeted by a thick pile of applications for Swedish protective passes. He signed all of them, commenting, "On the ruins of Stalingrad, I am signing protective passports. This is a historic moment." When someone asked him to extend the validity of his Swedish passport, Wallenberg replied, "I really don't think it's necessary, it's almost over."

He then asked Langfelder to drive him to the Town Hall. He found Szálai almost alone in the deserted, vaultlike shelter. The others had fled or had already changed uniforms to greet the new rulers. "As soon as the city is liberated," Wallenberg told his friend, "I want you to come with me to see Malinovsky. From there I will take you to Stockholm. I want to introduce you to the King of Sweden."

First, he had to reach the new power. Then he wanted to mobilize the population through a radio address. He knew his name carried enormous weight. He would personally announce the formation of what his colleagues insisted would be called the Wallenberg Institution for Rescue and Reconstruction. He was confident of his ability to do much more for these people. The Wallenberg empire and his secure, perhaps even brilliant future would have to wait a little bit longer. It was an audacious idea from a man who no longer took no as an easily acceptable answer. He could no longer return to being a mere diplomat, an apprentice banker, a young man who played by the cumbersome rules of bureaucracies. He had seen what the force of his own personality, intellect and imagination could accomplish.

21   The New Masters

The city's nearly two-month-long siege was shuddering to an end. Hidden loudspeakers, installed by the Russians, played the current popular song "You flee in vain, you hide in vain . . ." But the German suicide squad holed up in the Royal Palace ignored the song's message and hung on. Or perhaps they still believed that, at the last minute, those long-promised reinforcements would arrive, that the Reich would not abandon its soldiers. The armies of Marshal Rodion Malinovsky from the east and Marshal Fyodor Tolbukhin from the south had a pincerlike hold on the capital.

Hundreds of German soldiers now turned to the Hungarian people to provide them with civilian clothes. Many of them managed thus to survive the Soviets' capture of Budapest. Others did not do as well.

The garrison holding on the Vár came upon an underground escape route leading from the steep promontory to the exposed Széna Square below. One by one, as the bleary-eyed soldiers emerged from their underground tunnel, they were mowed down by waiting Soviet gunners. The next morning the residents of Buda awoke to find their city officially liberated. One of their busiest squares was bathed in the blood of German corpses, left there for the residents to dispose of.

The Soviet army was exhausted from the extended siege, frustrated that it had taken so much longer than anticipated. They blamed the population for sympathizing with and harboring the Nazis. Hungary had been Hitler's last ally. The residents of Budapest were regarded as suspect by the Red Army. "Partisan," they kept calling the mystified people.

There was a great deal of work to be done. The beautiful bridges that spanned the two banks of the city had been blasted by the retreating Germans. The city had no water or electricity. But there was an even greater need for manpower in the Russians' own ruined country. Long lines of forced laborers—"prisoners of war," the Russians called them—snaked east from Pest. Just about anyone would do for some *malenka robot*, "a little work." "*Davaj, davaj*," the Red soldiers quickly taught the residents, meant "Come on, move it." And off they went, some not to return for years. Others, more fortunate, got the message and jumped out of long ragged lines into icy streams or drain pipes and waited for the marching of feet to pass overhead.

The first wave of Russians were primarily interested in gold watches. Some of them walked around with four or five crawling up the arm of their uniforms. Alcohol, any kind, even rubbing alcohol, was their second passion. Their eyes went wide at the sight of the city's remaining bourgeois luxuries. They washed in toilet bowls and invaded the apartments of janitors—whom they referred to as *bourzoui*, or "bourgeois"—and who invariably lived on the ground floor. Thus they often missed the real luxury apartments on upper floors.

There were, of course, exceptions. One Soviet general set up his headquarters in a villa on Buda's Hill of Roses, not far from Eichmann's former residence. The general had brought with him his own white-toqued chef and dined nightly on the linen and silver which made up part of his gear. The Russian was soon invited to join his Hungarian neighbors' weekly game of bridge.

The second wave of "liberators" went wild. Their appetite for women became part of the city's legend. Nearly every female, young and old, had a horror story to tell. There was precious little affection between the population and the long-awaited Russian army. It was a relationship based on the uneasy truce between the conquered and the conqueror. Force, necessity and mutual resentment was the glue holding them together. Many of the country's historic prejudices about their powerful and not quite civilized eastern neighbor seemed to have materialized.

There were also stories of individual Russian soldiers' tenderness toward children and old ladies. Some of the new masters even showed a keen interest in art. When, in the workshop of the respected Rodin-inspired Hungarian sculptor Kisfaludy-Strobl, a

Russian officer discovered a lofty female figure, raising the palm branch of Peace and Glory, he wondered, "Who is this for?" In fact, the giant statue was intended to memorialize István, the son of Regent Horthy who had been shot down by the Russians. The officer had a better idea. Why not place the statue atop the Citadel, the highest peak overlooking the Danube? Let her serve as a memorial to the Army of Liberation. Today the muscular bronze owns the Buda skyline, the way the Danube dominates the ground.

Yesterday's heroes quickly became today's villains, as a new provisional government was set up under Russian "protection" in Debrecen, in the northeast. It was only the beginning. The Stalinization of Hungary would take four years to achieve. But the cornerstones were already being laid in January 1945.

The city's wits, never slow to respond, now asked, "What have been Hungary's three greatest national catastrophes? Answer: The Mongol invasion, the Turkish occupation and the Russian liberation."

Despite the unbelievable devastation, a great surge of life now flowed through the city. There was a determination to put the past behind and to rebuild what was once the pride of the Magyars. First the starving, unwashed, unshaven population had to get through the immediate ordeal. The sight of men and women stalking the rubble-filled streets with axes swinging was commonplace. All were searching for firewood, the only available fuel. They often settled for the parquet floors of deserted apartments. Some sacrificed antique furniture to keep warm.

Nobody was more grateful for the presence of the long-awaited Soviet liberators than the Jews of Budapest. Soviet troops crawled through air-raid shelters, which, in Pest, interconnect through cellars, to reach the International Ghetto, on January 16. The next morning, a division reached the Central Ghetto.

The terror inside the two ghettos did not subside until the Russians were actually inside. A handful of Arrow Cross and Nazis tried to shoot their way out, using Jews as shields. And 3,000 more Jews were killed during the painfully slow "liberation." The Russians found another 246 bodies in an advanced state of decomposition. But nearly 100,000 Jews had survived.

Now they staggered toward the six-foot-plank walls that had

trapped them inside for nearly three months. With hatchets, boots and fists they destroyed their prison. Moaning and weeping, the pale, stooped figures streamed out on the streets, forbidden them for so long. They were stunned by what they saw. Across the river there were only four recognizable buildings left of what was Buda. Nearly eight hundred other buildings were smoking piles of stone and ash. The search for children, husbands and wives began. The shock of returning to homes which were no longer there or had been requisitioned as Soviet barracks was blurred by the realization that they were alive, that they had survived.

As the Arrow Cross fled west they found time to carry out two more massacres. The Jewish hospitals in Buda, on Maros and Városmajor streets, were emptied of their patients, doctors and nurses. Several hundred more mindless executions were added to the Arrow Cross's long list of atrocities.

On the morning of January 13 Wallenberg was roused from his sleep by the persistent banging of a boot against a trap door in the Benczur Street cellar. The Russians, making their way underground, had arrived. There were twenty of them, low-ranking street patrols. They were neither friendly nor hostile, they were just doing their jobs. Wallenberg and the Hungarians were asked to show their papers. One of the Russians signaled that he, too, was Jewish. At the same time he put his index finger to his lips and pointed toward his preoccupied comrades.

Wallenberg, using the primitive Russian he had been practicing, pointed to his diplomatic papers, both in Swedish and Russian, and asked to speak to the division's commanding officer. Through a field telephone, one of the men contacted Major Dimitri Demchinkov. Within half an hour two officers arrived at Benczur Street. They shook hands with the Swede and were polite in their labored attempt to communicate with him. Using his Russian and their smattering of German they engaged in awkward conversation for nearly an hour. The Russians asked Wallenberg why he was still in Pest when all the other diplomats stayed in Buda. Wallenberg tried to explain his rescue mission for the Jews. They were visibly mystified, particularly about his insistence that he must reach the highest Soviet authorities. They agreed to drive him to their headquarters. Langfelder was already behind the wheel of the Stude-baker, which had been ready for days for a long trip. "*Auf Wieder-sehen,*" Wallenberg said to his friends.

He did return the next day. He had spent the night at the Russian headquarters on Erzsébet Királynö (Queen Elizabeth) Street. He came to pick up the rest of his belongings. An extremely polite, squat Russian in a greatcoat of faded olive drab, accompanied Wallenberg: Major Demchinkov. Wallenberg asked George Wilhelm to return several thousand dollars in Hungarian currency which he had given him for safekeeping. Wallenberg's mood was still calm, but not quite as relaxed as the previous day. Nor did he give off any signals of alarm. There was a certain edge in his voice when he said to Wilhelm, "I'm going to Debrecen. But I'm not sure if I'm going as their guest or their prisoner." It was too late for Wilhelm or anybody else to talk him out of going. He had already received Soviet permission to make the trip to Marshal Malinovsky's headquarters.

Under Russian escort, Wallenberg stopped off at the Tátra Street offices of the Swedish legation. He gave money to his Hungarian assistants. "I'll be back from Debrecen in about a week," he told them. "I'll establish contact with Russian headquarters and the new Hungarian government. Meanwhile, I want you to keep the opera-tion going." There was much more work to be done.

In front of the Swedish Hospital he had helped to set up near his office, Wallenberg slipped on the ice. Paul Nevi, the hospital's manager, helped him up. Just then two elderly men, with yellow stars still stitched to their overcoats, making their first hesitant steps as free men, passed by. "I'm glad to see," Wallenberg said to Nevi, "that my mission has not been completely in vain."

Wallenberg's childhood acquaintance, Lászlo Petö—the first familiar face he had spotted in the office of the Jewish Council the day he arrived in Budapest—planned to accompany him to Debrecen. Petö's mother did not like the plan. At the last minute the Hungarian apologized to his old friend and declined to make the journey. He walked with Wallenberg to his car. Langfelder was waiting behind the wheel. Petö stood for a long time in the middle of the rubble-filled Tátra Street as Wallenberg's blue Stude-baker, flanked by a Soviet motorcycle escort with sidecars, dis-appeared on the road east.

22   The Captive Guest

allenberg's elaborate leave-taking of his colleagues and friends was all accomplished under the watchful eye of his Soviet escort. The Swede and his Hungarian driver did not get very far beyond the Budapest city limits. There was no hint that they were actually prisoners, but they were no longer exactly free men, either. Their movements were subject to the approval of an absent authority. They were in that ambiguous zone between freedom and captivity which they themselves did not understand.

During one of his required stops at yet another link in the Russian chain of command, Wallenberg's car tires were slashed. Without his own car, he was far easier for the Soviets to control. The Russian officers continued for some time to be polite and to maintain the fiction of Debrecen as their eventual destination. They themselves were not certain as to the status of their "guest." That decision was being made elsewhere.

A new set of "escorts" was presented to Wallenberg. They were men of fewer words; they had a good command of both English and German. They seemed to be a tougher, more professional unit. They were not interested in the Swede's gold watch or in his money. There was no way Raoul Wallenberg, who was color-blind, could have noticed the red tabs on his new custodians' shoulder boards, nor could he have known that the tabs marked them as officers of the NKVD, the Soviet secret police. Nor was Wallenberg likely to know that, with the defeat of the Nazis, the raison d'être of the Grand Alliance was over. The Cold War had begun.

Wallenberg had been placed in the hands of a unit that took cues from the highest reaches of the Kremlin. In 1945 the NKVD was, quite literally, a state within a state. One special division, under the command of the feared Viktor S. Abakumov, was called SMERSH, a contraction of the Russian for "Kill the spies!" This elite group had carte blanche to do so. In Hungary the NKVD's mandate was to begin building a future Soviet satellite. There was no room for dissent or resistance from a population that had stuck out the war alongside the Nazis. The Soviets were keenly aware of the luke-warm support they received from the Hungarian population. The NKVD's first job was to root out the troublemakers, those who could cause them headaches later on. Hundreds of thousands of the capital's residents, still reeling from the ravages of life under-ground or in the ghetto had to submit to the merciless glare of Soviet interrogation.

With their usual speed and thoroughness, the NKVD unit in Budapest—as elsewhere a separate chain of command from the army—had begun to piece together the story of Raoul Wallenberg. His passports, often bearing his signature, were everywhere. There were thousands of fake Swedish protective passports in circulation, which had provided black marketeers with handsome profits. Not infrequently, the Soviets found them in the hands of Hungarian or German Nazi fugitives.

Shortly before the Soviet takeover, the Swedish Foreign Office had submitted a list of its Budapest diplomats to Moscow. A quick check turned up Wallenberg's record. He was a diplomat by con-venience only. He was the son of a capitalist dynasty, a quintessen-tial product of the "unproductive," exploiting class. He spoke half a dozen languages, including some Russian. He was educated in the United States. FDR's War Refugee Board had actually dispatched the businessman-architect to Budapest.

The young man had clearly dispensed money lavishly. Weren't thirty-two Budapest buildings flying the Swedish flag? Wallenberg's Hungarian associates did not see any reason to cover up the source of that funding: the American Jewish Joint Distribution Com-mittee. Several years later the NKVD would devote its time and energy to implicating a group of Jewish doctors in a plot to poison Stalin and the Kremlin's top echelon. The insidious doctors' plot, it was alleged, was funded by the Joint Distribution Committee. Already, in 1945, the Joint Distribution Committee was a cover for an international spy network, as far as the NKVD was con-cerned. And Wallenberg was the committee's man in Hungary.

From questioning his associates, the NKVD learned of the fantastic concessions the Swede had wrung from the Nazis. Nobody thought to cover up for Wallenberg. Why should they? He was a diplomat. He had immunity and was surely beyond the Russians' reach. He was also their hero. Nobody thought to mask that fact either. Weren't the Soviets on the same side?

But Wallenberg the hero, Wallenberg the worker of miracles, was precisely what the Soviet authorities did not need for the new order they planned to establish in Hungary. Raoul Wallenberg meant trouble. For a large portion of the city's population he had become the last court of appeal. For months there had been no laws, no civil rights, no executive or judiciary to take seriously. By 1945 the assumption of innocence and due process had become quaint period pieces. For hundreds of thousands of people, there was really only one place to turn for anything as exotic as fair play in this setting: Raoul Wallenberg. To the country's new masters, the man was dangerous. And they did not have to look very far to build a case against him.

There had been rumors among the Nazis that Wallenberg was not what he seemed. In December one of the Swede's Hungarian associates, Dr. Francis Zöld, an International Red Cross worker, had been alerted about Wallenberg's "connections." A Hungarian army officer, a family friend of Zöld's, saw him in Wallenberg's company. "Take my advice," the officer warned Zöld; "avoid Wallenberg. He's undercover for the Anglo-American secret services." Zöld ignored the advice. But among the dozens, hundreds of German and Hungarian Nazis hauled in by the NKVD, this piece of low-grade rumor was certainly not kept under wraps.

Lars Berg, the head of the Swedish legation's Section B, in charge of foreign interests in Hungary, was also under Soviet suspicion. Berg was taken into custody and interrogated. He was told he and Wallenberg were high-level Nazi spies. The Soviets did not find Berg's humanitarian "cover" convincing. He was accused of fabricating false documents for non-Jews, and of not actively serving the Russians' interests, which Sweden represented in Budapest. "Why would Berg and Wallenberg, neutrals and Christians, risk their lives for Jews?" he was asked. There was no real reason for Wallenberg, who was not even a diplomat, to stride into this nightmare, the Russians claimed, except as an agent. The fact that

Wallenberg's powerful cousins, Marcus and Jacob, were known to have acted as the intermediaries of the anti-Hitler underground's efforts to bring about a separate peace with the Anglo-Americans could not have helped Wallenberg's case.

The Russians' conspiratorial mindset did not stop with the Joint Distribution Committee. The Red Cross was also a prime suspect. George Wilhelm, Wallenberg's trusted Hungarian colleague, was also arrested and taken to the same dreary stone fortress where the Gestapo had had him interned. This time he was interrogated not about his Jewish blood, but about his activities for that well-known international network of spies, the Red Cross. Wilhelm did not provide the Soviets with any useful information about what his rescue work really covered up. Without having any formal charges leveled against him, he was thrown in a cell. But his former chauffeur, a Jew who owed his life to the Red Cross and to Wilhelm, came to his rescue. The chauffeur turned out to have been a member of Hungary's clandestine Communist party. He had good connections with the new hierarchy. He vouched for Wilhelm's innocence and won his release.

Wallenberg's fate was sealed in a matter of days. Russian machine guns were still pounding the last German soldiers when Wallenberg and Langfelder were driven under Soviet military escort to Budapest's Eastern Rail Road Station. His car passed through the familiar, nearly deserted streets. Only soldiers, in different uniforms and with broader faces and more Oriental features, patrolled the streets. Freshly dug graves were everywhere. But the city was clearly fighting to get back on its feet. Wallenberg would not be there to help.

Four soldiers and an officer made the long, monotonous train trip across the Rumanian countryside with Wallenberg and Langfelder. They were still only in protective custody. Despair had not yet taken hold. At the Russian-Rumanian border the group descended from the coach and dined together at a restaurant named Luther. It was not a memorable meal, but it was the last the Swede and the Hungarian would have as free men.

When their train finally pulled into Moscow the next afternoon, the status of the two captives was still not absolutely clear. Their armed escorts took the two men to Moscow's pride: the newly completed subway. They admired the glass and marble showcase of the

Soviet capital. Larger-than-life portraits of Stalin blanketed every building. Letters, each the size of a man, exhorted the population to DEFEAT IMPERIALISM! LONG LIVE LENIN! LONG LIVE STALIN!

But Wallenberg and Langfelder's tour of Moscow was brief. They were driven to the brightly lit Lubyanka Square. A five-storied former hotel flying a red flag, illuminated by a searchlight, dominated the square. The massive gray structure housed both the NKVD and hundreds of political prisoners.

It was perhaps only when Wallenberg and Langfelder had been marched past the impassive guards, past the steel-lined, vaulted threshold of Lubyanka, that the full meaning of their journey penetrated the tired travelers.

23   At Home

aoul Wallenberg was the only diplomat in Hungary that
the Swedish Foreign Office was not worried about, for
on January 16, 1945, on the eve of his journey to
Moscow's Lubyanka Prison, Soviet Deputy Foreign Minister
Vladimir Dekanosov dispatched an official note to Staffan Söderblom,
the Swedish envoy in Moscow. "First Secretary Raoul Wallenberg
of the Swedish Legation in Budapest has gone over to the Russian
side," the note read. "Wallenberg and his belongings have been
taken under Soviet protective custody." The source for the Soviet
official's message was General Tchernishev, commander of Budapest's Zuglo District. In the light of later developments, it is
apparent neither the general nor the minister cleared their information with the people who had final say over Raoul Wallenberg's
fate: the secret police.

Shortly after this reassuring word on Wallenberg, Alexandra
Kollontai, the colorful Soviet ambassador and prized social luminary
in the Swedish capital, invited the wife of the Swedish Foreign
Minister for tea. "Yes," she told Mme. Christian Günther, "Wallen-
berg is in Russian hands, safe and sound." Two weeks later Mme.
Kollontai, a former heroine of the Russian Revolution, entertained
Raoul's mother. She repeated the same soothing words to the
anxious Maj von Dardel.

From the other members of the Budapest Swedish legation, only
silence; they had spent the six weeks since "liberation" in a provin-
cial internment camp. They, too, crossed Rumania on their way to
Moscow. But Moscow was only a brief stopover for Minister
Danielsson and the other diplomats. When the train pulled into the
Western Rail Road Station—which, weeks before, had given

Wallenberg his first glimpse of Moscow—they were greeted by a large delegation from the Swedish embassy. Ambassador Söderblom approached the group with a bouquet of red roses and an expression of great agitation. "Remember," Söderblom whispered in Per Anger's ear when they boarded their Leningrad-bound express, "when you get home, not one bad word about the Russians!"

This man, so transparently intimidated by the Soviet authorities at whose pleasure he served, would be given the task of pressing the Kremlin about the missing Swede.

The tiny, delicate figure of Maj von Dardel stood out against the gray morning haze in Stockholm harbor when the group finally arrived home on April 18 by ship from Leningrad. Raoul's mother had been told her son was not among the diplomats who left Moscow. She refused to believe the official communiqué. Somehow, Raoul would be there. The sharp pain she felt as her eyes skimmed the sea of strange faces that morning was the beginning of an ache that would never leave her.

The returning diplomats found that they no longer spoke the same language as their colleagues at home. *Rysskräck,* "fear of Russia," was the strongest emotion in postwar Sweden. High-ranking Swedes were busily planning their exodus to Canada or America, so convinced were they that the Russian behemoth would not stop at the Baltic. The statue of King Charles XII, in central Stockholm, right arm extended and index finger pointing east, was said to be alerting his countrymen to the menace from the giant next door. The ruling Social Democrats were firm believers in a continued neutrality, based on past good relations with the Soviet Union. Little children who misbehaved were admonished, "Careful, or the Russians will get you!" The burden of Raoul Wallenberg's absence was a haunting embarrassment to both the Swedish Foreign Office and the Royal Palace.

Radio Kossuth, the voice of Russian-liberated Budapest, announced that spring that Raoul Wallenberg, secretary of the Swedish legation, was "most probably assassinated by agents of the Gestapo." It might have been a convenient and even a more or less credible way out for the Soviets. But reality, then and later, kept seeping through the cracks. The Soviets had not made up their minds what to do with the prize prisoner. The word "probably" inserted in the news bulletin left open the door for future use of the captive

Wallenberg. This kind of ambiguity would be the hallmark of the Soviets' approach to the Wallenberg case.

In Moscow, Ambassador Söderblom continued to make excuses for the Soviet authorities' silence. When, after several months, the Kremlin had still not declared itself on Wallenberg, U.S. Ambassador Averell Harriman, a figure of some stature in the Soviet capital, offered to intervene. Secretary of the Treasury Henry Morgenthau, Jr., had written the new director of the War Refugee Board, General William O'Dwyer: "Let [Secretary of State] Stettinius know I am personally interested in this man." Söderblom rejected the offer. "What good would the American's interference do?" he queried his home office. "The Russians," Söderblom told Harriman, "are doing everything they can already." With one exception, this was the last time Washington offered diplomatic support on behalf of Raoul Wallenberg for several decades.

Six months after Raoul Wallenberg vanished from the streets of Budapest, his former colleagues decided to celebrate their own safe return to Sweden. The akvavit flowed freely at the lavish smörgåsbord they enjoyed in Stockholm's fashionable Rosenbad restaurant. The diplomats, warmed by the occasion and happy to be reunited and at home, toasted and kidded one another. They recited humorous poems about their dramatic stay in war-torn Budapest. The danger had been great, and death imminent, but still, the doggerel rhapsodized, the Hungarian capital had its charm, its wine and its women. They told the tale of how one of them, following an evening's overindulgence, tried to take a dip in an empty swimming pool. All but one of us, the spoof went on, always managed to find something to relieve the gloom. Only Wallenberg could never be diverted. Only Wallenberg found nothing to laugh about. From the evening's light-hearted tone it is clear Raoul's former colleagues did not grasp the gravity of his absence. At another diplomatic party not long after this celebration, a Swedish diplomat, then posted in Paris, remarked, "No wonder Wallenberg doesn't want to come home. After all the tricks he pulled off in Budapest!" In the eyes of many in the Foreign Office, he had gone too far, broken too many rules and stepped on too many toes.

In late spring Ambassador Söderblom was still reluctant to press the Kremlin for more. The Swedish Foreign Office was still hiding behind the three-month-old note from Dekanosov confirming Wallenberg's well-being. Marcus Wallenberg, patriarch, along with Jacob, of the immensely powerful family, made a move. He spoke to Mme. Kollontai and urged her to prod Moscow for a reply, but Mme. Kollontai's queries were no longer answered by her superiors. (The following year Moscow confirmed what Stockholm society was already suspecting: Alexandra Kollontai had fallen out of favor. She was ordered to return to the Soviet capital. She had too many powerful friends in Stockholm and she was too energetic in speaking out about the growing anxiety of Raoul Wallenberg's mother. Mme. Kollontai pleaded poor health; she was ill with a high fever when the cable arrived informing her that her presence was no longer required in Sweden. "I have never said no to my government," she told her personal friend and physician, Dr. Nanna Svartz, who gave her an injection to enable her to make the journey to Moscow. Dr. Svartz, the eminent Swedish scientist who would play her own dramatic role in the Wallenberg story, accompanied her patient to Moscow.)

By the summer of 1945 the Big Three had sealed the shape of postwar Europe at the Crimean health resort of Yalta, Hitler and Himmler had both taken their own lives, and Adolf Eichmann was making his cautious way from Austrian to Italian monasteries, along the well-paved Odessa trail, to find a new life, and a new identity as Rudolf Klement, in Buenos Aires. It would take sixteen years for Jerusalem and justice to catch up with the brilliant engineer of death.

To Wallenberg's mother, it seemed that there was only one person in the world who cared about her missing son. Rudolf Phillip was a sharp-featured, chain-smoking Austrian Jew. He was a writer who had fled his native Austria one step ahead of the Nazis. First as a journalist, then as a man with an obsession, he regarded himself as Wallenberg's "white knight." Until Phillip's death in 1980 at the age of eighty, Wallenberg was his reason for being. Nina Lagergren, one of his very few friends, found the tiny room where the old man spent his reclusive last years dominated by pictures of Wallenberg. Fifteen suitcases crammed with articles, his own and others', about Wallenberg, made up his only real possessions.

Phillip was the first to begin the tedious and often frustrating task of searching for witnesses who emerged from the Soviet Union with information about Wallenberg. He wrung testimony out of dozens of released prisoners, contradicting the Soviets' own line on Wallenberg. Phillip was an explosive, insecure and unpredictable man, whose passionate involvement in the Wallenberg case was a mixed blessing for Raoul's mother.

A new Swedish Social Democratic government was elected this summer. The New Foreign Minister was Östen Undén, a Marxist professor of law. A plain, strong-faced man with a simple, straightforward manner, Undén had a remarkably trusting view of the great socialist experiment next door. To him, the Soviets were misunderstood by the rest of the world. Sweden, he felt, was in a position to help the Russians get their message heard in the West. And Wallenberg was a minor embarrassment.

Perhaps the most crucial period in Wallenberg's captivity, the first year, was thus spent in political and diplomatic footshuffling. A lack of understanding for Wallenberg's mission, and even a certain resentment of the man, characterized the Swedish Establishment.

One and a half years after Raoul Wallenberg crossed the threshold of Lubyanka, Ambassador Söderblom finally had the opportunity to face the Soviet leader and ask him about the Swedish diplomat. It was the Russians, not the Swedes, who ended up profiting from the exchange.

Josef Stalin was in an amiable mood when he received the nervous, smiling ambassador. "Of course we shall look into this matter for you, Mr. Ambassador," Stalin said with the beatific smile he reserved for potentially delicate moments. "I shall write down the name to make sure I remember." And so he did, putting the piece of paper with Wallenberg's name scribbled on it in the pocket of his marshal's uniform. "If, as you say," Stalin continued, "there is a chance that he is in the Soviet Union, our investigation will provide the answer."

Söderblom did not wish to end the rare interview with the powerful man on a low note. "I, personally," Söderblom volunteered, "think Wallenberg was a victim of robbers, or perhaps an accident in Budapest." The Generalissimo smiled and nodded and drew on his pipe. The audience was over. Söderblom had obligingly spared the Kremlin the trouble of fabricating their own version of the Wallenberg mystery.

Following his interview with the Soviet leader, the Swedish ambassador wrote Stockholm that he found Stalin "fit and in vigorous health. His short but well-proportioned body and his regular features made an especially agreeable impression. His tone of voice and demeanor gave an impression of friendliness."

Three months later the Soviet Foreign Ministry declared it would no longer accept inquiries about Raoul Wallenberg from the Swedish government. The directive came straight from the desk of Josef Stalin. There was no higher court of appeal.

It was not until the following summer, August 1947, that Foreign Minister Andrei Vyshinsky finally declared himself on Wallenberg. "Following an exhaustive investigation," the former prosecutor at the Stalinist purge trials, who used to wind up his courtroom denunciations with "Shoot the mad dogs!," concluded that "we are certain that Raoul Wallenberg is not in the Soviet Union and his name is not familiar to us." Referring to Dekanosov's hasty memo regarding Wallenberg's safety, he explained: "That information was indirect." The officer who was the source for this had not been found, Vyshinsky stated. "There is no Raoul Wallenberg in any Soviet prison or internment camp." Relying on the Radio Kossuth broadcast of March 1945, he added: "We draw your attention to the fact that Wallenberg in January, 1945, was in a war zone. He could have left this zone of his own free will. Or he could have fallen victim to an assassination attempt." Then, picking up Söderblom's own version, Vyshinsky summed up: "Our own hypothesis is that Wallenberg died during combat in Budapest, or that he was kidnapped by the Arrow Cross."

After two years of apathy, the Swedish public was beginning to stir. Rudolf Phillip compiled an impressive file of evidence contradicting the Soviet's line on Wallenberg. The feisty Austrian forced a meeting with Foreign Minister Undén. It was a confrontation more than a conference. Undén chose to treat Wallenberg as a controversial figure, not merely a diplomat of a neutral country whose immunity had been violated.

Undén told Phillip and the other members of the newly formed

Wallenberg Committee that the Swede could easily have been killed in the final struggle for Budapest. Guy von Dardel, Raoul's half-brother, pointed to the growing body of evidence contradicting that convenient theory. "But why, then," Undén asked heatedly, "would the Russians lock him up?" Birgitta Wylder-Bellander, another member of the committee, answered, "They seem to think that he was a spy." This was too much for the former Marxist professor of law. "Mrs. Bellander!" he bellowed. "Are you saying Vyshinsky is lying?" The lady nodded in silence. "But this is horrible!" The Foreign Minister was beside himself. "This is quite unthinkable!"

Undén continued to insist that diplomacy was a gentlemanly art played by men of honor whose words must be accepted at face value. Raoul Wallenberg would pay a high price for Östen Undén's lofty view of statesmanship.

In 1950 Per Anger was put in charge of the Foreign Office's moribund Wallenberg investigation. He was struck by Undén's boredom with the whole case. When the two men shared a compartment on the train between Stockholm and Oslo, Anger outlined his own views on Wallenberg, what he had done for the people of Budapest and why the Russians would regard him as dangerous. The only way to deal with the Russians, Anger told Undén, was to be tough. "Raoul wasn't the only diplomat they arrested in Budapest," he went on. "They imprisoned the Swiss attaché, Harald Feller. But his government got him free within a year. They offered a prisoner swap. It worked." Anger concluded with a suggestion: "Why not hold on to the next Soviet spy caught in Stockholm, and instead of expelling him, offer him as a trade for Raoul?"

Undén's face darkened at the suggestion. "The Swedish government," he told the young diplomat, "does not do such things." Anger had lost the minister's attention and interest. He had offended his dangerously idealistic view of how the world operated. After that, Anger gave up and requested a different posting.

If Wallenberg was a minor embarrassment to Stockholm, in Budapest he was already a folk hero. In August 1946 the Jewish Council of the city had obtained permission to rename Phoenix Street, in the heart of the district that once formed the International Ghetto, Wallenberg Street. In a ceremony attended by hundreds

of people who claimed they owed their lives to Wallenberg, a
plaque was unveiled:

To THE MEMORY OF RAOUL WALLENBERG, SWEDISH DIPLOMAT,
WHOSE HEROIC DEEDS SAVED TENS OF THOUSANDS OF
HUNGARIANS FROM THE FINAL DAYS OF NAZI TERROR.
RAOUL WALLENBERG DISAPPEARED DURING THE SIEGE OF BUDAPEST.

There is no Hungarian Wallenberg Committee, nor was there
ever one. The country was slowly undergoing its inevitable transformation into a Soviet satellite. Using its celebrated "salami tactics,"
the Hungarian Communist party gradually sliced away the splin-
tered opposition parties. By August 1947, with only 22 percent of
the voters behind them, the Communists had pieced together a
controlling majority in the Parliament. Hungary's metamorphosis
from a bourgeois democracy into a "People's Democracy" was
under way.

A bald, no-neck, barrel-chested man with a boundless appetite
for power gathered most of it in his pudgy hands. Mátyás Rákosi,
son of a prosperous country grocer, had once served in Béla Kun's
ill-fated Communist experiment. He had spent the time since either
in prison for Communist agitation or sitting at Stalin's feet, learning. In some ways he outdid the Master in imposing the rule of
terror on his own country. The secret police, the show trials and
public denunciations were all perfected by Rákosi. The West stood
by and let it happen. It had all been tacitly understood at Potsdam,
Yalta and Teheran. Hungary, the Axis' last friend, would drop into
Russia's "sphere of interest."

In this atmosphere of renewed uncertainty and fear of the midnight knock on the door, there was little Hungarian initiative on
behalf of Wallenberg. The climate was not ripe for action, not
when a large segment of the population was itself missing or
awaiting trial by a stacked court, or simply trying to go unnoticed
by the authorities.

So the people for whom he risked his life had to settle for a
symbolic gesture. In 1948 the Jews of Budapest commissioned
a statue of heroic proportions, depicting St. George slaying the
dragon, to memorialize Wallenberg. The sculptor, Paul Pátzay,

like a great many other people in Budapest, owed the survival of several close friends to Wallenberg. The statue, which bore Wallenberg's profile on its base, was to stand in St. Stephen's Park, one of the Gestapo's favorite collection centers for Jews awaiting deportation. On its pedestal the message read: "This monument is our silent and eternal gratitude to him and should always remind us of his eternally lasting humanity in an inhuman period."

It was one of those fresh April mornings when the Danube reflected only the gentle slopes of the Buda hills, not the burned-out ruins that still scarred the city's face. It seemed a good day to give thanks the war was over and the Nazis had been beaten. It was a good day to give thanks in the memory of one just man.

An anonymous phone call informed the head of the Jewish Council that no thanksgiving could take place—there was no statue left to unveil. Overnight, passers-by had seen Russian soldiers working with ropes and horses hauling the giant St. George off its stand. The authorities offered no explanation. It was another case of inexplicable disappearance.

Some years later the statue turned up, without an inscription, in front of a pharmaceutical factory in the town of Debrecen, Raoul Wallenberg's destination the day he disappeared from the streets of Budapest.

24   The Apprentice Inmate

Muscovites who pass the block-long Lubyanka commonly avert their eyes. They call it the tallest building in the Soviet capital. It is far from it, but folklore has it that from its barred cell windows, you can see Siberia. During Wallenberg's first night in the Lubyanka reception cell, he was, in all probability, too dazed, his thoughts spinning too fast and too far out of control, for any of this to penetrate. He may well have thought it was not really happening to him, that he was the spectator at a bad play, which would end by daybreak. Then he could resume being Raoul Wallenberg, Wallenberg of the now proven gifts, a man with both a distinguished past and a promising future.

All night long, prisoners were brought to the cavernous, cold chamber with its rows of trestle beds, supporting fifty equally bewildered souls. By morning they had been processed. Each had a personal file, a numbered journey through the Gulag. They could keep their own clothes, but all other reminders of a prior life —rings, watches, photographs—had been taken from them. Belts, deemed too dangerous, had been removed from trousers, which were now held up by shoe laces. When, the next day, the new inmates' heads were shaven, their transformation from proud, arrogant, aggressive, shy or outspoken human beings, to convicts, had begun. After this first night, Wallenberg would never see the faithful Langfelder again.

How long did the conviction that a mistake had been made, that his imprisonment was merely a temporary perversion of justice, keep Raoul Wallenberg from despair? In the early months as inmate of Lubyanka, the prisoner's real problems, depression and a gradual dehumanization, had not yet set in.

Wallenberg was busy. He had two cell mates. Gustav Richter had been Eichmann's representative in Bucharest. A few weeks earlier, Wallenberg and Richter would have been enemies. Richter had worked tirelessly to achieve the liquidation of Rumania's Jews. Now, finding each other face to face in the gray microcosm of prison, a world without choice or selection, they became friends. Otto Scheur also shared Lubyanka's cell 123 with them. Scheur, too, had served the Reich, as an army lieutenant on the Eastern Front. Each saw the others as the only humanity they had, and thus they formed some sort of a unit, if not rooted in affection, then at least based on a mutual adversity.

Wallenberg's two cell mates helped him compose a letter to the prison authorities. Drafted in the courtly German the Swede had used with the Nazis, Wallenberg stated what he considered his most basic rights. He wanted to communicate with the Swedish embassy in Moscow. Wallenberg was treating the Soviets as he had the Nazis: as a civilized, law-abiding, rational authority. With the Nazis, his tactic frequently gained amazing results. With the Soviets, it was a total failure. It was Wallenberg's first exposure to institutionalized apathy.

The neophyte inmate had other occupations. He had to unlock the mystery of inner prison communications, the lifeblood of the victims' imposed silence. Wallenberg did not take long to crack the code of "knocking." One tap equals "A", two taps "B", three "C" and so on down the painstaking prison alphabet. The water pipe in the corner of his cell was a perfect conductor for these knocking sessions. A toothbrush or a piece of petrified soap made good tapping instruments. The message had to be transmitted fast. The guards peered through the judas every two minutes. One cell mate could sit on the toilet and thus block the guard's vision to the tapper, who sat in a corner, one sleeve of his jacket arranged as though he were holding a book rather than sending a message. Wallenberg became an avid tapper, and thus did the startling word of a Swedish diplomat in the bowels of Lubyanka spread.

Through early spring Wallenberg retained his good spirits. He was communicative with his cell mates, and enjoyed regaling them with his exploits against Eichmann, their former superior.

Only once was Wallenberg interrogated by the NKVD during this period. The secret-police major who greeted him with a broad smile and shirt sleeves rolled up, ready for work, told him, "We

know all about you. You belong to that great capitalist family."
Wallenberg emerged from the interrogation confident. The major's
implication was too absurd to have serious meaning. "They seem to
think I am a spy," Wallenberg told Richter and Scheur. They
could not be building a real case against him, he concluded. It was
only a matter of time before the whole mistake would get cleared
up. Meanwhile, he worried about how his former companion
Langfelder was bearing up. Each time a prison guard came around
with cigarettes, Wallenberg asked that his ration be passed on to
Langfelder. It wasn't much, but it was all he could do for him.

The regime was monotonous, but it was not brutal. The captive's
level of frustration was probably still manageable. Wallenberg was
certainly no longer *asked* to do things, but ordered to "March!"
"Don't look around!" He lived not in a room, but in a cell. The
light that was left on day and night was meant less to illuminate
than to burn his eyes and expose "rash" moves. The light that
came through the crack in the wall, which was his window, was
not enough to tell either the time of day or even the season of the
year.

Early in March Richter was moved to another cell, and then
transferred to another well-known Moscow institution, Lefortovo
Prison. Before taking leave of each other, Wallenberg gave Richter
a slip of paper with his name and the Foreign Office, Stockholm,
scribbled on it. A guard found the tiny crumpled scrap on Richter
and took it away from him.

Wallenberg stayed alone with Scheur until the time came for
him to be marched down the endless padded corridors, past long
rows of olive-colored cell doors and out into the chill Moscow
night, to the waiting Black Maria. When the van door slammed
shut behind him, did the still naïve prisoner allow himself to think
the Swedish embassy and freedom were his destination? If he
did, the sight of the massive Lefortovo, a K-shaped fortress, would
have been all the more depressing. Lefortovo had a more permanent
feel, held a more routine dehumanization than Lubyanka. All
political prisoners pass through Lubyanka—that is where they are
registered and catalogued. Their records are permanently filed in
its basement. Thus Lubyanka has a temporary quality, which
allows the inmates to hope. Lefortovo no longer gave Wallenberg
that feeling.

Here, again, his cell mates were former Nazis. Jan Loyda had been a Czech interpreter, and Wilhelm Roedel a diplomat. Prison had made equals of them. They now shared each other's fate more than did their parents, wives or friends from another life. Together, using the prison's Russian library, they learned the language of their jailers.

Each saw the other learning to cope with a half life within four grimy walls, with never a moment's privacy. Each observed how the other dealt with that erosion of self-respect which comes from constantly being shouted at. "Get up! Interrogation!" or, "On your feet! Hurry up, to the courtyard!" Speed was always of the essence. They were never called by name, but only by the number assigned to them. They began not to live, but to exist as gray shadows. They were kept in storage, but for what?

Early in May, Wallenberg knew that the war was officially over. Guards came in and took the blackout shades off the Lefortovo windows. A thirty-gun salute shook the Moscow sky. From the tiny black patch which his cell wall allowed of the night to come through, Wallenberg could see the wild explosion of colors that burst into the familiar profile of Lenin over nearby Red Square. In New York, London and Paris, people were going wild. Soldiers were lifted high over crowds drunk with joy and relief. Raoul Wallenberg was not going to be part of anybody's homecoming. His celebration consisted of getting both his lunch and his dinner plates served at the same time. In Lefortovo, that only happens on May Day.

Even now, three months after he "vanished" from Budapest, it is clear the Soviets had not yet made up their minds what to do about the Swede. He was placed in the middle of a veritable foreign ghetto in Lefortovo. He and Langfelder alternated cell mates among a dozen or so former diplomats and officers of the Reich. As an avid knocker, Wallenberg formed links with prisoners above and below his own cell. His signature was five taps in a row. He had mastered tapping in both French and German.

In the summer of 1946 Wallenberg composed a letter to Josef Stalin. It was a genuine group effort between Wallenberg, Ernst Wallenstein, who had been scientific counselor at the German legation in Bucharest, and Bernhard Rensinghoff, economic counselor at the same legation. The three agreed that the letter should be in French, the language of diplomacy. In the most polite terms, Wallenberg requested the Marshal's permission to get in touch with his own embassy in Moscow. Wallenberg signed the letter with the formal and respectful *"Veuillez accepter l'expression de ma très haute consideration . . ."* Then he gave the letter to the prison guard to pass on.

The following night the routine ten o'clock bell, which is the prisoners' lights-out signal, was punctuated by the slamming of doors on the fourth floor of Lefortovo. "Hands behind your back! Head down!" the guard ordered Wallenberg. The flag man (one stood at the end of every corridor and signaled when a prisoner could proceed without running into another inmate) gave Wallenberg and his guard the go-ahead. The Swede was pushed into the locker of yet another Black Maria. He was driven across a pitch-black Moscow to the headquarters of the NKVD, half a mile from the Kremlin, on Lubyanka Square. Night is the traditional time for these sessions. The prisoner is even more tired than during the day. His defenses are down. The comfortably seated secret-police officer behind his desk has just arrived on his shift. He is fresh and alert and has the look of a man who has all night to get what he is after. The cavernous Lubyanka echoes with the sounds of screams, obscenities and the heavy tread of feet marching. Raoul Wallenberg was seeing the system with its kid gloves off.

The man behind the desk shoved his file toward him. "This contains all of the information we need about you," Wallenberg was told. "Proof of your guilt is that your own people are not interested in you. Neither the Swedish government nor the embassy here has shown the slightest concern about you."

It is an old but unassailable technique: isolate the prisoner even further . . . let him know he is forgotten. He might as well sign a confession if no one gives a damn about him, anyway. But Wallenberg's spirit was not that fragile. He continued to demand the right to get in touch with either the Swedish embassy or the Red Cross. The secret-police officer rejected both. "They aren't interested in you, believe me," he told the prisoner. "They would have gotten in touch with us long ago if they were."

Wallenberg was told he was a "political." "Your case is quite clear," his interrogator told him. "If you consider yourself innocent, it is up to you to prove it." When Wallenberg attempted to explain his rescue mission to save Budapest's Jews, the Russian cut him off. "Why would a rich Swede, a capitalist, a Christian, undertake that kind of work? Come on. You are a spy."

Wallenberg was sped back to his cell across town. The prisoner had plenty of time to ponder the line of questioning, as well as his jailer's new hostility. Perhaps he did not have the kind of support from his own people that would instantly prove his innocence. One thing he now understood. There was an almost pathological paranoia about his new adversaries. Their alliance with the West had been strictly a marriage of convenience. Had he perhaps been too careless in speaking out about his American funding, and FDR's personal support, when he was first taken captive? But how was he to know?

When he was led back to his own cell, he found Wallenstein and Rensinghoff, his prison family, anxiously waiting for his report. "I think I may have been forgotten by Sweden, and the rest of the world," he told them. "I wonder if any of the people I saved still remember?"

What Wallenberg did not understand was that in terms of logic and reason, and commonly accepted Western standards of justice, he was not in another country, he was on another planet: Stalin's Russia in 1946. Twenty million Russians had lost their lives in the war, though their leader insisted it was only seven million. The people knew better. Everybody was mourning someone. The first postwar census was proof. In the age groups older than eighteen at the end of the war, there were 32 million men left, compared with 52 million women. Stalin did not wish either his own people or his former allies to know just how drained and weak the country had emerged from the war. An entire generation had been wiped out on the battlefields of Stalingrad, Voronezh and Leningrad.

Instinctively, Stalin's method of dealing with the devastation was to inflict more devastation. The camps and prisons of the far north and Siberia began filling up. Fifteen million people populated that separate continent which came to be known as the Gulag. He institutionalized repression under the doctrine that the interests of the Soviet state took precedence over the letter of the law. The law itself could be dispensed with, as was frequently done by the NKVD whenever the "higher" interests of the state were in danger. Article 58 of the Soviet Legal Code, under which Wallenberg's "crimes" fit, became a handy umbrella for "counterrevolutionary actions" of all hues.

Stalin filled his camps not only with suspect foreigners. His paranoia demanded that returning Soviet officers and soldiers be dealt with—as prisoners of war, they had been "tainted," they had been exposed to the enemy. Instead of the warm welcome they had expected, they promptly found themselves under suspicion. Most, like Alexander Solzhenitsyn, were not even allowed to see their families before they were taken to Lubyanka or sent off to the even more accommodating Siberian fields. They were branded as traitors. They had disobeyed Stalin's orders, according to which they should not have allowed the Germans to take them alive. Civilians who had lived under German occupation were accused of collaboration. This postwar stocking of the Gulag ranks in the wake of two revolutions, a protracted civil war, massive compulsory collectivization of farmland and forced industrialization, as one more chapter in the violent epic of the forging of the Soviet state.

Raoul Wallenberg had no way of knowing any of this. He had of course not heard Winston Churchill, in March 1946, warn a rapt audience in Fulton, Missouri, of the "growing challenge and peril to civilization" from the "Communist fifth columns," threatening with a return to the "Dark Ages, to the Stone Age." The Iron Curtain, Churchill announced, had rung down, creating "two separate and hostile worlds, one free and the other captive."

To his captors, Raoul Wallenberg was one among hundreds of thousands of prisoners, distinguished by one trait only: he could yet be a useful pawn in a much bigger game. Unlike the Nazis, the Russians had no problems of space for their prisoners. Execution was the terrifying logic of the German quest for *Lebensraum*. Russian captives could be put to work rebuilding a ravaged country. They could clear the endless forests of Siberia, they could mine coal in the Donetz basin, and they could build roads in the Urals. The prisoner would be fed a minimal diet, just enough to permit him to meet his daily work quota, until he quietly died of exhaustion.

The Russian prisoner is treated more as a lost object than as a real villain. Apathy—the shrinking interest in a life of total monotony, when speech itself takes too much effort, burns too many calories—is a greater danger to the Soviet prisoner than sadistic guards or the firing squad.

Two years after he was led into Lubyanka, the Kremlin was not sure if Raoul Wallenberg had a future. They were in no great rush. In the summer of 1947, the clanging of steel doors again stirred the inmates on the third and fourth floors of Lefortovo out of their late-day trance. Ten of them—Richter, Loyda, Roedel, Scheur and six others—were led, one by one, to the interrogation chamber set up in Lefortovo's basement by the NKVD. Richter was first. "To whom have you spoken about Wallenberg?" the irritable NKVD major asked him. Richter named names. "What precisely did you tell them about the Swede?" Richter related the story of Wallenberg's amazing rescue of the remnants of Budapest's Jewish community. When the major was satisfied the German was holding nothing back, he was led away. He was not taken back to his old cell. For the next eight months Richter, and each of the others who underwent this interrogation, were placed in solitary confinement. The same treatment was accorded the former cell mates of Vilmos Langfelder.

In the following month—August—the long-awaited statement of the Soviet Foreign Minister was issued. "Raoul Wallenberg," it said, "is not in the Soviet Union, and he is unknown to us."

Thus, from a protected "guest," Wallenberg was transformed into a phantom. "It is correct that the Russian Foreign Ministry on January 14, 1945, received a short message, based on indirect statements by one of the commanders of a military force fighting in Budapest, that Wallenberg should have been found in the Benczur Street." Vyshinsky explained: "At that point it was impossible to verify the message, as the fighting in the city continued for another month . . . careful investigations have been made, which, however, have not given positive results, and the Russian officer who gave the statement has not been found." Yet another case of a mysterious disappearance.

Henceforth Raoul Wallenberg became the almost invisible prisoner of the Gulag. He was never long in any of the many "islands" that form the Archipelago. He was constantly on the move. No sooner did word of his presence in the Vorkuta region seep out than he was sighted at Vladimir Prison, about a hundred miles east of Moscow. It is not unusual for Soviet inmates to be transported from one place to another. They have even adopted a word from the military for this: "etapes," they call it, or stages in the prisoner's journey. Its purpose is to give the general impression of mobilization. If the country is not perpetually in a semi-war situation, why then would it have such an immense prison population? Seeing long columns of prisoners, whether lined up in front of the Trans-Siberian Rail Road, or mounting convoys of roadside trucks, instills this mood of "a country on the alert" in the population. It also serves the purpose of making it more difficult to trace prisoners. The transport also takes a great deal of planning and manpower and provides thousands of jobs.

For the prisoner, the transport is hell. He is whisked from a routine which he has mastered, and to a certain extent, tamed, into the unknown. He must leave behind the few precious articles he may have accumulated. He does not know where he is going: to the permafrost of Siberia or a desert in Kazakhstan, or beyond the Arctic Circle, where they mine nickel or pan gold. Often the convict does not have the right clothes for the trip, nor is he likely to be issued them, until after he has settled in his new "home." Then he is given the shabby castoffs of a dead prisoner from the prison storehouse.

The transport starts when the convicts are shoved quickly into Black Marias. Everything must always be accomplished "On the double!" Up to forty prisoners are squeezed in the tight embrace of these closed trucks, which were designed to hold one-fourth that number. After a half-hour of barely breathing, inhaling fumes and feeling every bump on the road, the prisoners are hurried onto airplanes (the only way to reach the camp at Yakutsk in northern Siberia, where Wallenberg was once sighted) or freight trains, the most common prison transport. Bodies are interwoven with bodies during stifling journeys across the vast Soviet landscape.

Since official penal statistics are classified as state secrets, it is difficult to say how many prisons and camps there are today in the Soviet Union. Amnesty International has the designations and locations of 330. From satellite photographs, the CIA calculates that the Soviet prison population is just under 2.5 million today. Of those, roughly 10,000 are believed to be political, or prisoners of conscience.

Raoul Wallenberg has experienced "etape" several dozen times in his life in the Gulag. He has, according to a score of eyewitnesses, crisscrossed the Archipelago several times in trains, planes,

Black Marias and trucks. He has been dispatched from solitary confinement in Moscow to hard labor in Wrangel's Island, just beneath the Arctic Circle. Like a piece of unwanted luggage, he has been searched, squeezed and commanded to go faster, ever faster. He has seen the gates of camps swing wide open and slam shut behind him, dozens, perhaps hundreds of times. He has been marched every ten days to the bathhouse in the company of only his guards, because Wallenberg is a special case and Wallenberg must, at all cost, be prevented from communicating with other inmates. Wallenberg has watched the tiny stream of yellow light that never changes trickle into his cell. How many times did he wonder, Why?

25   The Silent Prisoner

"T" hey just want me to disappear. Simply vanish into the
night. That would suit them best." That was how Raoul
Wallenberg once described his own view of his captors'
attitude toward him. By 1947 he had become a very cumbersome
prisoner. By then the Swedes were making life a little less comfortable for the Kremlin.

Wallenberg was now in perpetual motion. It is an elementary law
of physics: an object in motion is more difficult to trace than one
that is stationary. Wallenberg was seldom stationary. His potential
usefulness at some later date was his protective shield at a time
when "losing" an unwanted inmate to overwork, overinterrogation,
undernourishment or even the firing squad was a very small event.
Sometimes, though, the enormous bureaucracy that runs the
General Administration of Labor and Prison Camps, more familiarly
known as the Gulag, makes mistakes. Around Christmas time in
1947, the Gulag committed one such bureaucratic blunder in the
prison life of Raoul Wallenberg.

André Shimkevich remembers the approximate date because in
prison there are two ways to tell time. If you are exceptionally cold,
since not all cells are heated, and if the ground is frozen under
your feet as you perform your daily twenty-minute shuffle in the
tiny exercise yard, then it is winter. If your rations include a bit
more fat and some sugar, you are also being prepared for a cold
snap—or for transport to Siberia. André Shimkevich had just
received his extra sugar rations when he was told to prepare to move.

Shimkevich was a seasoned veteran of eighteen years in the
Gulag. He no longer reacted in any particular way when the guards
barked, "On your feet!" He was a journeyman prisoner who had
passed into a world of his own. He was immune to the whims of

his captors, having squeezed all feeling, all hope, out of himself. That was his way of getting through.

The heavy steel-reinforced door of his new cell swung open. The guard pushed Shimkevich in and slammed the door behind him shut. A lone prisoner sat on the cot in the corner. The man looked as Shimkevich imagined he himself must have appeared: frail and gaunt, with a complexion that had taken on the pallor of prison. His clothes hung on his shrunken form. Like most convicts, the man could have been any age.

What Shimkevich calls "the Great Silence" reigned in their cell block. The two cell mates were practiced at sign language. Following the prisoners' unwritten protocol, it was the man whose cell had been invaded that initiated communication. He spelled the international word for "diplomat": consul. André Shimkevich, plugged into the Lubyanka grapevine, had heard tapped messages of the presence in the great fortress of a Swedish diplomat named Wallenberg. His cell mate now mouthed the name. Then he held up first five, then eight fingers. Code 58. Espionage. Shimkevich felt somewhat in awe of this near-legendary figure. Wallenberg was a name nearly as well known in Lubyanka as in Stockholm.

Compared to Shimkevich, the Swede, an inmate of less than two years, was in fair condition. Shimkevich did not decline when Wallenberg offered him a portion of his daily bread. "Bread," Shimkevich explains, "is like a religion in prison. You eat it crumb by crumb. Sometimes you deliberately let a few crumbs drop on the ground so you can pick them up later and make it last longer."

By the prisoner's well-practiced combination of lip reading and signing, Shimkevich told the Swede his own story. He was the stepson of the French cubist sculptor Jacques Lipchitz. In 1929, as an idealistic, left-leaning student, he had gone to Russia. At that time Lenin was the prophet of a large body of French university students. A pilgrimage to the Promised Land wrapped a cloak of immeasurable prestige around a Left Bank intellectual. Shimkevich never had a chance to parade his new-found wisdom before his friends. He was arrested during the height of a wave of Stalinist hysteria and charged, under the immensely flexible Code 58, with suspicion of spying. In those days, foreigners in Soviet custody had little chance of ever walking out.

At the end of his second day with Wallenberg, their cell door swung open and an agitated guard told Shimkevich to get ready to move. Shimkevich had never before spent only two nights in a cell. A mistake, his prisoner's third sense told him, had been committed; Wallenberg was clearly not meant to share his cell with another foreigner.

Shimkevich had good connections. Through her husband, his mother mobilized the members of the leftist intelligentsia of Paris. The poet Louis Aragon and others fired off letters to get the young man out of prison. André Shimkevich, product of a class of fellow travelers and sympathizers, could have meant no harm to the Soviet state, the letters stated. It took twenty-seven years, but the Frenchman was eventually pardoned in 1958.

He walked out of Lubyanka a middle-aged cynic whose youthful ideals had been replaced by a thick skin and an impenetrable coat of irony. His right hand, a crumbled collection of bones that will never heal, was Shimkevich's most conspicuous reminder of the energetic hours his captors spent trying to get a confession out of him. They never did.

On his way home from Moscow to Paris, André Shimkevich obeyed the prisoner's primary code of conduct. He decided to try to locate Maj von Dardel and tell her everything he remembered about her son. By train and boat, he journeyed to Stockholm. In his Parisian's rapid-fire French, today he tells a strange tale of a candlelit dinner in a palace he can no longer identify, somewhere in Stockholm. Wallenberg's mother was present, and others whose names have been erased from his memory by twenty-three years. As he was shown around the grand setting, Shimkevich remembers admiring a clock on the kitchen wall. His host immediately presented the former prisoner with it. The clock, shaped like a frying pan, continues to tell time in Shimkevich's apartment in Paris.

Mostly Shimkevich recalls the discomfort he felt throughout the evening. It was his first real dinner as a free man. The company, the conversation, the food, the china and silver on which it was served, swirled around his prisoner's head, blurring more precise details. The dinner was Shimkevich's repayment for another, much humbler meal he had once shared with the son of these well-bred, well-meaning people.

In Stockholm there is no record of the Frenchman's nocturnal visit. No documents show any follow-up to Shimkevich's revelation in 1958, which must have been a crucial year in the prison life of Raoul Wallenberg. It was less than a year earlier that the Kremlin had finally admitted that Wallenberg had indeed been taken prisoner twelve years earlier. But according to the Kremlin, he had died of a heart attack after two years at Lubyanka. The date of Wallenberg's death was given as July 1947, six months before the Swede shared his bread with the Frenchman.

The picturesque town of Vladimir claims a proud chapter in Russia's past. Once, during the Middle Ages, it was the capital of the vast country. Today it is a place where tourists and the faithful swarm to admire its beautiful twelfth-century Cathedral of the Assumption. Not far from the serene onion-domed cathedral, and the pious who wait for hours to admire the altar inside, is the building that is Vladimir's major claim to fame today. Vladimir Prison looks like a great many other innocuous official buildings in the Soviet Union. It has five stories, small windows and very few entrances. There are no signs advertising its true function. It is a prison reserved for "politicals" deemed of special danger to the state. Prisoners are transferred here from labor camps if they have proved recalcitrant or if they require relentless surveillance. At intervals throughout the fifties, Raoul Wallenberg was an inmate of Vladimir.

Wallenberg has never been an ordinary prisoner. He was not supposed to communicate with anyone after 1947, his official date of death. Vladimir is equipped for assuring the strictest isolation. But the Wallenberg myth proved elusive to the control of the Gulag's ablest administrators.

One by one, German, Swiss, Italian and American prisoners, pardoned during Khrushchev's period of tentative thaw, reported the presence of the Swede in Vladimir Prison. Taken individually, their testimony is thin. Together, the weak threads form a fabric of some durability.

It was mostly in the Vladimir hospital that these foreign prisoners broke through Wallenberg's nearly perfect isolation. In a prison hospital, security tends to be less stringent. The Swede had become adept at giving rapid signs.

Otto Schoggl, another Nazi captive, received one such hurried message. Schoggl was in the prison infirmary following a stomach operation in early 1955. He was put in a cell with a prisoner who knew their exchange would be cut short. He had been through the drill countless times before. "If you get out," he whispered to the Austrian in an accented German, "tell them you met a Swede from Budapest. That's all. They'll know the rest." The two spent only one night together. The next morning a red-faced, ill-tempered guard kicked open their cell door. "Who put you in here?" he bellowed at the Austrian. "On your feet! Out!" Another error.

Wallenberg mostly tapped his messages to fellow inmates at Vladimir. A Swiss businessman, ten years Wallenberg's senior, fell into Stalin's net, like Shimkevich, for being in the wrong place at the wrong time. Emil Brugger, a six-year veteran of the Gulag, was as keen a "tapper" as Wallenberg himself. In 1954 he was in the Corpus II wing of Vladimir, a nearly hermetically sealed section for foreign prisoners. Brugger was not sure he received the right message when it came through the pipe. He tapped back, "Repeat, please," in German. The same message was tapped anew: "Wallenberg, Swedish Legation, Budapest." For two months the Swede and the Swiss communicated thus, sharing with each other, in the prisoners' elliptical code, the circumstances of their arrest, and their subsequent odyssey through the Soviet penal system. Neither man had ever been tried or sentenced. Both lived in the suspended animation of those with an open-ended term.

Brugger was proud of his contact with this prison legend and spoke of his "conversations" with Wallenberg to a handful of others at Vladimir. They were not all under quite the same canopy of silence as the Swede. Thus did Wallenberg's presence there spread through the Gulag and to the outside world.

This was the mid-fifties. Raoul Wallenberg was an inmate of ten years' standing. He had not, according to his tapped efforts at communication, sunk into irreversible despair. He was not allowed to either write or receive letters. But he was not yet resigned to his permanent injustice. Word of the death of Josef Stalin had spread like a warm blanket over the prison population. Through the intricate grapevine, Wallenberg learned that henceforth prisoners would no longer be executed. He had survived the harshest period of Soviet history. Perhaps now something would happen to end the nightmare. But the only change in Wallenberg's life was more "etapes," more transports. The authorities were taking fewer chances that his trail would be picked up. Somehow it always was, several steps too late.

Two years before, in 1953, during one of those endless, claustrophobic journeys between two islands of the Gulag, between Verchne Uralsk Prison for "politicals" near the Ural Mountains and Alexandrovski Central Prison in the Russian heartland, General Gennadi Kuprianov had met Raoul Wallenberg. For three weeks the Swede and the general shared a train compartment with dozens of other "important" inmates. Crowded into sleeping cars meant to hold half the number, they shared the daily humiliation of body searches. The former general, like the former diplomat, hardly even noticed the deliberate debasement of the transport. The isolation, the perpetual weariness, the lack of food, above all, the near-total absence of human contact, had worked miracles in transforming both prisoners. Bit by bit, the two men, one frail and gaunt, the other square and close to the ground, traced the jagged road that brought each to the train that was speeding them to still another camp or prison.

General Kuprianov, one of the scores of Stalin's officers who had helped to thwart Hitler's Operation Barbarossa, had been decorated during the war as a Hero of the Soviet Union. Peace turned out to be even more perilous than war for the general. Relations between the former Allies, Washington and Moscow, had never been chillier than in 1948. On August 4 the Soviets blockaded Berlin, cutting off two and a half million people from the outside world and from all their sources of supply. It was also during the summer of 1948 that the final and inevitable split between Stalin and his most powerful European ally, Marshal Tito, was sealed. Stalin now reversed his previous orders to his army to demobilize. Simultaneously with the rearmament policy he announced, Stalin, true to instinct, began a purge of the upper reaches of his army. It was in this sweep that the former Hero of the Soviet Union, General Gennadi Kuprianov, was caught. He was, along with many others, charged with hatching a plot to overthrow the Generalissimo, with the help of fellow officers in Leningrad. He was arrested, charged with treason and sent wandering through the Gulag. All of this Kuprianov related to Wallenberg.

The two prisoners were separated after this trip and did not see each other again for two years. In 1955 they were both in the infirmary of Vladimir Prison. Both prisoners had developed stomach problems from years of inedible food combined with almost constant nervous tension. Kuprianov and Wallenberg both waited in vain for Khrushchev's era of reform to touch their prison lives. It had not, except in small ways. There was more fish in their daily watery soup. There was even meat now on special days. But the two men were still too important to be treated as normal offenders, with even minimal rights. Wallenberg did not have the right to exist.

The following year they met again in that most porous place in the prison: the infirmary. Kuprianov and Wallenberg both needed dental work at roughly the same time. But now the guards were more alert. The two friends had only an instant to exchange glances before the general was rushed out of the dentist's waiting room.

Around this time, unknown to the prisoners, an upheaval was under way behind the impenetrable walls of the Kremlin. A short, bald, plain-spoken man with a fondness for the language of the farmyard decided it was time to smash the cult of Stalin. The god of some thirty years standing had failed them. In his cataclysmic secret party speech, Nikita Khrushchev submitted that war was no longer the inevitable means to world socialism. Different roads could be taken to achieve a People's Democracy. The KGB (formerly the NKVD) would no longer exist as a state within a state. Thousands of political prisoners, stockpiled and forgotten for decades, were now free to pick up the pieces of their shattered lives.

General Gennadi Kuprianov was among those who were rehabilitated. He was no longer considered an enemy of the people and had the right to wear his cherished decorations once more. Kuprianov walked out of Vladimir Prison in the now completely threadbare uniform in which he had been arrested eight years before. He took the first train to his hometown, Leningrad.

This was not the end of the general's relationship with the recently humbled KGB. Thirteen years later, in February 1979, Kuprianov received the familiar green summons from the KGB. The colonel who greeted the pensioned general was courteous and smiling. The general must guard against speaking to Western journalists about his life in prison, he warned the older man. The foreign press, he continued, was a well-known cover for infiltrators of all shades. They would distort whatever the general told them.

"It is a dangerous practice, which only serves the cause of the imperialists and the Zionists," the KGB officer concluded.

The old soldier had been attentive but continued to look at the colonel with a blank expression on his lined face. He had spoken to no Western journalists. Someone, it turned out, had done the speaking for him. The general had mentioned his meetings with the Swedish prisoner to another former inmate of the Gulag. The man in question, a Russian Jew, had since emigrated to Israel. Through him the Kuprianov-Wallenberg connection had found its way into a Russian émigré paper. The KGB only cared about one thing: the connection which some people in the West had apparently noticed between a man as clearly living as the sturdy, avuncular general and a prisoner who was officially dead.

Kuprianov walked out of his first interrogation stunned. So things had not fundamentally changed since he was dragged before a kangaroo court and presented with a list of trumped-up charges. What pained him most was the thought of Wallenberg. The Swede must still be in Soviet custody. Kuprianov recalled Wallenberg saying he was serving a twenty-five-year term for espionage. By his calculation, Wallenberg should have been released in 1970. Why hadn't he?

Four months later the general received his second green summons. He was greeted by the same colonel, and again they were alone, but this time the KGB officer was conspicuously less solicitous, less respectful of the general's rank. "You have been pandering to the agents of the Zionists," the officer accused Kuprianov. He unfolded a faded, dog-eared copy of an article in the conservative Stockholm daily, *Svenska Dagbladet*, and jabbed his index finger at a photograph that accompanied the article. It showed a considerably younger Kuprianov, resplendent in army greatcoat and Hero of the Soviet Union decoration. "You are collaborating with these agents who mask as reporters!" the colonel shouted. The article linked him to Wallenberg, and described three meetings between the two inmates. "You," the KGB officer continued, "who have been rehabilitated must help to refute these American-Israeli provocations!"

The general was not a political man. He had retired from the service of his country and looked forward to spending the time still left him in the company of his wife. They had missed eight years together. He was the kind of man who spoke his mind, he knew no other way. "We have already acknowledged the crimes of Beria," he stated simply, referring to the execution in 1953 of the dreaded secret-police chief. "Why can't we then also acknowledge the crime against Wallenberg?"

This logic was too much for the officer of the KGB. "We are not here to discuss the possible crimes of Beria, but the crimes of the American and Israeli intelligence agencies against the Soviet Union!" he exploded at the startled old man. "You must go home now," the general was told, "and compose your denial of these false reports." The general did not wish to mislead the agent. "But I cannot deny the truth. I cannot say, 'No, I have not met the Swede,' when I met him on three different occasions."

Kuprianov was told to return the following day with his denial. He went home to his wife that evening and told her he was not sure how he would bear up under further grilling. But he had no intention of fabricating a denial. He was too old to start playing their games now.

The following day when he arrived at the colonel's office, there was no longer any pretense of respect accorded the general. The rehabilitated Hero of the Soviet Union had been cut down to what Stalin had once called him: a traitor to his own people. This time the KGB interrogator was not alone.

"Where is your denial?" the colonel asked.

"I have none to make," Kuprianov answered with all the naïveté of those not accustomed to lying.

"In that case," the KGB officer offered, "you can sign this one. We have prepared it for you."

Kuprianov's tired eyes skimmed the official document set before him. It denied any knowledge of the prisoner Wallenberg in the Soviet Union. "I cannot sign this. It is not true." Kuprianov did not return to his wife that evening.

Five days later she received her own summons. "Your husband is ill," a voice at the other end told her. "You may visit him in the police hospital." When she arrived at Leningrad's KGB head-quarters it was not to the hospital, but to the morgue that she was led. The cause of the general's death was given as an infarct of the heart, the same cause given for Wallenberg's death thirty-two years earlier.

When she returned home, the widow found her apartment ransacked. Upholstery had been slashed, drawers emptied of their contents. The general's private papers and the meticulous journal he always kept were the only objects missing. He had recorded all his prison experiences, including his meetings with Wallenberg.

Shortly thereafter, Kuprianov's widow received her final call from the KGB. "If any Western journalists try to reach you," the anonymous caller told her, "do not turn them away." She was to get their names and fix an appointment to see them. "Then," said the KGB, "you must ring us." The elderly lady had seen enough. She did not wish to follow her husband to the KGB morgue. She did as she was told. The journalist who called did not make it to the appointment she had set up for him. He had picked up something in her voice.

A close friend and sometime secretary of Kuprianov's was already on her way from Leningrad to Vienna, on an exit visa she had waited for many years to obtain. She carried with her notes from the general's diary.

26   Dead or Alive

T he tall, pale Swedish Prime Minister faced the sturdy Ukrainian with his rosy complexion and legendary temper across the baize-topped Kremlin conference table. "Raoul Wallenberg," Tage Erlander declared on this day in April 1956, "is casting a giant shadow over Swedish-Soviet relations." The Prime Minister had gone to Moscow armed with a thick file of sworn testimony. Thanks to the hyperactive Rudolf Phillip, the Swedes now had affidavits from the newly released German, Austrian and Italian POWs describing encounters with Wallenberg for two years following his abduction. The Swedish public had shaken off its indifference to the fate of the missing diplomat and was putting pressure on the government to stop swallowing Moscow's humiliating, casual attitude toward the Wallenberg case.

Tage Erlander thought the moment ripe for some progress. Khrushchev's thunderbolt—destruction of the Stalin myth—had shaken the Kremlin and caused ripples throughout the world. Konrad Adenauer, the Chancellor of West Germany, had recently negotiated the release of those of his countrymen still captive in the Soviet Union. The Swiss and the Austrians had achieved the same results. Sweden was beginning to smart under the Wallenberg impasse.

Prime Minister Tage Erlander also handed over a letter to Communist Party Chairman Nikita Khrushchev. It was from Maj von Dardel for her son.

Dear beloved Raoul,

After many years of despair and infinite sorrow, we have now advanced so far that the leaders of the governing parties,

Prime Minister Erlander and Interior Minister [Gunnar] Hedlund, are going to Moscow to see to it that you may at last return. May they succeed and may your sufferings come to an end. We have never given up hope of seeing you again, despite the fact that all our efforts to contact you have, to our great sorrow, been unsuccessful. From the other prisoners who have returned, and who have shared cells with you, we have got some information about your life in prison in Russia, and via Major Richter we have got greetings from you. . . . There is a room waiting for you when you return with the Prime Minister.

Whether the prisoner ever received his mother's letter is not known.

De-Stalinization—the process begun after the tyrant's death in 1953—had turned out to be mostly an in-house clean-up operation. Lavrenti Beria, the universally loathed chief of state security, was led before a firing squad. Viktor Abakumov, the tall, black-haired head of SMERSH counterintelligence, had three stars ripped off his commissar's uniform. Then, he too, met the same fate he had meted out so freely to others. It was Abakumov's agents in Budapest who had taken Wallenberg out of the hands of the military and ultimately pronounced him an enemy of the Soviet people. But Abakumov did not act alone. At some point he needed the blessing of the Kremlin's highest reaches. The people who once gave Abakumov their approval were still in power.

Khrushchev referred to crimes committed by "certain people" in his secret party speech. Nowhere did the new Party Chairman say there was anything wrong with the system itself. Nor did he condemn a state that can dispense with due process, trial by jury, which can lock people up just in case they might be useful some day. That would have required a repudiation of all that the Soviet state stood for. An admission of that nature would have amounted to a more fundamental revolution.

Raoul Wallenberg was quite possibly the Soviet's most important prisoner. His name and his legend were too powerful to release. In at least one new Soviet province, Hungary, Wallenberg would present dangerous competition to the Communist party's most jealously guarded possessions: legitimacy and power. Free,

Wallenberg would be a living indictment of a system that had not fundamentally changed. What is more, it had no plans to change. The captive's mother, her life a ruin, had opposed the Swedish Prime Minister's confrontation with Khrushchev. Maj von Dardel felt it would be dangerous for the Swedes to show their hand to the Soviets at that point. Sweden was now regularly receiving evidence about Wallenberg. While Erlander had brought the file from 1945 to 1947, the rest of the testimony was still in the hands of a couple of Swedish Supreme Court justices, who were meticulously screening each scrap of the more current evidence and testing its veracity. Mrs. von Dardel feared the Soviets would find a way to turn the Swede's limited dossier to their own advantage.

Ten months later the Kremlin was ready with its reply. The long-awaited word came in the form of a memorandum from Deputy Foreign Minister Andrei Gromyko:

> In pursuance of the Swedish Government's request, the Soviet Government instructed the pertinent Soviet authorities to pursue the material concerning Raoul Wallenberg which had been received from Swedish quarters at the Swedish-Soviet Negotiations in Moscow. . . . In the course of perusal and testing of said material, the Soviet authorities have made a careful search of the archives . . . similarly many persons have been questioned who could have had anything to do with circumstances mentioned in the material received from Sweden.
>
> As a result, it has not been possible to find any information whatsoever concerning Wallenberg's sojourn in the Soviet Union. It has transpired that none of those heard knew of any person by the name of Wallenberg. In this connection, the competent Soviet authorities have undertaken to search page by page the archive documents from all wards in certain prisons. As a result of such search of archive documents from the health services in the Lubyanka Prison, a document has been found which there is good reason to consider as referring to Raoul Wallenberg.
>
> This document has the form of a handwritten report, addressed to the former minister of the state security of the

Soviet Union, Abakumov, and written in the hand of the
health service director of said prison, A. L. Smoltsov, reading
as follows:

I report that the prisoner Walenberg [sic], who is well
known to you, died suddenly in his cell this night, probably
as the result of a heart attack. Pursuant to instructions
given by you that I personally have Walenberg under my
care, I request approval to make an autopsy with a view to
establishing the cause of death.

Smoltsov, Chief of Prison Sanitary Ward   July 17, 1947
Colonel in Medicine Service

On this report the following notation is found in Smoltsov's
handwriting:

I have personally notified the Minister and it has been
ordered that the body be cremated without an autopsy:
[signed] Smoltsov

It has not been possible to find any other information what-
soever having the character of document or testimony, all the
more so since the aforementioned A. L. Smoltsov died on May
7, 1953. On the strength of what has been cited above, the
conclusion should be drawn that Wallenberg died in July
1947.

Wallenberg was apparently arrested along with other persons in the area for military operations by Soviet troops. At
the same time it may be considered indisputable that Wallenberg's subsequent detention in prison, as well as the incorrect
information about him supplied by certain leaders of the security organs to the Soviet Union's Foreign Ministry over a
period of years, comprised the result of Abakumov's criminal
activities. In connection with gross crimes committed by him
it will be recalled that Abakumov, who engaged in activities
implying the violation of the laws of the Soviet Union, and
who had sought to inflict upon the Soviet Union all kinds of
damage, was executed in accordance with the verdict handed
down by the Supreme Court of the Soviet Union.

The Soviet Government presents its sincere regrets because
of what has occurred and expresses its profound sympathy to

the Swedish Government as well as to Raoul Wallenberg's relatives.

[signed] Andrei Gromyko

Twelve years and one month after Wallenberg's arrest, the Soviets had a near-perfect alibi. There was no body; it had been cremated. The guilty, Abakumov and his direct superior Beria, had both already been dealt with by Soviet justice. There were no witnesses. Smoltsov, the prison hospital director, was dead. And there was no death certificate.

A closer examination of the Gromyko memorandum reveals it to be full of inconsistencies and fabrications. Cremation was an unheard-of method of disposing of dead prisoners, according to Soviet prison specialists. In the late forties, mass graves were the common means used, as there was only one known crematorium in the Soviet Union. The fact that Gromyko claimed it took twelve years of thorough search and questioning to locate any trace of Wallenberg's death in Lubyanka stretched the Swedes' credibility even further. As mentioned earlier, Lubyanka is the central clearing house for all prisoners. It is here that new arrivals to the Gulag are processed, their photographs and fingerprints taken, and a file set up. The prisoner's file never leaves Lubyanka. It is a brown manila folder with the inmate's name and number and the status of his case stamped plainly in the top right-hand corner. Some prisoners have caught a glimpse of their file left on a policeman's desk upon the prisoner's release. The file contains details of the prisoner's itinerary through the Gulag, as well as copies of any correspondence he may have sent or received. Lubyanka Prison is known for a great many things; sloppy filing is not one of them.

The date of Wallenberg's alleged death, given as July 17, 1947, is equally suspicious. It was the same month that all those prisoners, since released, who had shared cells or had any contact with Wallenberg or Langfelder, were interrogated on the subject of the two men. Following their interrogations they were warned not to talk about them. To underline the message, each was then placed in solitary confinement. From that time on, Wallenberg and Langfelder started their endless journeys through the Gulag.

In spite of all these precautions, the Soviets still left themselves a small opening. Gromyko had phrased his memo carefully:

". . . there is good reason to *consider*" that the cremated prisoner was Wallenberg. "Wallenberg was *apparently* arrested" and "the conclusion *should be drawn* that Wallenberg died in July 1947." The tone of the statement is not the unambiguous, positive stance the Kremlin normally strikes in its denials. In 1957, the Kremlin had not completely ruled out a future shift in Wallenberg's fortune.

Four days after the Gromyko memo was issued, the United States Senate Internal Security Subcommittee held a special closed-door session. The senators grilled Yuri Rastvorov, a former KGB officer who had recently defected to Washington. Under questioning, Rastvorov disputed the official Soviet account of Wallenberg's death. The secret police, he stated, did not arrest foreigners without the permission of the highest government leaders, including the Foreign Minister. As to the Kremlin's "sudden" discovery that Wallenberg had indeed been their prisoner, Rastvorov stated under oath, "It is ridiculous to believe that the Soviet government would take twelve years to locate the records of the Wallenberg case." The defector also shed some light on de-Stalinization. Abakumov, he claimed, had not been arrested as an accomplice in Beria's "criminal activities." He had been arrested in 1951 at Beria's urging—not for excessive brutality, but for committing "social crimes." The former counterintelligence chief had reportedly accumulated several million rubles' worth of "public property" in West Germany.

Though the prisoner's mother was not altogether surprised by the Gromyko memo, it was a fresh wound. She never relented, however, in her pursuit of more witnesses and more testimony to bolster her government's case vis à vis the Kremlin. If the purpose of the Soviet memo was to defuse Swedish interest in the case, it missed its mark.

The mother's conviction that her son was still languishing in the Gulag was not shaken in the least. But the Foreign Office still treated her as an unwelcome intruder. Foreign Minister Undén frequently referred to her trying to get Sweden "to declare war on Russia" for the sake of her son. And when Mrs. von Dardel called on the newly appointed Swedish Secretary-General of the United Nations, she received the same cold, cautious response. "As a Swede," Dag Hammarskjöld told her, "I am in no position to put this case before the Russians. It is a question of retaining an impartial role among the Big Powers."

The Swedish monarch, Gustav VI Adolf, shared Hammarskjöld's embarrassment at the continued persistence of Mrs. von Dardel. When the King's private secretary, Carl-Fredrik Palmstierna, a distant relative of Wallenberg's, approached the monarch about the possibility of a royal plea for his release, he was asked, "What do you expect me to do? We can't just ransack the Russian prisons, or declare war, for the sake of Wallenberg!"

It was Wallenberg's fellow countrymen whose pressure, more than anything else, forced the Swedish government to pursue his tracks. Two years after the Gromyko memo, Stockholm presented Moscow with new evidence pointing to Wallenberg's imprisonment in Vladimir Prison in the fifties. The Kremlin's answer set the tone for the next twenty years of fruitless dialogue between the two countries. Moscow stuck to the Gromyko memo of 1957. The Vladimir testimony of the fifties was deemed unreliable. The Soviet position was that the testimony of Wallenberg's former cell mates was not credible, as they were prisoners of war.

While two capitals debated his existence, the prisoner himself continued his weary trail through the Gulag. A feisty, potbellied, balding Pole, a rare Jewish officer in the Polish army, released from both a Soviet prison, in 1959, and later from the Soviet Union to Israel, reported sighting the Swede in Vladimir Prison. Abraham Kalinski, arrested in Moscow in 1944, caught a glimpse of the solitary bent figure of Wallenberg in the exercise yard. The daily ten minutes represents the prisoner's only break from the dead air and permanent semidarkness of his cell. Kalinski knew it was the Swede, because their paths had crossed before.

In 1951 the Pole had picked up the rumor of the former diplomat's presence in the Verchne Uralsk "luxury establishment" for political prisoners, where Kalinski himself was serving time. Wallenberg had been described to the Pole as a "noble and naïve Swede who does not understand why he was under suspicion for spying." The two prisoners did not see each other until they shared a prison transport between Alexandrov Central and Vladimir Prison.

At Vladimir it was a fellow inmate, a Georgian Social Democrat named Simon Gogoberidze, who alerted Kalinski that the famous Swede was a fellow inmate. Wallenberg, Kalinski learned, was in cell number 23, in solitary confinement. The guards took no chances in permitting any contact between the Swede and other inmates. But once, on the way to his weekly bath, the Pole's guard did not wait for the full all-clear signal, a combination of finger snapping and keys clicking, before he allowed Kalinski to proceed. Kalinski and Wallenberg fixed a split-second glance on each other, before they were rushed off in opposite directions.

In 1967 the former Polish officer traveled to the Georgian capital of Tbilisi to visit his prison friend Simon Gogoberidze, who had just been pardoned. From the Georgian he learned that Wallenberg had still been at Vladimir when Gogoberidze was released earlier in the year.

To back up his testimony, Kalinski produced a postcard for the Swedish Foreign Office. It was dated October 1959, and postmarked "Vladimir, the USSR." Written in Yiddish, it was addressed to Kalinski's sister, who was living in Haifa at the time. "Have met a Swede," Kalinski wrote, "who saved the Jews of Rumania." The Pole, now settled in the Israeli resort of Naharya, claims that changing "Hungary" to "Rumania" was his way of evading the censors.

27 "Now, Dear Colleague ..."

S tockholm is in some ways a very small place, and for many decades Dr. Nanna Svartz has occupied a central position in its Establishment. This delicate, birdlike woman with her snow-white, closely cropped hair, is one of Sweden's most prominent physicians and researchers. Her social connections are the best. Her patients include the powerful, the wellborn and the wealthy. Dr. Svartz did not always have an easy time of it. But unlike a great many women in her overwhelmingly masculine field, Nanna Svartz had strong male support, to ensure that the professional plums she merited dropped in her lap. Fredrik von Dardel, Raoul Wallenberg's stepfather, head of the Karolinska Hospital, was her mentor. In the mid-fifties he asked Dr. Svartz to look after his wife. The years of waging a lonely campaign to free her son had taken their toll on Wallenberg's mother.

Then, in January 1961, Dr. Svartz was invited to deliver a lecture at one of the many international medical congresses in which she frequently participates. The congress was held in Moscow, a city Dr. Svartz knew well. In 1946 she had accompanied her friend and patient, Soviet Ambassador Alexandra Kollontai, when she was ordered by Stalin to return from Stockholm.

During a break between sessions of the congress, Dr. Svartz engaged an old acquaintance in conversation. Dr. Alexander Myasnikov, a Soviet researcher and head of several hospitals, as prominent in Moscow as Dr. Svartz is in Stockholm, had had many conversations with Dr. Svartz over the years. Myasnikov had once confided to her that among his patients was Communist Party Chairman Nikita Khrushchev. Their conversation, as always, was in German.

Dr. Myasnikov was somewhat taken aback when, after dispensing with the latest professional news and gossip, Dr. Svartz lowered her voice and said, "Now, dear colleague, I have something more personal, and far more important to ask of you. Forgive me, but there is a man, a Swede, the son of my close friends, who may be in your country. His name is Raoul Wallenberg. There is a good chance that, by some error, he is in one of your prisons."

Prior to going to Moscow, Dr. Svartz had prepared for more than just a lecture on internal medicine. She had also scrupulously studied the Swedish Foreign Ministry's voluminous Wallenberg file. Now she proceeded to give the Soviet scientist a capsule version of Wallenberg's assignment to Budapest, his subsequent Red Army protective custody, the Soviet denial of his presence in Russia, followed ultimately by the Gromyko memo admitting that Wallenberg had been taken prisoner but alleging his death ten years earlier. Dr. Svartz had a sure command of the facts in the thick file. She spoke quickly of the many sworn statements contradicting the official Soviet line. She did not have much time for subtleties or subterfuge. She was afraid that at any moment he might cut her off. "Have you any personal knowledge of the case?" she whispered.

To her barely concealed amazement, Myasnikov nodded. "I certainly do know about this case," he replied. "I have in fact examined the man in question myself. What is it you wish me to do in this matter?"

Dr. Svartz, her voice unsteady from excitement, said, "The main thing is that Wallenberg be returned home, no matter what his condition."

Myasnikov knitted his bushy eyebrows and said, "Ah, yes, but the man is in very poor condition." Then his voice dropped to a barely audible whisper. "Raoul Wallenberg is a patient in a mental hospital, here in Moscow." Myasnikov said he would call one of his associates, a man with higher party rank than himself, who was also a participant in the congress. Myasnikov wanted him to be involved in this delicate discussion.

Myasnikov did not return to the antechamber of the conference hall where he and Dr. Svartz had been engrossed in conversation. Instead another man, a prominent figure both in the party and in the medical profession, now sat down and faced the nervous Swedish doctor.

"Write down the name of the man you are after, and where he was serving." Svartz did as she was told. Then, striking a doctor-to-doctor tone, she said, "You know, his mother is my patient. Her case would be well served if only she had some certainty about her son. No matter how sick he is today, it would be a blessing for her, and for all of Sweden, if he could be cared for in his own country."

The man asked that his involvement be kept confidential, but said he would do everything in his power to help. Svartz took his hand in both of hers. "The entire Swedish nation would be grateful to the Soviet Union if Wallenberg would be allowed to return home. It is a matter that lies very close to the heart of our government." Dr. Svartz then mentioned she had struck up a friendship with Soviet Vice Premier Vladimir Semionov, during his stay in Stockholm.

"My advice, then," the Russian told her, "is that you get in touch with Comrade Semionov. Speak to him about the possibility of taking Wallenberg home yourself."

Dr. Svartz felt as though she were at the center of a miracle. She did not stay for the remainder of the medical congress. She rushed back to her hotel room and immediately started dialing the number of the Soviet Foreign Ministry. When she finally got through, she was told that Comrade Semionov had gone abroad. Disappointed, but still elated from what she felt was an imminent breakthrough, Dr. Svartz went off to the banquet that evening.

Dr. Myasnikov spotted her in a room full of physicians from all over the globe. "Well, have you spoken to Semionov?" he asked, pulling her aside. Svartz explained why she had not succeeded in reaching the Vice Premier. "Then you must write to him," Myasnikov advised. He was less than enthusiastic about Svartz using either his or his higher ranking colleague's name in her letter. Finally he agreed and gave her permission to do so. "My colleague and I have spoken since your conversation, and we both agree that a possible transportation to Sweden of the man in question, if he is still alive, has to be organized through diplomatic channels." Nanna Svartz said she was in full agreement.

The Swedish doctor then left the Soviet capital for Stockholm. She was confident that it was all only a matter of time and some delicate diplomatic maneuvering. The prisoner's tracks had finally, after sixteen frustrating years of silence and denials, been traced.

She, Professor Nanna Svartz, was responsible for the clouds parting. As her plane touched down in Stockholm she felt exhilarated.

The next day she strode confidently across the Persian-carpeted office of the Prime Minister. Tage Erlander was accompanied by Foreign Minister Östen Undén, the man who had once said it was bad form to question the Soviets' word. Times had changed. The Social Democrats were under fire from the Moderate Party for foot-dragging and naïveté in their handling of the Wallenberg case. Undén was prepared for a more energetic stand on the prisoner's behalf.

Dr. Svartz gave a full accounting of her conversations with Myasnikov and his superior, who still insisted on anonymity. The three Swedes agreed she must waste no time in following up this breakthrough with a letter to Myasnikov, urging a meeting at his earliest convenience. Svartz was also to write to Semionov in the Foreign Ministry. She was to inquire how the latest investigations into Wallenberg's whereabouts were proceeding, and about the possibility of taking Wallenberg home.

Erlander and Undén requested that she not breathe a word of any of this, not even to Raoul's mother and stepfather, until the matter was concluded. Meanwhile Erlander would draft his own letter to the Soviet ambassador in Stockholm, referring to the doctor's conversations. Striking an unusually human note, Erlander wrote: "It is a generally accepted principle that members of the same family who have been separated and mutually wish for contact shall be given all available information about each other and that they shall be given the opportunity to join each other. The principle is not only generally accepted in theory. It has also come to be more and more put into practice. I appeal urgently to your Government and to the Chairman of the Council of Ministers, Mr. Khrushchev, personally to take this into consideration in dealing with this matter."

Svartz's own letter to Myasnikov was answered almost immediately. In a matter of days the Swedish doctor was back in Moscow, facing her old colleague. This time Myasnikov was not alone. He identified the man who accompanied him only as a "colleague."

"When may I visit Raoul?" Dr. Svartz began.

"That," Myasnikov replied, "will have to be arranged on a much higher level. Unless," he added, "Wallenberg is dead."

"But, then," Dr. Svartz rejoined, "he must have died quite recently."

Later, when the Soviet and Swedish doctors were momentarily alone, Myasnikov reproached her for having spoken to Swedish officials about their first conversation. He did not attempt to deny it took place, but he was clearly less forthcoming this time. Guarded reserve had replaced his eagerness to help. Myasnikov kept one eye fixed on the rest of the room. "It was my poor German," he whispered to the amazed Swede. "You must have misunderstood me. I knew nothing of the Wallenberg case until you spoke of it." Then, as the two friends walked out of the hotel lobby where they had been talking, and plunged into the noisy Moscow street traffic, Myasnikov told her, "You have made my life most unpleasant. I was summoned by Chairman Khrushchev and asked to give a detailed breakdown of our conversation. But he already knew, anyway. He was furious at what I told you." The agitated Myasnikov left the Swede, who was shaken and disillusioned.

Dr. Svartz's phone calls to the Foreign Ministry, to her friend Semionov, were not returned. Myasnikov was unavailable for any further conversations. Svartz again returned to Stockholm empty-handed.

For the next year Nanna Svartz continued to bombard Moscow with letters. They were no longer answered. From the Soviet perspective, it was as though she and Myasnikov had never had their dramatic conversation in the first place.

When Dr. Svartz was again invited to lecture in Moscow, she extended a warm hand of greeting to Dr. Myasnikov. He, cold and guarded, held up his palm. "You and I can have no further private conversations on the subject most in your mind." That was all. As far as Alexander Myasnikov was concerned, their friendship had been terminated.

Prime Minister Erlander now turned to Nikita Khrushchev for help. "Foreign Minister Undén and I have discussed the most suitable way of transferring Wallenberg to Sweden," he wrote in a tone of almost defiant confidence. "We have found that the best way would be if a Swedish physician were permitted to come to Moscow and discuss with his Soviet colleagues arrangements for transportation, medical care, etc." The letter, hand-delivered by the Swedish ambassador in Moscow, was a startling departure from the Swede's previous, carefully managed diplomatic efforts on Wallenberg's behalf. The Soviet leader did not take the time to answer in writing. He merely raised one shoulder in a scornful shrug and told the waiting ambassador, "There is nothing to add to the Gromyko memo."

By this time, it is doubtful if the prisoner was still in the Moscow clinic where Myasnikov examined him in 1961. He may, in fact, already have been dispatched to the far end of the Soviet Union. A former SMERSH agent, arrested in 1945, since released, and emigrated to Israel, reported sighting Wallenberg at the notorious Wrangel's Island Prison in 1962. Efrem Moshinsky claims to have communicated with the Swede in this island fortress off the northern tip of Siberia, in the east Siberian Sea. No camp is more remote for a prisoner condemned to oblivion. Others besides Moshinsky have reported sighting Wallenberg at Wrangel's Island. One of them, a Hungarian-born former inmate of the Gulag, claims he met Wallenberg in a camp for foreigners in Irkutsk, near Lake Baikal, in the south. Wallenberg told the Hungarian he had just been transported there from Wrangel's Island.

The Soviets were clearly taken aback by the Swedes' new persistence. When Foreign Minister André Gromyko visited Stockholm in 1964, Wallenberg was all the Swedes were interested in discussing. Gromyko, the author of the only Soviet document dealing with the Swedish prisoner, said there was nothing new to add to his previous statement. Dr. Svartz, he added, must have misunderstood Dr. Myasnikov. This time, though, the Soviets were prepared to be a degree more accommodating. Moscow offered to arrange a meeting between the two colleagues.

Shortly after Gromyko's offer, Myasnikov sent a letter to Dr. Svartz. "As you will surely recall," he wrote, "I told you that I know nothing about Mr. Wallenberg, have never heard his name and have not the slightest idea whether or not he is alive." Myasnikov even denied that he had ever been Chairman Khrushchev's personal physician. "As everyone knows full well," the Soviet doctor wrote, "N. S. Khrushchev is in absolutely good health and I was never his doctor. Owing to some misunderstanding inconceivable to me, this short talk with you (it was carried out in the German language which I may not fully master) has come to be erroneously interpreted in official Swedish circles." In closing, Myasnikov wrote: "I learned later on that Mr. Wallenberg had died already in 1947, and that our Government at a later date had informed the Swedish Government and the deceased's family accordingly."

Nikita Khrushchev's visit to Stockholm in June 1964 was the Soviet leader's last foreign trip before his sudden fall from power. It was not an altogether pleasant stay. Newspaper headlines framed in black screamed at him in Russian, "Where is Wallenberg?" He did not come with a new answer. Nor could he keep Wallenberg's name off the agenda. Khrushchev's way out of an uncomfortable situation was well practiced. He unleashed a temper tantrum and shifted blame from himself to both Stalin and Stockholm. "You are threatening to poison normal relations between our countries!" he berated the Swedish leaders. "Deeply tragic things happened during the Stalin period. You should not expect me to account for them all. I do not wish to expose myself to this interrogation any further." He concluded, "These questions have all been answered long ago."

But Erlander held his ground. He was facing elections that fall, and Wallenberg was high on the list of campaign issues. Erlander's public statement on Wallenberg showed how far his government had evolved since the days when the prisoner was primarily an embarrassment.

The fate of Raoul Wallenberg has deeply engaged Swedish opinion. We have sought to convince the Soviet leadership of the extraordinary seriousness with which Swedish quarters look upon this question. An essential part of our negotiations with the Soviets during this time has come to concern the Wallenberg case. Unfortunately, the result has been negative. The Soviet leaders firmly assert that Raoul Wallenberg is not in the Soviet Union . . . either in prison, in a hospital or somewhere else. We have not achieved the result we have sought. Today, we make public our account. . . . In a democratic country the individual citizen should be able to rest assured that the community will spare no efforts for his protection. As long as there is a possibility this effort must continue and be pursued. In its effort to find a solution to the Wallenberg case, the Government has felt the support of a unanimous Swedish public opinion.

It is a matter of speculation how Moscow would have responded if, nearly twenty years earlier, the Swedes had struck this unequivocal tone.

Several months after the assumption of power by a collective of faceless and cautious men in the Kremlin, a meeting was finally arranged between the two estranged professors of medicine. It was a strained and formal reunion between Professors Svartz and Myasnikov, inside the Kremlin's Foreign Ministry. The Swedish ambassador and two representatives of the Soviet government flanked the two colleagues. This time each spoke in his own language. The Kremlin had provided interpreters.

In her slow, methodical style, Dr. Svartz outlined her long interest in the Soviet Union, dating back to her friendship with Alexandra Kollontai. Svartz then described her long-standing relationship with Myasnikov, a relationship carried out entirely in German. Nanna Svartz launched into why she doubted the truthfulness of the Soviets in the Wallenberg case. "According to the Gromyko note," Dr. Svartz went on, "he is supposed to have died on July 17, 1947. Is it not surprising, then, that ten days later, on July 27, 1947, all prisoners who had been in contact with Wallenberg and his chauffeur were interrogated in both Lubyanka and Lefortovo?" Svartz also noted the remarkable uniformity of the sworn testimony transmitted to Stockholm by these former prisoners. "All this seems strange considering the fact that on August 18, 1947, Foreign Minister Vyshinsky dispatched a note to Stockholm saying that Wallenberg was unknown to Soviet authorities. Within the course of one month it would have happened that Wallenberg had died. Within ten days, there would have been interrogations on Wallenberg in two different prisons, not by prison personnel, but by secret police, indicating that Wallenberg was well known. Those interrogated were then placed in solitary confinement for months. Then came the announcement the next month he was not known to Moscow." This story, Dr. Svartz concluded, simply did not hold up under the bright light of scientific analysis. "That is why I have felt compelled," she told the Soviets, "to become involved in the Wallenberg case." Additional testimony placing Wallenberg in Vladimir Prison in the fifties only compounded the mystery, she added; it did not diminish it.

As to her colleague's allegedly shaky grasp of German, Dr.

Svartz said, "I have never had any difficulty understanding you, in all the years we have known each other. It would be wrong of me to say anything else." She then gave the Soviets an opportunity to save face. "Perhaps," she ventured, "Wallenberg has in recent years been in places unknown to the Kremlin. But it should be possible through a very thorough investigation to extract information to achieve a final answer. In Sweden, and throughout the world, this would be interpreted as a truly great action by the Soviet government."

Then it was the turn of the agitated, perspiring Dr. Myasnikov to speak. "The first time I heard the name Wallenberg," he began, "was from Dr. Svartz. How could I have known of the man, since I have nothing to do with prisoners, prison hospitals or with the military? I can only say again that Dr. Svartz misunderstood me." Then Myasnikov reproached his colleague of many years for false pretenses. "I was under the impression that we were speaking in a humane spirit," he said. "I had no idea Dr. Svartz was on an official or semiofficial errand. Otherwise I would have summoned an interpreter to write down what was being said." Myasnikov ended by saying the person in question was probably dead.

Myasnikov, whose words were intended for a different audience from the one he faced, repeated his lines like an automaton. In the end, there was no point in prolonging the performance. The two physicians rose, shook hands, and never laid eyes on each other again. Alexander Myasnikov died several months later. The cause of death was given as cardiac arrest. The same cause the Gromyko memo had given for Raoul Wallenberg's death in 1947.

28   The Tracks Reappear

O n September 16, 1965, under the hot blaze of television lights, Prime Minister Tage Erlander broke his government's best-kept secret to his countrymen: one of Sweden's most respected physicians had come within a hair's-breadth of reaching Raoul Wallenberg. Erlander laid out the frustrating course of the Nanna Svartz–Alexander Myasnikov story. The Prime Minister was forced to admit that, once again, the Kremlin had got the better of the Swedes. Raoul Wallenberg had apparently survived three successive Soviet regimes: Stalin's Terror had given way to Khrushchev's thaw, which, in turn, was toppled by Brezhnev and Kosygin's faceless bureaucracy. Wallenberg's captivity seemed immune to shifting Kremlin politics and a growing Soviet accommodation with the West.

Erlander had fought a stubborn battle with the Soviets. He had tasted both the temper and the scorn of the Politburo. Having achieved nothing, he was now ready to give up. "The Swedish Government considers useless further approaches to the Soviets on the subject of Raoul Wallenberg's disappearance twenty years ago." The case was closed.

For Wallenberg's mother, this was the beginning of a period of near-total despair. She felt betrayed by her old friend and physician, Nanna Svartz, who, for years, had kept her in the dark about Myasnikov's dramatic disclosure. Feeling there was nobody she could really trust, nobody who really cared, she stopped talking about her missing son. But she did not abandon her personal campaign to gain his freedom. She tried every door and every source of authority. She wrote a letter to the Soviet Ministry of Justice, an institution others in her place might regard as a contradiction in terms. Mrs. von Dardel appealed to the Soviets' humanity. "I am 83 now and my husband, Raoul's stepfather, is 89. For both of us, it would be a great happiness if we, before our death, could embrace our beloved son. Give us that happiness." Assuming that somebody in the Kremlin read her letter, he certainly did not choose to give the grieving mother either that happiness or a reply.

In the spring of 1973 Maj von Dardel turned in another direction for help. "I have followed with great admiration your persistent and successful campaign for peace in the Far East," she wrote Secretary of State Henry Kissinger. "I am now approaching you regarding my son, Raoul Wallenberg." She reminded Kissinger that it was an American minister, Herschel Johnson, who originally presented the official request to her son about the Budapest mission.

> The Swedish Government is at present not willing to request further inquiries by the Soviet authorities into the fate of my son. The tragic uncertainty as to what really happened to my son after his imprisonment, I beg of you, who by your outstanding efforts liberated thousands of prisoners, to inform me whether you consider yourself able to undertake anything in order to shed light on the fate of my son, and, should he still be alive, to restore him to liberty.

Mrs. von Dardel's letter was answered by one of Kissinger's assistants. A coded taped memorandum was drafted for the U.S. ambassador in Moscow, Walter J. Stoessel. Both carried the same message:

> Since 1965, the Swedish Government has been unwilling to make further inquiries regarding Mr. Wallenberg, despite the unsatisfactory nature of the Soviet response. As Mrs. von Dardel points out, her son had gone to Budapest in 1944 at the request of the then U.S. Minister to Sweden, to lead an operation for the rescue of the Hungarian Jews, and his efforts saved thousands of Jews from death. . . . We believe we should reply to Mrs. von Dardel's request in a sympathetic manner, and offer to make inquiries of the Soviet Foreign Ministry, without, however, encouraging her hopes that this effort will be successful.

Neither the letter to Wallenberg's mother nor the taped message to the American ambassador in Moscow was ever sent. Henry Kissinger disapproved both. They were returned to their author with the notation "Rejected by Kissinger, 10.15.73." There was no official explanation for his refusal, but relations between Stockholm and Washington had reached their lowest point in 1973. Swedish Prime Minister Olof Palme aroused Kissinger's animosity by his relentless criticism of America's Vietnam intervention, particularly President Richard Nixon's unauthorized bombing of Cambodia. Once again, Raoul Wallenberg was the pawn in a larger game.

Mr. Palme did not show more interest in Wallenberg's imprisonment than Henry Kissinger. When he sat down with Alexei Kosygin in 1976 to negotiate a number of issues outstanding between their two countries, Wallenberg's name was not on the agenda. The Palme administration's one-word description for the status of the prisoner's case was *"utagerad,"* Swedish for "settled" or "taken care of."

Maj von Dardel spent her final years in bitter isolation. Occasionally her despair would give way to momentary hope. When Simon Wiesenthal, whose dogged persistence cracked Eichmann's near-perfect cover, told her, "I will help you find your son," she stirred from her gloom. But those with the power to move institutions out of their inertia—the Wallenbergs, Kissinger, Palme and, of course, ultimately, the Kremlin—all considered her a nuisance. She would spend days not moving from her telephone, waiting for the Foreign Office to return her calls. They were largely ignored. Finally, despairing of ever learning more about her first-born son, Maj Wallenberg von Dardel died early in 1979, at the age of eighty-seven, two days before the death of her beloved Fredrik, who had gone almost completely blind. They did not live to see the world take an interest in Raoul—thirty-five years too late.

In 1979 a Tel Aviv dentist, newly arrived from the Soviet Union, became Wallenberg's latest messenger from the Gulag. She was a Soviet Jew named Anna Bilder, a strapping, fresh-faced woman with the young's gift for beginning life anew. In 1977 she had received a startling phone call from her father, who was still in Moscow. Jan Kaplan, a former administrator of an operatic conservatory, had been picked up by the KGB two years earlier on black-marketeering charges. His real crime had been to apply for an exit visa to Israel. Kaplan suffered from a weak heart, so he was released after eighteen months in Lubyanka. "How did you get through all that time?" Anna Bilder asked her father. "Oh, you can survive for a long time in there," Kaplan answered. "In fact, I met a Swede in the Butyrki prison hospital who has survived thirty years."

Anna Bilder had never heard of Raoul Wallenberg and was far more concerned about her father than about some "Swede who survived thirty years" in Soviet prisons. She did write to relatives in Detroit about her father's release and their conversation. It was through the Russian émigré grapevine that Abraham Kalinski eventually picked up the story. Once in Israel, the former Polish army officer called on Dr. Anna Bilder. He then reported the new lead to the Swedish embassy in Tel Aviv. But by now Jan Kaplan was no longer available to answer questions. A smuggled letter informed Anna Bilder of her father's rearrest.

Jan Kaplan's wife, Eugenia, alone and afraid, had taken the extremely risky step of smuggling a letter to her daughter in Israel. It was just this sort of courage, approaching a foreigner in the Moscow synagogue and asking him if he would mind taking a letter out of the country, that got her husband in trouble with the KGB. But Mrs. Kaplan didn't have many options left. She wanted her daughter's help to get her husband free.

> My dear Anna [she wrote], The same thing has happened to your father. For the past year and a half, he has been imprisoned . . . I had lost all hope after having been summoned to Lubyanka by the KGB, where I was told all this happened because of a letter concerning a Swiss or a Swede named Wallenberg whom your father knew in the prison infirmary. Your father had written to you about this Wallenberg and tried to get it to you through some tourists in the synagogue. Since then, your father has been in Lefortovo and Lubyanka and I have now lost all hope of ever seeing him again.

Kaplan, like Kuprianov, had been effectively obliterated as a potential witness in the Wallenberg case. But Mrs. Kaplan's letter resulted in the first official Swedish communication on the subject of Raoul Wallenberg in fourteen years. The Swedes requested an interview with Jan Kaplan, wherever he might be. The Soviet reply was familiar: "Raoul Wallenberg died in 1947. There is nothing more to add."

The Swedes no longer took their cues from Moscow. Prime Minister Ola Ullsten declared the case alive and open. Henceforth Stockholm's view would be that Raoul Wallenberg is alive until the Soviets prove otherwise. The burden is on Moscow to establish a credible explanation of his alleged death. The Kremlin's flimsy string of contradictions and vague denials of three decades was finally and permanently rejected.

By 1980 the entire world decided it was time for outrage. Sweden became the target of a global gaze. Guy von Dardel and Nina Lagergren picked up their mother's struggle. Unlike her almost obsessively private campaign, they launched a frontal attack on the Kremlin. With their support, Wallenberg committees have sprouted around the world. There are now several thousand people working nearly full time at the dual task of telling Wallenberg's story and putting pressure on the Soviets to tell theirs. A committee of U.S. senators, including Daniel Patrick Moynihan of New York, Claiborne Pell of Rhode Island, and Rudolph E. Boschwitz of Minnesota, and the newly elected California Congressman Tom Lantos (it was Lantos' wife, Annette, who started American action on Wallenberg's behalf in 1978; as a child in Budapest she had been rescued by the Swede), sponsored legislation making Raoul Wallenberg an honorary American citizen. On October 5, 1981, President Reagan signed the resolution by which Wallenberg joins the Marquis de Lafayette's descendants and Winston Churchill in being thus distinguished. It is more than a symbolic memorial to the man. The members of Congress hope to have more impact on the Kremlin when pressing for further information regarding the whereabouts of an American citizen, honorary or not.

At Yad Vashem, Jerusalem's Documentation Center and Memorial to the Holocaust's six million victims, Raoul Wallenberg has been deemed the most outstanding of the "Righteous Gentiles"—non-Jews who risked their lives to save the Nazis' intended victims.

Only in Hungary, the scene of both his epic and its tragic conclusion, is Raoul Wallenberg still a nonperson. Very few Hungarians look up to read the faded and chipped plaque in his honor on the street that still bears his name, only a few blocks from the headquarters of the Communist party. The block, still pockmarked by the small-arms fire of 1945 and 1956, like half a dozen others running east and west toward the Danube, once sheltered "his" Jews and flew the flag of his country.

No Hungarian regime is on record for having requested a single piece of information regarding its citizen Vilmos Langfelder, Wallenberg's friend and driver, who vanished from the streets of his city in January 1945.

Langfelder's trail went cold in 1947, in Lefortovo. In 1978 Wallenberg's was picked up again on the outer limits of the Gulag, in Blagoveshensk, just north of Manchuria, across the Sino-Soviet border. The word of the presence of "an old Swede in the Blagoveshensk Special Psychiatric Hospital in very poor condition" filtered to the West through an underground Soviet publication based in Munich. The source, as is often the case, is vulnerable, still in the Soviet Union and out of the reach of Western interrogators. But a great many Soviet prison experts feel a psychiatric hospital would be the ideal place to dispatch a man slated for nonexistence. It is a sealed-off, controlled environment where the inmate risks few unplanned contacts: Blagoveshensk, one of the newer of such institutions, was constructed for the purpose of dealing with the rise in the dissident's movement, following the Soviet invasion of Czechoslovakia. Like the other psychiatric hospitals in the Gulag, it is not by any definition of the word a hospital. It is administered by the Soviet Penal System, not by the Ministry of Health. It is distinguished from a regular prison, such as Vladimir or Lubyanka, by the presence of doctors alongside the jailers. But under their white coats, these doctors wear the drab green of army officers. State security and not the prisoners' health is their chief concern.

Under Stalin, political prisoners considered a term in a psychiatric hospital a lucky break. The regimen there tended to be easier than in forced-labor camps and less grim than the isolation of a maximum-security prison. More recently, former inmates of such institutions have brought nightmarish reports of their existence under the supervision of these jailers in white coats. Prisoners are prescribed liberal doses of a drug known as Aminazine, a common treatment for schizophrenics. For those not suffering from schizophrenia, it causes symptoms similar to Parkinson's disease: uncontrollable trembling followed by numbness. Sanity under such care is considered a distinct disadvantage.

Other, more recent reports from the Gulag no longer place Wallenberg in this particular circle of Dante's Hell. Wallenberg was sighted by still another dissident group in a Moscow prison hospital. And, again, in the Leningrad region there were reports of an old Swede, barely alive. Wallenberg has become so intertwined with the fabric of Gulag lore that as time passes it becomes increasingly difficult to separate reality from the legend and from the wishful thinking that has permeated his case.

Epilogue

I n the late fall of 1979, Stockholm offered Moscow a deal. Stig Bergling, a former Swedish Defense Ministry employee, had just been convicted as a KGB spy. He was given a life sentence for feeding his masters in Moscow a regular diet of Swedish military secrets for the past decade. Bergling's base of operations had been the Middle East, where he was a member of the Swedish battalion of the United Nations' Peacekeeping Force. Stockholm proposed Stig Bergling as an exchange for Raoul Wallenberg. The Kremlin barely acknowledged receipt of the offer. Bergling was a "blown" agent, of no further use to his employers in Moscow. The fact that the offer was made is significant. Twenty years earlier Foreign Minister Östen Undén had dismissed the suggestion that the next Soviet agent caught in a compromising situation be offered up for Wallenberg. "Sweden," Undén pronounced, "does not do such things."

How many opportunities were lost in the crucial years, before the Soviets entangled themselves too deeply in a thick web of deceptions and contradictions, before Wallenberg became too old, too ill, too spent to be released to a closely observing world?

In 1978 the Russians had arrested a Swede of Latvian origin named Lajmonis Niedre. He was charged with spying in his native Latvia. The Soviets released him a year later for what they gave as "health reasons." Upon his return to Stockholm he related to the world press what a high-ranking Soviet official had said to him. In Russia there were four alternatives, Niedre was told, to closing a case involving a foreign prisoner:

1. Exchange him for someone held in the West
2. Respond to a plea from his country on humanitarian grounds

3. Free him on grounds of his being an invalid

4. Retry his case

The Soviet official told Niedre that the Kremlin preferred the first two methods. They may have opted for the third in Niedre's case, since it coincided with fresh revelations in 1979 about Wallenberg, reportedly still alive somewhere in the Gulag. The Soviets may have wished to avoid aggravating an already tense situation between the two countries.

Twenty years ago, appealing to something other than the Soviets' humanity may have worked in the Wallenberg case. In 1979 Raoul Wallenberg would have been sixty-seven years old. By the most optimistic reports, the prisoner would have been a frail shell of the man the world remembers today. At Wallenberg's expense, Sweden has learned a painful lesson: the price demanded to maintain one's neutrality can sometimes be too high. The scorn with which the Kremlin treated Stockholm's queries about Wallenberg was not altogether unjustified given the Swedes' lack of conviction following his imprisonment. The dim memory of an early-nineteenth-century Russian invasion, Sweden's first and last, is not sufficient explanation for the country's spineless behavior on behalf of its captured diplomat.

Not only did Wallenberg fall victim to his countrymen's *rysskräck*, a near-pathological fear of Russia; he was also hurt by his name. Succeeding Swedish Social Democratic governments were not likely to be forceful in their campaign for the freedom of a man named Wallenberg. Had his name been Larsson or Persson he may have had a better chance of early support. Those of his powerful relatives who might have exerted pressure on his behalf chose not to do so.

Wallenberg's own legacy to his countrymen is a generous one. Sweden now claims a genuine hero of international stature, matched by perhaps only a handful in recent history. More, his name and what it represents stand like a wall between Sweden and Soviet hopes for its Finlandization. In his silence, Wallenberg has taught his countrymen, and the world, volumes about the Soviet system.

Wallenberg's name is now synonymous with mystery. Neither the man's singular achievement nor his subsequent tragedy is well served by this. Both need to be observed under a stronger, colder light. Otherwise they are threatened with dissolving into the mists of twice-told tales. Before Raoul Wallenberg melts into folklore, before the monuments are built, it is vital to attempt to draw some kind of meaning out of his seemingly absurd fate. A world which for thirty-five years was indifferent to his imprisonment should not now slide into hero worship. That would be too easy, and Raoul Wallenberg would not be comfortable with it.

Wallenberg fell victim to events comprehensible only with the benefit of hindsight. There was no way the young Swede could have predicted them. Another, more cautious man may have escaped his fate. But Wallenberg was concerned less with his own safety than he perhaps ought to have been. He also had little understanding of the forces already at play in Hungary in the winter of 1945.

The Red Army was in the process of "liberating" Hitler's last ally from the Nazis' grip. "Liberation" is a euphemism for invasion. That much Wallenberg understood. What he could not foresee was that invasion in this case would be solidified into permanent occupation. The new masters of this weak and demoralized country were supplied with more than assault rifles and Stalin organs—they came with a grand plan. The NKVD constituted the advance men of the master scheme. Stalin had achieved a perfect monolith in his own country; now he was about to apply the same formula to the newly liberated lands of Eastern and Central Europe.

Stalin was the master of patience. He was not a man who took risks. Absolute control was achieved in small doses, in the same methodical way he had sliced away the opposition in the Soviet Union. Stalin knew that conquest by a foreign army is not the same thing as a popular revolt. The Red Army's "liberation" of Hungary did not set off an uprising of workers and peasants clamoring for the Dictatorship of the Proletariat. That was the scenario depicted in Marxist-Leninist texts. It did not happen in Hungary or anywhere else. Communism, Stalinism, succeeded thanks to the irresistible force of Soviet tanks, guns and terror. It was imposed by Stalin's puppets, who enjoyed only the most meager support among their own countrymen.

A man like Wallenberg will always be a danger to the Soviet system. He was not fighting for his own cause. He could not be dismissed as just another counterrevolutionary agitator. He wanted nothing for himself. His hold on the people of Budapest was based on the power of a single man who faced down the seemingly indestructible machine of the state. This is not something the Kremlin can live with. The Soviets could not even tolerate a monument raised in his honor by the people of Budapest. The statue, like the man, was removed by Soviet soldiers. The Soviets knew what they were doing when they spirited him away from the country they were about to shape in their own image.

The Soviet state, like any other giant enterprise, is, above all, a bureaucracy. Bureaucrats do not, as a whole, like to make decisions. Decisions require a degree of courage and responsibility, qualities in short supply among public servants on both sides of the Great Divide. If Wallenberg survived the years of rampant Stalinist terror, it was probably more as a result of bureaucratic inertia than anything else. He also had potential. He was a very big catch. Dead, he was of no use to anybody. Alive, who could say when he might serve his purpose? After Stalin, they stopped executing political prisoners. Instead, they put them in storage. That was one of the few real concessions made by the party to an exhausted and terror-weary population.

The revelations of Dr. Nanna Svartz were a crucial indicator of his prestige in the Gulag. Dr. Alexander Myasnikov, the distinguished Soviet scientist and personal physician to N. S. Khrushchev, told her he had also examined Wallenberg. This clearly was no ordinary prisoner. But Dr. Myasnikov also said the Swede was in poor shape and in a mental institution. Stockholm replied by demanding his immediate release.

Would they have fared better had they held off until Sweden had something the Soviets wanted? Or should Stockholm have enlisted Washington's support and together struck a quiet deal with the Soviets? There have surely been things the Soviets wanted as badly in the last three decades as the West now, finally, wants Wallenberg. The technique was never tested. Not by Sweden, the country of his birth; not by the United States, which enlisted him for the Budapest mission; not by Israel, the home of many of the people he rescued.

In the 1980s they are raising monuments and heaping honors on Raoul Wallenberg. Simon Wiesenthal, the tireless hunter of Nazis, has taken time off from pursuing the criminals to try to follow Wallenberg's tracks. Those who for thirty-five years were not heard from weep now about the debt they owe this man. Even Marcus Wallenberg broke his silence and faced a gathering of the world's press in Stockholm. "A great power," the tall, gaunt elder of the most powerful family in Sweden declared, "must have the courage to admit it has made a mistake."

Are the old men in the Kremlin listening? Or do they think this outrage belated, the honors, the monuments too slow in coming, for them to be troubled? Do they feel that in the fate of Raoul Wallenberg there is a degree of complicity between three Soviet regimes—Stalin's, Khrushchev's and now Brezhnev's—and the world, which held its fire for thirty-five years?

Afterword

I really thought I would be with you for Christmas. Now I must send you my best wishes for Christmas by this means, along with my wishes for the New Year. I hope the peace so longed for is no longer so far away. . . . Lots of kisses to Nina and her little girl.

H alf a century has passed since Raoul Wallenberg wrote those lines to his mother, Maj von Dardel. Despite all her efforts, she did not live to see her eldest child alive again. His sister Nina Lagergren has also devoted much of her life to searching for his tracks in the Gulag Archipelago. Nina's "little girl" turns fifty this year.

More than a decade has passed since I wrote this book, during which a number of sobering revelations have forced me to abandon my initial guarded optimism about Wallenberg's chances of walking out of the Gulag a free man. Resignation and sadness have replaced outrage. To a certain extent the question I raised regarding the complicity between the Kremlin and the world over the fate of Raoul Wallenberg has been answered in the affirmative. In the end, tragically, the Kremlin's silent old men, though long since dead, prevailed.

With stunning speed, the Cold War ended in 1989 and the seemingly invincible Soviet Empire collapsed. Yet one of its most tragic victims did not come home. In its final days, however, the sclerotic Soviet state released some of its awful secrets. Eager to break with the past, the new managers—it is not yet clear whether they are masters—of the Kremlin began to scrape away fifty years of lies. Slowly, the painful truth about Raoul Wallenberg has emerged.

In the wake of the hard-liners' failed coup of August 1991, Soviet reformers moved quickly to unbolt the door to the old regime's innermost sanctum: the Lubyanka. The official in charge, Vadim V.

Bakatin, one of a new breed of spymasters, briskly, if selectively, eased the KGB's long-standing policy of silence and deception. Two years earlier, Bakatin, then minister of the interior, had allowed Wallenberg's sister and brother, Nina Lagergren and Guy von Dardel, to review prison records. Their reward was mostly heartache. Nina held in her hand her missing brother's diplomatic passport, his diary, his address book, his cigarette case, and a pile of crumpled dollars and old Hungarian pengö. These were the first concrete reminders that her brother had once passed through the same chambers and corridors where she and Guy were now politely received. The dusty objects had tumbled by chance from a shelf in the KGB's archives—or so they were now informed. "It was tremendously emotional," she recalled, "just to see Raoul's handwriting again." They were given the original handwritten report from Col. A. L. Smoltsov, head of the Lubyanka Prison medical service, to Minister of State Security Viktor Abakumov, requesting instructions regarding the disposition of Wallenberg's body. Meager compensation for so many years of hopes and prayers.

As far as Lagergren and Von Dardel were concerned, the Lubyanka's style may have changed under its new chief, but the substance had not. The agency was still retailing the Big Lie: a trim and athletic thirty-four-year-old prisoner died of a sudden heart attack in 1947.

Accustomed to disappointment, however, Wallenberg's brother and sister pressed on. Their extraordinary resilience was bolstered by the more than 20,000 pages of testimony involving 3,000 names and witnesses, compiled by the Swedish Foreign Ministry, one-third of the information dating from 1979 or later.

Any lingering suspicion that the Russians were still toeing the old Soviet line—whether deliberately or not—was soon confirmed. Two years later, in June 1993, Izvestia, the Russian daily recast in a reformist mold, published an article entitled, "Wallenberg Is Dead: Unfortunately There Is Sufficient Proof." But it is difficult to dismiss lightly an article supported by so many credible details—and the hard ring of truth. Its author, Ella Maxsimova, cites specific Soviet security files that confirm Wallenberg's stay in the Lubyanka and Lefortovo. Far more startling, however, is the picture it paints of the agitation within Stalin's inner circle regarding Raoul Wallenberg. The Kremlin apparently knew from the beginning who Wallenberg was and what he had done in Budapest. *Izvestia* quotes a recently declassified memorandum from Andrei Vyshinsky, then deputy foreign minister, to Vyacheslav M. Molotov, deputy premier, dated May 14, 1947. It is the most telling and incriminating document involving Raoul Wallenberg to have come to light and is thus worth quoting at length:

> At the end of 1944, the Swedes addressed to the Peoples' Commissariat of Foreign Affairs of the USSR a request to take under its protection the first secretary of the Swedish Mission in Budapest, Raoul Wallenberg. On January 16 [1945] the mission was informed that Wallenberg had been found and taken under protection by Soviet military authorities. On April 24, 1945, the Swedes informed the Peoples' Commissariat of the USSR that among the members of their mission who had left Budapest, Wallenberg was missing, and asked us to locate him. These requests from the Swedish side were repeated several times, both in writing (eight notes) and orally (five meetings). On June 15, 1946, former Swedish Ambassador to the Soviet Union Soderblom was received by Comrade Stalin, whom he asked to issue instructions to establish the fate of Raoul Wallenberg.
>
> Several times in 1945 and 1946, through oral and written means, we directed our requests to SMERSH, and later to the Minister of State Security for clarification on the fate and whereabouts of Wallenberg. As a result of our efforts, in February of this year [1947] Comrade Fedotov [Molotov's deputy], in his talk with Comrade Novikov [of the Ministry of Foreign Affairs], informed us that Wallenberg was now at the disposal of the Ministry of State Security and promised to report to you personally on further actions to be undertaken by the Ministry of State Security.
>
> Since to the present day the case of Wallenberg remains without progress, I request that you direct Comrade Abakumov to submit a summary of the substance of the case and *suggestions for liquidation* [italics mine].

Soviet authorities were aware of Raoul Wallenberg's presence in Budapest as early as 1944 because, ironically, the Swedes themselves had asked the Soviets to "protect" him while he was in

Hungary. Former Soviet spymaster and one-time Deputy Director of Foreign Intelligence Pavel Sudoplatov writes in his 1994 memoirs, *Special Tasks,*

> We knew he [Wallenberg] had a heroic image among world Jewish leaders. Wallenberg could not have been detained without direct orders from Moscow. If he was arrested accidentally, as might occur during the fierce fighting in Budapest, local SMERSH authorities were bound to report the incident to Moscow. Now it is known that Nikolai Bulganin, the then deputy commissar of defense, signed the order to detain Wallenberg in Hungary in 1945 and passed it on to Abakumov, head of SMERSH.

Sudoplatov claims the KGB's Wallenberg files "disappeared" in 1947 but not before the deputy head of SMERSH, Lieutenant General Aleksandr Belkin, had inspected them. Belkin reported that in 1945 SMERSH agents in Hungary were informed that Wallenberg was an "established asset" of German, American, and British intelligence. They were further instructed to report Wallenberg's movements to Moscow and to "assess and study his contacts with German authorities, both national and local."

The Soviet perception of Wallenberg was further skewed by a Soviet agent in place in Budapest. The agent, a Russian émigré named Kutuzov, had been recruited by SMERSH in the 1920s. Kutuzov, using a job with the International Red Cross as his cover, observed Wallenberg's astonishing rescue of Hungarian Jews. There was only one explanation the Soviet agent could provide for Wallenberg's remarkable success in negotiating with the Nazis for the lives of thousands of Jews: the Swede was a Nazi collaborator. "Kutuzov's interpretation," Sudoplatov recalls, "was that Wallenberg was playing a double game. Thus Wallenberg had left himself open to forced recruitment as our agent: join us or be exposed as a German agent. This was how the plan must have been formulated to recruit Raoul Wallenberg and through him promote the cooperation of his family with Soviet representatives in Scandinavia."

In late 1993, the CIA finally opened its own Wallenberg files. They, too, lend support to the theory that, as far as the Kremlin was concerned, Raoul Wallenberg was not a humanitarian caught in the war zone; he was an enemy agent—an agent with potential. The once secret American documents reveal that Iver Olsen, chief of the Stockholm office of the War Refugee Board, and the man who had recruited Wallenberg, was also an agent for the wartime Office of Strategic Services, the forerunner of the CIA. For paranoid Stalinist observers, it was a very short distance from Olsen's under-cover work to the certainty that Wallenberg was serving the same clandestine cause.

If turning Wallenberg into a double agent was what SMERSH had in mind, they were doomed to failure, given all we know of the man. The records indicate how hard the Soviets applied themselves in trying to force Raoul Wallenberg to betray his country and himself. Newly released prison documents record that a notorious interrogator named Lieutenant Colonel Dmitri Koppelyansky re-peatedly worked Wallenberg over, from the time of his arrest in 1945 until 1947. The last entry for Wallenberg is dated March 11, 1947. Two years in a Stalinist hell, intimidation, and very probably torture at Koppelyansky's hands—these had not turned Wallenberg into a Soviet agent. "By early July 1947 Wallenberg's case was stalled," Sudoplatov notes. "Wallenberg had refused to cooperate. . . ." In Vyshinsky's bloodless words of May 1947, Wallenberg's case "re-mains without progress."

A similar conclusion—that by 1947 the Soviets deemed the Swede a lost cause—was reached by the 1989 International Com-mission to Investigate the Fate of Raoul Wallenberg. One of its members, Dr. Vadim Birstein, asserted in his final report:

> We know through our recent archival investigation that in July of 1947 *something extraordinary happened* [italics mine]. Every person who had ever been a cellmate of Wallenberg or Lang-felder [Vilmos Langfelder, Wallenberg's Hungarian driver] was interrogated on the 22nd of July. On the basis of the archival data and the testimony of witnesses, we can reconstruct the details of this interrogation. . . . After being interrogated, every person was isolated in a "box," or very small cell, for one or more months. From the testimonies and memoirs of witnesses we know the theme of these interrogations: establishing what his cellmates knew about Wallenberg and Langfelder.

"However," Dr. Birstein concludes, "the main task of the inter-rogations was to terrorize each of these men, who were strictly

forbidden to utter the names of Wallenberg or Langfelder at any
time in the future."

The degree of terror instilled by these interrogations is made
clear by a report of the deputy director of Lefortovo Prison, Major
Eremin, to the chief of the prison department of the KGB, about
a Finnish soldier named Pelkonnen. "This is to inform you that
on 14th August, 1947, at 2:55 P.M., prisoner Pelkonnen—who
was kept in Box Number 4 of Lefortovo Prison . . . as di-
rected . . . suddenly stood up from the bed, jumped up to the win-
dowsill and, with the purpose of committing suicide, threw himself
down, intending to break his skull on the radiator and hit the back
of his head against the cement floor." Following his release, Pelkonnen refused to pronounce the name Wallenberg. He died only three
years ago in his native Finland.

The man who was the object of this campaign of terror, Raoul
Wallenberg, was under an unofficial death sentence by 1947. Sudoplatov claims that Vyshinsky's use of the word *liquidation* in his
letter to Molotov says as much. "To me," Sudoplatov asserts, "it is
clear that this was not a suggestion to close the case, but one to
eliminate Wallenberg. The term 'liquidation' in such top secret
documents meant physical elimination." Wallenberg was not only
useless, he was an "unwanted witness."

Not until ten years later did the Soviet government, faced with
mounting Swedish pressure, announce that Wallenberg had died of
a heart attack in 1947. At the time, they could hardly go further.
Bulganin, the man who had allegedly ordered Wallenberg's arrest in
1945, was prime minister. Molotov, though no longer the foreign
minister, was still a ranking party member. Conveniently absent
from the scene, having been executed for "Stalinist excesses," was
Abakumov, the minister of state security. Abakumov was chosen as
the scapegoat. A report prepared for Andrei Gromyko, the new
foreign minister, evaluated the effect that acknowledging Wallenberg's death would have: "If an answer is given immediately it would
be certain to provoke a hubbub around 'the Wallenberg Affair.' "
But it also concluded that the hubbub would soon subside and
ultimately "do nothing to change our relations with Sweden."

The Soviets therefore informed the Swedes that according to the
Lubyanka records the medical examiner had requested instructions
as to whether he should perform an autopsy, in order to determine

the cause of death. In reply, Abakumov personally ordered the body to be cremated. Thus did a Stalinist regime, in a final act of cruelty, ensure that the precise circumstances surrounding Wallenberg's end would remain permanently obscure. Thus, too, did it forestall the bitter relief and final acceptance that come with the acknowledgment of certain death. Several months later, the Kremlin informed Hungary that Langfelder had also died in the Lubyanka on March 2, 1948.

The present head of archives in Russia, General Anatoly Kryushin, confirmed to *Izvestia* the possibility of an "execution without sentencing." "Otherwise," Kryushin noted, "they would not have scratched Wallenberg's name out of the prison records, and there would have been a medical certificate, an autopsy, and a record of cremation."

Despite decades of sightings, there is a growing body of evidence testifying to Wallenberg's unquiet death at the hands of Stalin's henchmen. But how then explain the persistent rumors of the Swede's existence in the Gulag well beyond 1947? There is no logical explanation. Both inside the Gulag's boundaries and outside of them, legend and hope transformed Wallenberg into an avatar of all that is good and brave in humanity, all that must endure. Among those who owe him their lives and those who have in some way been transformed by his courage, there is a stubborn reluctance to let go of the possibility that somewhere he is alive. People around the world feel burdened by the weight of an unpaid debt. They feel a moral duty not to abandon Raoul Wallenberg a second time. The overwhelming evidence now suggests that the loyalty his memory inspires is not in the least misplaced. For, if anything, the newly opened archives only confirm the ineffable courage of a man who did not bend before the murderous machinery of not one but two of the century's most brutal totalitarian orders.

Kati Marton
September 1994
New York City

Chapter Notes

PROLOGUE

This account of the beginning of the death marches is based on the eyewitness testimony of Susan Tabor, today librarian at Hebrew Union College, New York, as told the author in July 1981.

1 THE LEGACY

Wallenberg family history and lore provided by the Swedish television commentator and author Åke Ortmark, who has just published a work comparing the Wallenbergs, the Medicis, the Rockefellers and the Rothschilds, entitled *Power and Guilt.*

The Wallenbergs' view of themselves and their society, as well as a personal glimpse into how they live, was described to the author by Berit Wallenberg in Stockholm, May 1981. Miss Wallenberg, a distinguished art historian, is a cousin of Raoul Wallenberg.

Details of the Wallenbergs' reaction to the disappearance of their cousin supplied by Lars Åke Nilsson in Stockholm, June 1980. Nilsson was for a number of years charged with the Swedish Foreign Office's investigation of the Wallenberg case. He is currently posted at the Swedish embassy in London.

Nina Lagergren described in one of the several interviews she granted the author the effect of the powerful family's indifference to Wallenberg's plight on the prisoner's mother.

Jacob Wallenberg's apparent remorse . . .   This scene was described to the author by Erik Sjöquist in May 1981 in Stockholm. Sjöquist, who attended the funeral of the old couple, is correspondent for the Stockholm afternoon paper *Expressen* and has followed the Wallenberg story longer than any other journalist. He is the author of several books on the subject.

Marcus Wallenberg's lack of interest in joining an international effort to free Wallenberg was described to the author by Simon Wiesenthal during an interview in Vienna in July 1981.

Karl Goerdeler's abortive attempt at an eleventh-hour anti-Hitler uprising is described by William Shirer in his meticulously documented work *The Rise and Fall of the Third Reich*, pp. 373, 1046 and 1072.

The NKVD officer's greeting of Wallenberg . . . This is part of the Swedish Foreign Office's Wallenberg file, Vol I, based on the collected testimonies of eyewitnesses and former Wallenberg cell mates.

2 THE YOUTH

Raoul Wallenberg's parents . . . Their story, as well as the childhood memories of Raoul, were related to the author by Wallenberg's sister during the course of several visits to Stockholm in 1980–1981. Nina Lagergren also permitted the author's use of the family's correspondence in this chapter and throughout the book.

Raoul Wallenberg's impressions of his powerful family members were related to the author in Stockholm, in May 1981, by Gösta Hagströmer and Rolf Klintberg, childhood friends of Raoul, and, in the case of the former, a maternal cousin.

3 THE SLOW AWAKENING

The Wannsee Conference is depicted in detail by Lucy S. Dawidowicz in her important work *The War Against the Jews, 1933–45*, pp. 182–186.

Zyklon B and the development of the Auschwitz crematoria are described by Arthur D. Morse in *While Six Million Died: A Chronicle of American Apathy*, pp. 48–50.

The Bermuda Conference: Henry Feingold's *The Politics of Rescue*, pp. 125, 174, 197–207 and 208–247, and Morse, *op. cit.*, pp. 50–63. Both of these are thoroughly documented accounts of the

Roosevelt Administration's inertia during much of the Holocaust. They are equally convincing in their depiction of Breckenridge Long's unsuitability for the task of dealing with the problem of rescue.

Walter Lippmann's ambivalence toward the Jews: Ronald Steel's *Walter Lippmann and the American Century*, pp. 186–196 and 330–333.

Why the Allies chose not to bomb Auschwitz in the light of mounting evidence pointing to the camp's true purpose is described and documented by Martin Gilbert, an Oxford historian, in his *Auschwitz and the Allies*.

The War Refugee Board . . . How it was set up and the unorthodox methods it employed are well described in Morse, *op. cit.*, pp. 313–323.

4   THE RIGHT MAN

The search for the "right man" . . . The author has drawn heavily upon the painstaking documentation of Jenö Lévai in this chapter and elsewhere. Lévai, a Hungarian journalist and historian of the Holocaust, interviewed the participants in the Wallenberg drama shortly after the events occurred. His three works, *Raoul Wallenberg, Eichmann in Hungary* and the *Black Book of the Martyrdom of Hungarian Jewry*, translated from the original Hungarian into English, are indispensable original sources for profiling the period. They contain most of the relevant documents, eyewitness reports and correspondence between the chief participants.

Reaction of Herschel Johnson and Iver Olsen to Raoul Wallenberg . . . Based on their correspondence with Washington, available both in the records of the U.S. Department of State and in the War Refugee Board's archives at the Franklin Delano Roosevelt Memorial Library in Hyde Park, New York.

5   THE JOURNEY STARTS

Wallenberg's personal reaction to his mission was described to the author by Nina Lagergren during the course of interviews in Stockholm in June 1980, and January and July 1981.

The exchange of letters between the King of Sweden and the Regent of Hungary is reproduced in Lévai, *Black Book* . . ., p. 231.

Wallenberg's arrival in Hungary was depicted by eyewitness accounts of survivors of the period, including the author's parents, Endre and Ilona Marton, who have provided many of the precise details of life in Hungary under the Nazis.

6   AN ADMIRAL WITHOUT A FLEET

The Teleki suicide is described in a carefully documented account of the Horthy period in the historian Mario Fenyö's *Hitler, Horthy and Hungary*, especially pp. 9–10. Teleki embodied all that was wrong with Hungary . . . The author's father earned his Ph.D. under Teleki and provided material for this portion.

The trauma of the Treaty of Trianon . . .   Described by the historian George Schöpflin of the Eastern European Department of the London School of Economics during an interview with the author in London, May 1981.

Béla Kun and the rise of Hungarian anti-Semitism was portrayed by an important actor of the time. In an interview in Washington, D.C., in March 1980, Aladár Szegedi-Maszák, a member of Regent Horthy's Foreign Ministry who participated in secret negotiations for a separate peace between Hungary and the Allies, and later became Hungary's last ambassador in Washington prior to the Communist takeover in 1947, gave vital insights into this period.

Horthy's painful meeting with Hitler at Klessheim Castle . . . Described in the Regent's own *Memoirs*, p. 212.

Horthy's bodyguard, Peter Hain, the bloodthirsty head of the newly formed Hungarian Gestapo . . .   Described in Lévai, *Black Book* . . ., p. 99.

7   THE NAZIFICATION OF HUNGARY

Budapest had been caught sleeping . . .   Described in detail in Fenyö, *op. cit.*, ch. 9, p. 148, and in Horthy, *op. cit.*, throughout.

Aladár Szegedi-Maszák, who was among the Gestapo's first victims after the German takeover and then interned at Mauthausen, also provided the author with details of the German occupation.

Only one shot was fired . . . See Fenyö, *op. cit.*, pp. 174 and 189. Also Paul Ignotus' readable and concise history of the country from Árpád to the present, *Hungary*.

Eichmann in Budapest . . . See Lévai, *Eichmann in Hungary*, pp. 67–70, and his *Black Book* . . ., pp. 79–88.

Eichmann and his lieutenants . . . Lévai, *Black Book* . . ., pp. 108–110.

Eichmann appearance and manner . . . Described to author by Elizabeth Eppler, librarian of the Institute of Jewish Affairs, May 1981, London. Ms. Eppler was a member of Budapest's fledgling Zionist underground in 1944.

Eichmann's trade in human lives . . . See Lévai, *Eichmann in Hungary*, p. 190, and Morse, *op. cit.*, p. 353–358.

8   HUNGARY'S JEWS: DOWN THE SLIPPERY SLOPE
The gradual dehumanization of Hungary's Jews is described in several works of both fiction and nonfiction:
István Bibo's *Zsidokérdés* (The Jewish Question) is an excellent if difficult-to-read (even with good command of Hungarian) account of the flowering of anti-Semitism in the period between the world wars, which was encouraged by official propaganda.
Maria Ember's *Hajtü Kanyar* (Hairpin Curve) is a fictionalized account of the degradation of provincial Jews prior to their liquidation. György Moldova's *A Szent Imre Indulo* (The St. Imre March) is another Hungarian novel dealing with the passage of Budapest's Jews from a key role in society to the ghetto. These books are all relatively recent attempts on the part of Hungarian authors to grapple with the thorny subject of Jewish suffering and Hungarian guilt.

The rapid rise of the Jewish bourgeoisie in pre–World War II Hungary and its conspicuous success is brilliantly described in Oscar Jászi's classic, *The Dissolution of the Hapsburg Monarchy*, pp. 172–175.

Jews could no longer rely on any segment of Hungarian society . . . George Schöpflin of the London School of Economics, a native of Hungary, described this phenomenon to the author in May 1981.

232   NOTES

. . .

The gradual development of some sort of Jewish consciousness in the cosmopolitan atmosphere of prewar Budapest . . . Described to the author by Elizabeth Eppler, whose Zionism was first nurtured in this environment.

9   THE PROVINCES ARE PURIFIED
On the first day of the Jewish passover, Hungarian gendarmes . . . Jenö Lévai describes in a straightforward, journalistic style the step-by-step ritual of deportation in his *Eichmann in Hungary*, especially pp. 75–76. Lévai's account is rich in documents and only suffers from his somewhat sycophantic treatment of the "Red liberators," under whose regime his works were published.

The Diary of Éva Heyman . . . This small volume of the impressions of a thirteen-year-old girl whose Jewishness was only thrust upon her by the Nazis was published by Yad Vashem, the Jewish Documentation Center in Jerusalem. Éva's mother survived the Holocaust and edited her daughter's journal, which had been preserved by the family's Christian maid. It is impossible to check the diary's authenticity; however, a sharply drawn and moving picture of the daily humiliation of provincial Jews emerges through the consciousness of this precocious thirteen-year-old.

The capital could have no illusions about the Royal Hungarian Government's . . . Secretary of State László Endre's interview extolling the virtues of a Nagyvárad (Éva Heyman's town) free of Jews is reprinted in Lévai, *Black Book* . . ., p. 138.

Hungary's Roman Catholic Primate . . . See pp. 350–351 in Morse, *op. cit.*, for more on the limited concern regarding reports of Jewish extermination shown by certain elements of the Church, including Pope Pius XII.

10   THE SUMMER BEFORE THE FALL
It was not the same city . . . The author's parents, former Budapest residents, described the changes the capital underwent during this period. Edith Wohl Ernster, whose father, Hugo Wohl, was one of Wallenberg's most trusted assistants, provided details of how these changes gradually reduced the Jews' freedom of movement, in interviews with the author in Stockholm, January and June 1981.

Wallenberg was imbued with a conviction . . . Drawn from Per Anger's description to the author in Stockholm, January 1981, and from Anger's own book, *With Raoul Wallenberg in Budapest.*

Wallenberg's attitude toward Jews . . . Edith Wohl Ernster to author, in Stockholm, June 1981.

Wallenberg at the Jewish Council headquarters . . . Described by László Petö to Jenö Lévai, in Lévai's *Raoul Wallenberg*, pp. 52–53.

He was lavish with money . . . See p. 67, *ibid.*, for copy of letter Wallenberg wrote to Kálmán Lauer, and p. 53, Wallenberg requests more funds from Stockholm.

Wallenberg formed a special section within the legation . . . From the author's interview with Agnes Mandl Adachi, March 1980, New York. Mrs. Adachi was a member of Wallenberg's staff.

Wallenberg's letter in the diplomatic pouch of July 18 . . . See Jacques Derogy, *Le Cas Wallenberg*, p. 76.

Wallenberg's most significant achievement . . . Per Anger to the author during an interview in Stockholm, January 1981.

He instilled in Jews some kind of confidence . . . See p. 87 of Derogy, *op. cit.*, which reprints Wallenberg's letter regarding the Jews' apathy toward their own fate.

Wallenberg's own self-confidence . . . *Loc. cit.*, Wallenberg's memo to his Foreign Office regarding Allied propaganda.

Wallenberg and Horthy . . . Lévai, *Raoul Wallenberg*, p. 74.

Wallenberg turns thirty-two years old . . . Derogy, *op. cit.*, p. 88.

A summons to SS headquarters . . . This episode is described in a letter written by Wallenberg's assistant László Hegedüs to Maj von Dardel, from Prague, June 1946, and made available to the author by Agnes Mandl Adachi.

In a letter to the War Refugee Board . . . This and other correspondence to Iver Olsen is part of the WRB's archives in the Franklin Delano Roosevelt Memorial Library, Hyde Park, New York.

I'll try to be home several days before the Russians . . . Lévai, *Raoul Wallenberg*, p. 83.

11   OCTOBER 15
The abduction of the Regent's son is described in detail in Fenyö's *Hitler, Horthy and Hungary*, pp. 230–233. See also Shirer's *The Rise and Fall* . . ., pp. 19, 1066–1069, 1090, 1092, for a description of the master kidnapper, Otto Skorzeny.

The young man had no way of knowing . . . See C. L. Sulzberger's *A Long Row of Candles*, p. 526 (illustration).

Now the silver-uniformed figure . . . For a solid, if somewhat dry, description of the Szálasi movement and its lackluster founder, the author relied on Miklós Lacko's *Nyilasok, Nemzetiszocialisták*, as well as *A Szálasi Puccs*, by Agnes Rozsnyoi.

12   THE CRUCIBLE
"I can assure you I am well . . ." Raoul's letter home, courtesy Nina Lagergren.

He was not by nature a man who embraced . . . Thomas Veres, the photographer who accompanied Wallenberg on many of his most dramatic missions, provided this description in an interview with the author in New York, July 1981.

He insisted that his colleagues wear sensible shoes . . . Edith Wohl Ernster to author, Stockholm, June 1981.

With the Nazis, natural authority worked . . . Nina Lagergren described to the author Wallenberg's uncanny gift of mimicry, something he often used in Budapest when dealing with the Germans and the Arrow Cross. Baroness Elisabeth Kemény confirmed this in her lengthy interview with the author in Munich, July 1981.

It started with a blood bath . . . The description of Miklós Kalmár, who is currently editor of a Hungarian-language Jewish newspaper in New York and was once protected by Wallenberg, to the author in New York, July 1981.

Wallenberg's memo to his staff . . . Agnes Mandl Adachi, who worked for Wallenberg, to the author in interview, March 1980, New York.

Minister Danielsson worried that Wallenberg . . . From Baroness Kemény and Per Anger to the author.

Neither a new identity nor a new . . . From the Wallenberg file of Yad Vashem Documentation Center, Jerusalem.

13 THE BARONESS
This chapter represents the personal recollections of Baroness Elisabeth Kemény, as told the author in Munich during the week of July 6, 1981, and in subsequent correspondence. The baroness, who has lived with her son in Germany since shortly after the war, has until now kept her relationship with Wallenberg a private matter. Recent reports of her presumed love affair with Wallenberg, as well as her would-be Jewish background as the reason for her involvement in his rescue mission (both untrue, she alleges), have persuaded her to tell her own version of the events.

14 "I WANT TO SAVE A NATION"
Captain Nándor Batizfalvy . . . Testimony of the Hungarian army officer to Jenö Lévai, taken shortly after the events described. See Lévai, *Raoul Wallenberg*, pp. 145–150.

For those who made it that far . . . Per Anger to author, and in his book, *With Raoul Wallenberg in Budapest*, p. 68.

Wallenberg tries to instill courage into defeated death marchers . . . From two eyewitness accounts: Dr. Johny Moser, self-described Wallenberg "errand boy," as told to Wallenberg's stepfather, Fredrik von Dardel (made available to author courtesy Nina Lagergren), and Natalia Ozoran, rescued from the death march by Wallenberg, whose testimony was assembled by Jenö Lévai; see his *Raoul Wallenberg*, p. 293.

"I want to save a nation" . . . Wallenberg to Miriam Herzog, Israeli citizen, as told to the BBC during an interview with Ms. Herzog in Tel Aviv for a BBC documentary, spring 1980.

Eichmann was still not ready to give up . . . From the testimony
of Dieter Wisliceny before the Nuremberg Military Tribunal.
Wisliceny was hanged in a Bratislava prison in 1947, but not before
he wrote his own revealing biography of his commanding officer,
Adolf Eichmann. Parts of this biography have been reprinted in
Hungarian by Lévai in various volumes of his documentation of the
Hungarian Holocaust and provide useful background on Eich-
mann. (For a translation, see *Eichmann in Hungary*, pp. 247–264.)

15　PLAYING FOR TIME

As much as Wallenberg needed the sleep . . . Testimony of Tibor
Vándor as told to Jenö Lévai. See Lévai, *Raoul Wallenberg*, pp.
290–291.

The imaginary typhoid epidemic . . . Related by Paul Nevi, administrator of the Swedish Hospital, which Wallenberg helped to
set up, and who was among the last to see Wallenberg when the
Swede was already in Russian custody, in January 1945. *Ibid.*, pp.
149–150.

Wallenberg at the synagogue . . . Described to the author by Dr.
Francis Zöld, whose diligent correspondence provided a great deal
of crucial information for this book. Dr. Zöld, on the faculty of the
University of California at Claremont, was a member of the International Red Cross Special Transport Group that worked side by
side with Wallenberg.

The boy was called Junior . . . This is another incident related
by a member of Wallenberg's Humanitarian Action Group to Jenö
Lévai.

16　THE PHOTOGRAPHER

This account of the relationship between Raoul Wallenberg and
his photographer, Thomas Veres, was related by Veres to the author in New York, July 1981. Veres is today a successful commercial photographer in New York City.

17　THE REIGN OF TERROR

Wallenberg's love of order . . . Told to the author by Edith Wohl
Ernster, whose father was a close colleague of Wallenberg's, in
Stockholm, January 1981.

George Wilhelm had little love left for life . . . Told to the author by George Wilhelm in Brussels, Belgium, July 1981.

Wallenberg frequently turned the dissent between the three powers to his own advantage . . . Related to the author by George Wilhelm, Brussels, July 1981.

Wallenberg wanted to meet Eichmann . . . Told to the author by Lars Berg, in Stockholm, January 1981, and from Berg's description in his book, *What Happened in Budapest.*

That Wallenberg found the work . . . Letter courtesy of Nina Lagergren.

The Semestyen family's execution by the Arrow Cross . . . Related by their father, Adrás Semestyen to Jenö Lévai. See Lévai, *Raoul Wallenberg,* p. 156.

The sight of the Danube . . . Related to the author by Agnes Mandl Adachi, whose own return to her native Hungary was marred by such an episode.

18 EICHMANN'S FINAL DAYS

The siege . . . Described to the author by Endre and Ilona Marton, who survived this period in various cellars scattered around Budapest.

"You'd better take your Jews" . . . The testimony of Paul Szálai, former Arrow Cross police officer who was later cleared of all charges of collective guilt by a Hungarian People's Court. His last-minute cooperation with Wallenberg was critical to the survival of the city's Jews. Gábor Vajna, the Interior Minister, like Szálasi, the chief of state, and 262 other members of the Arrow Cross hierarchy were subsequently found guilty of murder and either hanged or executed by a firing squad.

The messenger had reached Wallenberg . . . Related to the author by Thomas Veres, who accompanied Wallenberg on this mission.

Wallenberg's memorandum to German headquarters . . . Reprinted by Lévai, *Raoul Wallenberg,* pp. 210–211.

"I've never been closer to the end than in there" . . . From the eyewitness testimony of a member of the Humanitarian Action Group as told to Jenö Lévai. *Ibid.*, p. 176.

Miklós Kalmár was a Budapest Jew who was trying to save himself . . . Related to the author by Kalmár in New York, June 1981.

Eichmann leaves Budapest . . . Reported by members of the Jewish Council (Miksa Domonkos and Lajos Stöckler) to Jenö Lévai. See his *Eichmann in Hungary*, pp. 179–180.

19   THE SIEGE

That he was still keenly interested in his own future . . . Letter courtesy of Nina Lagergren.

There were no days off . . . Thomas Veres to the author, New York, July 1981.

Per Anger's skepticism about Wallenberg's tactics . . . Related to the author in an interview in Stockholm, January 1981.

Wallenberg's unsuccessful attempt at a weekend off . . . Described by his secretary, Mrs. Lászlo Falk, to Jenö Lévai. See his *Raoul Wallenberg*, p. 296.

Wallenberg and Anger summoned to the Foreign Ministry . . . See Anger, *op. cit.*, pp. 76–83.

Father Kun liked to oversee the torture . . . See Lévai, *Black Book* . . ., p. 412. Kun was convicted of murder and sentenced to death by a Hungarian People's Court after the war.

Szálai, Wallenberg's last ally . . . See Lévai, *Raoul Wallenberg*, p. 185.

Wallenberg's memo to Arrow Cross regarding food . . . See Lévai, *Black Book*, p. 410.

Wallenberg's lengthy memo regarding conditions in the ghetto . . . *Ibid.*, p. 405.

The planned pogrom . . . Described by Szálai before a Hungarian People's Court and reproduced in detail both in Lévai's *Black Book* and his *Raoul Wallenberg*, p. 205.

20 WALLENBERG ON THE RUN

"Big Danube" was the code word . . . This account of the violation of Wallenberg's own offices is based on the testimony received
shortly after the war of a member of the Swede's staff, Imre Terner,
as told to Jenö Lévai. See Lévai, *Raoul Wallenberg*, p. 222.

For now there was nothing more Wallenberg could do . . . This
description of Wallenberg at the Hazai Bank was provided the
author by Edith Wohl Ernster, who was among those taking shelter
in the bank.

He was not content to listen to the BBC's nightly reports . . .
Wallenberg's perilous journey to the Géllert Hill was described to
the author by photographer Thomas Veres, who accompanied him.

Wallenberg spent the next three days . . . This is based on the
author's interviews in Brussels and New York, July 1981, with
George Wilhelm and Stephen Radi, two men who also waited for
the "liberators" in the Benczur Street villa, along with Wallenberg.
They were with him when the first Russian soldiers appeared in
the cellar and have been able to describe in detail Wallenberg's
final days in Budapest.

Wallenberg tells Szálai he will introduce him to the King of
Sweden . . . Based on Szálai's interview with Jenö Lévai. See
Lévai, *Raoul Wallenberg*, p. 227.

21 THE NEW MASTERS

Description of the Russian liberation of Budapest provided by members of the author's family who survived the events.

Wallenberg's childhood acquaintance . . . Lászlo Petö's testimony
as told to Jenö Lévai, in Lévai's *Raoul Wallenberg*, pp. 233–234.

22 THE CAPTIVE GUEST

Wallenberg's elaborate leave-taking . . . The description of the
Swede's trip from Budapest to Lubyanka Prison, including his
Rumanian stop, are based on testimony collected by the Swedish
Foreign Office in what constitutes the largest single file there: the
Wallenberg Papers. In the early years of Wallenberg's imprison-
ment, it was an Austrian journalist, Rudolf Phillip, who interro-

gated newly freed Soviet prisoners on the subject of Wallenberg. Later the Swedish Foreign Office took over the task and continues to the present recording their testimony, however tenuous the claimed link to Wallenberg. The Foreign Office has published three so-called White Books on Raoul Wallenberg: the first one appeared in 1957 and presents a remarkably detailed account of Wallenberg's first twelve years under Soviet custody. The other volumes followed in 1965 and 1980, respectively. The following chapters draw heavily on these documents as well as on the author's own interviews with members of the Swedish Foreign Office and Soviet prison specialists.

The NKVD's separate chain of command . . . Based on the author's interviews with George Wilhelm and Lars Berg, who were both arrested by the Soviet secret police in Budapest following "liberation."

Wallenberg and the NKVD . . . See Isaac Deutscher's brilliant work, *Stalin*, p. 604, for a description of the mentality of the Swede's captors.

23   AT HOME
From the other members of the Budapest legation . . . Interview with Per Anger in Stockholm, January 1981.

Söderblom to Anger . . . See Anger, *op. cit.*, p. 145.

"Rysskräck" . . . Sweden's mood of fear following World War II described to the author by Lars Persson, editor of the Stockholm daily *Expressen*, in interview held in London, spring 1980.

Radio Kossuth announced that spring . . . Archive material of newspapers from various countries reporting the story of Wallenberg's disappearance from the first days until the present, courtesy of Radio Free Europe, Munich.

In Moscow, Ambassador Söderblom . . . Interview with Lars Åke Nilsson, who was for several years charged with the Wallenberg investigation of the Swedish Foreign Office, and who is currently posted at the Swedish embassy in London: June 1980 interview in Stockholm.

Six months after Wallenberg vanished . . . This account of the diplomats' homecoming was provided by a highly reliable participant who wishes to remain anonymous.

In the eyes of the Foreign Office . . . Told the author by Carl-Fredrik Palmstierna, former private secretary to the King of Sweden, currently Court librarian.

Alexandra Kollontai's gradual eclipse . . . Described to the author by Nina Lagergren. See also Deutscher, *op. cit.*, pp. 162, 183, 212, 226–228, 438.

Rudolf Phillip was a sharp-featured, chain-smoking . . . Nina Lagergren to the author, May 1981, Stockholm.

Östen Undén becomes Foreign Minister . . . See Anger, *op. cit.*, pp. 152–155.

Söderblom and Stalin . . . Swedish Foreign Office White Books on Raoul Wallenberg, Vol. I.

Vyshinsky on Wallenberg . . . *Ibid.* See also Deutscher, *op. cit.*, pp. 370, 543, 589–590.

Undén faces the Wallenberg Committee . . . See Anger, *op. cit.*, p. 153.

Per Anger and Undén . . . *Ibid.*, pp. 153–155.

In Budapest, Wallenberg is a folk hero . . . Lévai, *Raoul Wallenberg*, p. 256–266.

Mátyás Rákosi collects all power in his hands . . . From the author's childhood memories of the dictator (as a member of the Communist Youth, Young Pioneers, the author was taken to May Day parades where Rákosi was also present), and from Paul Ignotus' excellent study, *Hungary*, pp. 193–220.

The statue vanishes . . . From newspaper accounts, courtesy of RFE, Munich.

24 THE APPRENTICE INMATE

All night long prisoners were brought in . . . This account is based on interviews with former Soviet inmates (André Shimkevich, who also passed through Lubyanka, and the author's mother and father, inmates of Hungary's own version of Lubyanka, the Fö Utca Maximum Security Political Prison, in Budapest).

Wallenberg was busy . . . Swedish White Books, Vol. I, based on the testimony of Gustav Richter and Otto Scheur, released former cell mates of Wallenberg.

Early in May, Wallenberg knew the war was over . . . See Alexander Solzhenitsyn's *The First Circle* and the *Gulag Archipelago, 1918–1956*.

But two years after they led him into Lubyanka . . . Swedish White Books, Vol. I.

25 THE SILENT PRISONER

André Shimkevich remembers . . . The author's interview with the Frenchman in Stockholm, January 1981.

Two years before, in 1953 . . . The story of General Kuprianov was related to the author during the course of two interviews with Simon Wiesenthal, January 1981, in Stockholm, and July 1981 in Vienna. Wiesenthal was in possession of precise notes reproducing Kuprianov's journal, delivered to him by Kuprianov's secretary and friend. Wiesenthal would only identify her as "I.L." She is a recent Soviet émigrée, now settled somewhere in the United States, but with relatives still living in Leningrad, whom she wishes to protect. Wiesenthal, who has many years of experience examining witnesses, says he is satisfied with the veracity of "I.L.'s" detailed testimony.

26 DEAD OR ALIVE

Tage Erlander and Khrushchev . . . Based on newspaper accounts of their meeting, as well as on archive material from the Swedish Foreign Office.

Maj von Dardel's letter to her son . . . Courtesy of Nina Lagergren.

De-Stalinization . . . See *Prospects for Soviet Society*, by Allan Kassof, pp. 64–65. 322–328, 330–331, 342–346.

The captive's mother opposed the Swedish Prime Minister . . . Nina Lagergren to author.

Gromyko's memorandum . . . From the Swedish White Books on Wallenberg, Vol. I.

The prisoner's file stays with him . . . Letter of Andrei Sakharov to Wallenberg's half-brother, Guy von Dardel, May 1980.

The United States Senate Internal Security Subcommittee . . . UPI, February 11, 1957.

The mother's conviction . . . Nina Lagergren to the author.

Dag Hammarskjöld on his neutrality in the Wallenberg case . . . Carl-Fredrik Palmstierna to the author in Stockholm, June 1980.

Kalinski knew it was the Swede . . . Lars Åke Nilsson to the author, June 1980, Stockholm.

27 "NOW, DEAR COLLEAGUE . . ."

This chapter is based on the detailed reporting of the events by Dr. Nanna Svartz in the Wallenberg file of the Swedish Foreign Office, Vol. III. Additional material was made available to the author by Erik Sjöquist, the Swedish journalist who spent many hours questioning Dr. Svartz for his books on the Wallenberg case.

28 THE TRACKS REAPPEAR

Tage Erlander faces the Swedish public with the Nanna Svartz story . . . Based on newspaper reporting of the events from the archives of RFE.

For Wallenberg's mother this was the beginning . . . Nina Lagergren to the author.

Maj von Dardel's letter to Dr. Henry Kissinger . . . United States State Department Archive material obtained under the Freedom of Information Act.

In 1979 a Tel Aviv dentist . . . Swedish White Books, Vol. III.

The word of the presence of "an old Swede" . . . From Ludmilla Thorne, Freedom House, New York. July 1981, to the author.

But under their white coats these doctors wear . . . Alexander Podrabinek and Viktor Nekipelov (Soviet prisoners), *The Silent Asylum*.

EPILOGUE

In 1978 the Russians arrested a Swede . . . See Anger, *op. cit.*, p. 157.

Bibliography

Amnesty International Report: *Prisoners of Conscience in the USSR: Their Treatment and Conditions.* 1980.

Anger, Per, *With Raoul Wallenberg in Budapest* (New York: Holocaust Library, 1981).

Bibo, István, *A Zsidókérdés Magyarországon* (The Jewish Question in Hungary) (London, 1960).

Berg, Lars, *What Happened in Budapest* (Stockholm, 1947).

Dardel, Fredrik von, *Facts Around a Fate* (Stockholm, 1970).

Dawidowicz, Lucy S., *The War Against the Jews 1933–1945* (New York: Bantam Books, 1979).

Derogy, *Le Cas Wallenberg* (Paris: Editions Ramsay, 1980).

Deutscher, Isaac, *Stalin: A Political Biography* (London: Oxford University Press, 1949, 1966).

Ember, Maria, *Hajtü Kanyar* (Hairpin Curve: The Story of the Provincial Hungarian Deportations) (Budapest, 1974).

Feingold, Henry L., *The Politics of Rescue: The Roosevelt Administration and the Holocaust, 1938–1944* (Rutgers, N.J.: Rutgers University Press, 1970).

Fenyö, Mario, *Hitler, Horthy and Hungary* (New Haven: Yale University Press, 1972).

Gilbert, Martin, *Auschwitz and the Allies* (New York: Holt, Rinehart & Winston, 1981).

Herman, Victor, *The Gray People* (New York: Independent Publishing House, 1980).

Heyman, Éva, *The Diary of Éva Heyman* (Jerusalem: Yad Vashem, 1964).

Horthy, Miklós, *Memoirs* (New York: Robert Speller and Sons, 1957).

Ignotus, Paul, *Hungary* (London: Ernest Benn Ltd., 1972).

Jászi, Oscar, *The Dissolution of the Hapsburg Monarchy* (Chicago: University of Chicago Press, 1929).

Kassof, Allan, *Prospects for Soviet Society* (New York: Praeger, 1967).

Lacko, Miklós, *Nyilasok, Nemzetiszocialisták, 1935–1944* (The Arrow Cross and the National Socialists) (Budapest, 1976).

Lévai, Jenö, *Black Book of Martyrdom of Hungarian Jewry* (Zurich: Central European Times, 1948).

———, *Zsidosors Magyarországon* (The Fate of Jews in Hungary) (Budapest: Magyar Teka, 1948).

———, *Raoul Wallenberg* (Budapest, 1948).

———, *Eichmann in Hungary* (Budapest, 1948).

Moldova, György, *A Szent Imre Indulo* (St. Imre's March). A semifictional account of the Budapest ghetto by one of Hungary's most respected contemporary authors. (Budapest, 1976).

Morse, Arthur D., *While Six Million Died* (New York: Random House, 1968).

Palmstierna, Carl-Fredrik, *Feather in My Hand* (Stockholm, 1976).

Podrabinek, Alexander, and Nekipelov, Victor, *The Silent Asylum* (Moscow, 1977). *Samizdat* material.

Rauch, Georg von, *A History of Soviet Russia* (New York: Praeger, 1967).

Rozsnyoi, Agnes, *A Szálasi Puccs* (The Szálasi Coup) (Budapest, 1977).

Schöpflin, George, "Jewish Assimilation in Hungary: A Moot Point" (Haifa: University of Haifa, 1976).

Seton-Watson, Hugh, *From Lenin to Khrushchev* (New York: Praeger, 1967).

Shirer, William L., *The Rise and Fall of the Third Reich* (New York: Simon & Schuster, 1960).

Solzhenitsyn, Alexander, *The Gulag Archipelago* (New York: Harper & Row, 1973).

Speer, Albert, *Inside the Third Reich* (New York: Macmillan, 1970).

Steel, Ronald, *Walter Lippmann and the American Century* (Boston: Little, Brown, 1980).

Sulzberger, C. L., *A Long Row of Candles* (New York: Macmillan, 1969).

Swedish Foreign Office White Books on Raoul Wallenberg, 3 vols. (Stockholm, 1957, 1965, 1980).

Száraz, György, *Egy Elöitélet Nyomában* (In Quest of a Judgment) (Budapest, 1976).

Index

ABOUT THE AUTHOR

Born in Hungary, Kati Marton is the author of *An American Woman*, *The Polk Conspiracy: Murder and Cover-Up in the Case of CBS Correspondent George Polk* (currently being turned into a feature film), and most recently, *A Death in Jerusalem: The Assassination by Jewish Extremists of the First Arab/Israeli Peacemaker*. Former Bonn bureau chief and foreign correspondent for ABC News, Ms. Marton has also reported for National Public Radio, the *Times* of London, the *Washington Post, Newsweek,* and *Vanity Fair*. She lives in New York City with her daughter Elizabeth and her son Christopher.